THE MAN SHAKESPEARE

BY FRANK HARRIS

Fiction

THE BOMB
ELDER CONKLIN
MONTES, THE MATADOR

Plays

MR. AND MRS. DAVENTRY
SHAKESPEARE AND HIS LOVE

THE MAN
SHAKESPEARE

AND HIS TRAGIC
LIFE-STORY

BY

FRANK HARRIS

NEW YORK
MITCHELL KENNERLEY
MCMIX

Copyright 1909 by
Mitchell Kennerley

I DEDICATE THIS BOOK TO MY FRIEND,

ERNEST BECKETT (NOW LORD GRIMTHORPE),

A MAN OF MOST EXCELLENT DIFFERENCES,
WHO UNITES TO A GENIUS FOR PRACTICAL THINGS
A PASSIONATE SYMPATHY FOR ALL
HIGH ENDEAVOUR IN LITERATURE AND ART

The Man Shakespeare

vii

INTRODUCTION

THIS book has grown out of a series of articles contributed to " The Saturday Review " some ten or twelve years ago. As they appeared they were talked of and criticized in the usual way; a minority of readers thought " the stuff " interesting; many held that my view of Shakespeare was purely arbitrary; others said I had used a concordance to such purpose that out of the mass of words I had managed, by virtue of some unknown formula, to re-create the character of the man.

The truth is much simpler: I read Shakespeare's plays in boyhood, chiefly for the stories; every few years later I was fain to re-read them; for as I grew I always found new beauties in them which I had formerly missed, and again and again I was lured back by tantalizing hints and suggestions of a certain unity underlying the diversity of characters. These suggestions gradually became more definite till at length, out of the myriad voices in the plays, I began to hear more and more insistent the accents of one voice, and out of the crowd of faces, began to distinguish more and more clearly the features of the writer; for all the world like some lovelorn girl, who, gazing with her soul in her eyes, finds in the witch's cauldron the face of the belovèd.

I have tried in this book to trace the way I followed, step by step; for I found it effective to rough in the chief features of the man first, and afterwards, taking the plays in succession, to show how Shakespeare painted himself at full-length, not once, but twenty times, at as many different periods of his life. This is one reason why he is more interesting to us than the greatest men of the past, than Dante even, or Homer; for Dante and Homer worked only at their best in the flower of manhood. Shakespeare, on the other hand, has painted himself for us in his green youth with hardly any knowledge of life or art, and then in his eventful maturity, with growing experience and new powers, in masterpiece after masterpiece; and at length in his decline with weakened grasp and fading colours, so that in him we can study the growth and fruiting and decay of the finest spirit that has yet been born among men. This tragedy of tragedies, in which "Lear" is only one scene—this rise to intensest life and widest vision and fall through abysms of despair and madness to exhaustion and death—can be followed experience by experience, from Stratford to London and its thirty years of passionate living, and then from London to village Stratford again, and the eternal shrouding silence.

As soon as this astonishing drama discovered itself to me in its tragic completeness I jumped to the conclusion that it must have been set forth long ago in detail by Shakespeare's commentators, and so, for the first time, I turned to their works. I do not wish to rail at my forerunners as Carlyle railed at the historians of Cromwell, or I should talk, as he talked, about "libraries of inanities . . . conceited dilettantism and pedantry . . . prurient stupidity," and so forth. The fact is, I found all this, and worse; I waded through tons of talk to no result. Without a single exception the commentators have all missed the man and the story; they have turned the poet into a tradesman, and the unimaginable

tragedy of his life into the commonplace record of
a successful tradesman's career. Even to explain
this astounding misadventure of the host of critics
is a little difficult. The mistake, of course, arose
from the fact that his contemporaries told very
little about Shakespeare; they left his appearance
and even the incidents of his life rather vague.
Being without a guide, and having no clear idea
of Shakespeare's character, the critics created him
in their own image, and, whenever they were in doubt,
idealized him according to the national type.

Still, there was at least one exception. Some
Frenchman, I think it is Joubert, says that no great
man is born into the world without another man
being born about the same time, who understands
and can interpret him, and Shakespeare was of
necessity singularly fortunate in his interpreter.
Ben Jonson was big enough to see him fairly, and
to give excellent-true testimony concerning him.
Jonson's view of Shakespeare is astonishingly accurate and trustworthy so far as it goes; even his
attitude of superiority to Shakespeare is fraught
with meaning. Two hundred years later, the rising
tide of international criticism produced two men,
Goethe and Coleridge, who also saw Shakespeare,
if only by glimpses, or rather by divination of kindred genius, recognizing certain indubitable traits.
Goethe's criticism of " Hamlet " has been vastly
over-praised; but now and then he used words
about Shakespeare which, in due course, we shall
see were illuminating words, the words of one who
guessed something of the truth. Coleridge, too, with
his curious, complex endowment of philosopher
and poet, resembled Shakespeare, saw him, therefore, by flashes, and might have written greatly
about him; but, alas, Coleridge, a Puritan born, was

brought up in epicene hypocrisies, and determined to see Shakespeare—that child of the Renascence —as a Puritan, too, and consequently mis-saw him far oftener than he saw him; misjudged him hideously, and had no inkling of his tragic history.

There is a famous passage in Coleridge's " Essays on Shakespeare " which illustrates what I mean. It begins: " In Shakespeare all the elements of woman-hood are holy "; and goes on to eulogize the instinct of chastity which all his women possess, and this in spite of Doll Tearsheet, Tamora, Cressida, Goneril, Regan, Cleopatra, the Dark Lady of the Sonnets, and many other frail and fascinating figures. Yet whatever gleam of light has fallen on Shakespeare since Coleridge's day has come chiefly from that dark lantern which he now and then flashed upon the master.

In one solitary respect, our latter-day criticism has been successful; it has established with very considerable accuracy the chronology of the plays, and so the life-story of the poet is set forth in due order for those to read who can.

This then is what I found—a host of commenta-tors who saw men as trees walking, and mistook plain facts, and among them one authentic witness, Jonson, and two interesting though not trustworthy witnesses, Goethe and Coleridge—and nothing more in three centuries. The mere fact may well give us pause, pointing as it does to a truth which is still insufficiently understood. It is the puzzle of criti-cism, at once the despair and wonder of readers, that the greatest men of letters usually pass through life without being remarked or understood by their contemporaries. The men of Elizabeth's time were more interested in Jonson than in Shakespeare, and have told us much more about the younger than the

greater master; just as Spaniards of the same age
were more interested in Lope de Vega than in Cervantes, and have left a better picture of the second-
rate playwright than of the world-poet. Attempting
to solve this problem Emerson coolly assumed that
the men of the Elizabethan age were so great that
Shakespeare himself walked about among them unnoticed as a giant among giants. This reading of
the riddle is purely transcendental. We know that
Shakespeare's worst plays were far oftener acted
than his best; that " Titus Andronicus " by popular
favour was more esteemed than " Hamlet." The
majority of contemporary poets and critics regarded
Shakespeare rather as a singer of " sugred " verses
than as a dramatist. The truth is that Shakespeare
passed through life unnoticed because he was so
much greater than his contemporaries that they
could not see him at all in his true proportions.
It was Jonson, the nearest to him in greatness, who
alone saw him at all fairly and appreciated his
astonishing genius.

Nothing illustrates more perfectly the unconscious wisdom of the English race than the old
saying that " a man must be judged by his peers."
One's peers, in fact, are the only persons capable of
judging one, and the truth seems to be that three
centuries have only produced three men at all capable of judging Shakespeare. The jury is still
being collected. But from the quality of the first
three, and of their praise, it is already plain that
his place will be among the highest. From various
indications, too, it looks as if the time for judging
him had come: " Hamlet " is perhaps his most
characteristic creation, and Hamlet, in his intellectual unrest, morbid brooding, cynical self-analysis and dislike of bloodshed, is much more typical

of the nineteenth or twentieth century than of the sixteenth. Evidently the time for classifying the creator of Hamlet is at hand.

And this work of description and classification should be done as a scientist would do it: for criticism itself has at length bent to the Time-spirit and become scientific. And just as in science, analysis for the moment has yielded pride of place to synthesis, so the critical movement in literature has in our time become creative. The chemist, who resolves any substance into its elements, is not satisfied till by synthesis he can re-create the substance out of its elements: this is the final proof that his knowledge is complete. And so we care little or nothing to-day for critical analyses or appreciations which are not creative presentments of the person. "Paint him for us," we say, "in his habit as he lived, and we will take it that you know something about him."

One of the chief attempts at creative criticism in English literature, or, perhaps it would be fairer to say, the only memorable attempt, is Carlyle's Cromwell. He has managed to build up the man for us quite credibly out of Cromwell's letters and speeches, showing us the underlying sincerity and passionate resolution of the great Puritan once for all. But unfortunately Carlyle was too romantic an artist, too persuaded in his hero-worship to discover for us Cromwell's faults and failings. In his book we find nothing of the fanatic who ordered the Irish massacres, nothing of the neuropath who lived in hourly dread of assassination. Carlyle has painted his subject all in lights, so to speak; the shadows are not even indicated, and yet he ought to have known that in proportion to the brilliancy of the light the shadows must of necessity be dark. It is not for me to point out that this romantic painting of great men, like all other make-believes and hypocrisies, has its drawbacks and shortcomings: it is enough that it has had its day and produced its pictures of giant-heroes and their worshippers for those who love such childish toys.

The wonderful age in which we live—this twentieth century with its X-rays that enable us to see through the skin and flesh of men, and to study the working of their organs and muscles and nerves— has brought a new spirit into the world, a spirit of fidelity to fact, and with it a new and higher ideal of life and of art, which must of necessity change and transform all the conditions of existence, and in time modify the almost immutable nature of man. For this new spirit, this love of the fact and of truth, this passion for reality will do away with the foolish fears and futile hopes which have fretted the childhood of our race, and will slowly but surely establish on broad foundations the Kingdom of Man upon Earth. For that is the meaning and purpose of the change which is now coming over the world. The faiths and convictions of twenty centuries are passing away and the forms and institutions of a hundred generations of men are dissolving before us like the baseless fabric of a dream. A new morality is already shaping itself in the spirit; a morality based not on guess-work and on fancies, but on ascertained laws of moral health; a scientific morality belonging not to statics, like the morality of the Jews, but to dynamics, and so fitting the nature of each individual person. Even now conscience with its prohibitions is fading out of life, evolving into a more profound consciousness of ourselves and others, with multiplied incitements to wise living. The old religious asceticism with its hatred of the body is dead; the servile acceptance of conditions of life and even of natural laws is seen to be vicious; it is of the nobility of man to be insatiate in desire and to rebel against limiting conditions; it is the property of his intelligence to constrain even the laws of nature to the attainment of his ideal.

Already we are proud of being students, investigators, servants of truth, and we leave the great names of demi-gods and heroes a little contemptuously to the men of bygone times. As student-artists we are no longer content with the outward presentment and form of men: we want to discover the protean vanities, greeds and aspirations of men, and to lay bare, as with a scalpel, the hidden motives and springs of action. We dream of an art that shall take into account the natural daily decay and up-building of cell-life; the wars that go on in the blood; the fevers of the brain; the creeping paralysis of nerve-exhaustion; above all, we must be able even now from a few bare facts, to re-create a man and make him live and love again for the reader, just as the biologist from a few scattered bones can reconstruct some prehistoric bird or fish or mammal.

And we student-artists have no desire to paint our subject as better or nobler or smaller or meaner than he was in reality; we study his limitations as we study his gifts, his virtues with as keen an interest as his vices; for it is in some excess of desire, or in some extravagance of mentality, that we look for the secret of his achievement, just as we begin to wonder when we see hands constantly outstretched in pious supplication, whether a foot is not thrust out behind in some secret shame, for the biped, man, must keep a balance.

I intend first of all to prove from Shakespeare's

works that he has painted himself twenty times
from youth till age at full length: I shall consider
and compare these portraits till the outlines of his
character are clear and certain; afterwards I shall
show how his little vanities and shames idealized
the picture, and so present him as he really was,
with his imperial intellect and small snobberies; his
giant vices and paltry self-deceptions; his sweet
gentleness and long martyrdom. I cannot but think
that his portrait will thus gain more in truth than
it can lose in ideal beauty. Or let me come nearer
to my purpose by means of a simile. Talking with
Sir David Gill one evening on shipboard about the
fixed stars, he pointed one out which is so distant
that we cannot measure how far it is away from
us and can form no idea of its magnitude. "But
surely," I exclaimed, " the great modern telescopes
must bring the star nearer and magnify it?" "No,"
he replied, " no; the best instruments make the star
clearer to us, but certainly not larger." This is
what I wish to do in regard to Shakespeare; make
him clearer to men, even if I do not make him larger.

And if I were asked why I do this, why I take
the trouble to re-create a man now three centuries
dead, it is, first of all, of course, because he is worth
it—the most complex and passionate personality
in the world, whether of life or letters—because,
too, there are certain lessons which the English will
learn from Shakespeare more quickly and easily than
from any living man, and a little because I want to
get rid of Shakespeare by assimilating all that was
fine in him, while giving all that was common and
vicious in him as spoil to oblivion. He is like the
Old-Man-of-the-Sea on the shoulders of our youth;
he has become an obsession to the critic, a weapon to
the pedant, a nuisance to the man of genius. True,

Introduction

he has painted great pictures in a superb, romantic fashion; he is the Titian of dramatic art: but is there to be no Rembrandt, no Balzac, no greater Tolstoi in English letters? I want to liberate Englishmen so far as I can from the tyranny of Shakespeare's greatness. For the new time is upon us, with its new knowledge and new claims, and we English are all too willing to live in the past, and so lose our inherited place as leader of the nations.

The French have profited by their glorious Revolution: they trusted reason and have had their reward; no such leap forward has ever been made as France made in that one decade, and the effects are still potent. In the last hundred years the language of Molière has grown fourfold; the slang of the studios and the gutter and the laboratory, of the engineering school and the dissecting table, has been ransacked for special terms to enrich and strengthen the language in order that it may deal easily with the new thoughts. French is now a superb instrument, while English is positively poorer than it was in the time of Shakespeare, thanks to the prudery of our illiterate middle class. Divorced from reality, with its activities all fettered in baby-linen, our literature has atrophied and dwindled into a babble of nursery rhymes, tragedies of Little Marys, tales of Babes in a Wood. The example of Shakespeare may yet teach us the value of free speech; he could say what he liked as he liked: he was not afraid of the naked truth and the naked word, and through his greatness a Low Dutch dialect has become the chiefest instrument of civilization, the world-speech of humanity at large.

FRANK HARRIS

LONDON, 1909.

BOOK I

SHAKESPEARE PAINTED BY HIMSELF

CHAPTER I

"AS I passed by . . . I found an altar with this inscription, To The Unknown God. Whom therefore ye ignorantly worship, him declare I unto you." This work of Paul—the discovery and proclaiming of an unknown god—is in every age the main function of the critic.

An unknown god this Shakespeare of ours, whom all are agreed it would be well to know, if in any way possible. As to the possibility, however, the authorities are at loggerheads. Hallam, " the judicious," declared that it was impossible to learn anything certain about " the man, Shakespeare." Wordsworth, on the other hand (without a nickname to show a close connection with the common), held that Shakespeare unlocked his heart with the sonnets for key. Browning jeered at this belief, to be in turn contradicted by Swinburne. Matthew Arnold gave us in a sonnet " the best opinion of his time ":

" Others abide our question. Thou art free.
  We ask and ask—Thou smilest and art still,
  Out-topping knowledge."

But alas! the best opinion of one generation is in these matters often flat unreason to the next, and it may be that in this instance neither the opinion of Hallam nor Browning nor Arnold will be allowed to count.

3

The Man Shakespeare

As it is the object of a general to win battles, so it is the life-work of the artist to show himself to us, and the completeness with which he reveals his own individuality is perhaps the best measure of his genius. One does this like Montaigne, simply, garrulously, telling us his height and make, his tastes and distastes, his loves and fears and habits, till gradually the seeming-artless talk brings the man before us, a sun-warmed fruit of humanity, with uncouth rind of stiff manners and sweet kindly juices, not perfect in any way, shrivelled on this side by early frost-bite, and on that softened to corruption through too much heat, marred here by the bitter-black cicatrice of an ancient injury and there fortune-spotted, but on the whole healthy, grateful, of a most pleasant ripeness. Another, like Shakespeare, with passionate conflicting sympathies and curious impartial intellect cannot discover himself so simply; needs, like the diamond, many facets to show all the light in him, and so proceeds to cut them one after the other as Falstaff or Hamlet, to the dazzling of the purblind.

Yet Shakespeare's purpose is surely the same as Montaigne's, to reveal himself to us, and it would be hasty to decide that his skill is inferior. For while Montaigne had nothing but prose at his command, and not too rich a prose, as he himself complains, Shakespeare in magic of expression has had no equal in recorded time, and he used the lyric as well as the dramatic form, poetry as well as prose, to give his soul utterance.

We are doing Shakespeare wrong by trying to believe that he hides himself behind his work; the suspicion is as unworthy as the old suspicion dissipated by Carlyle that Cromwell was an ambitious hypocrite. Sincerity is the birthmark of

4

genius, and we can be sure that Shakespeare has depicted himself for us with singular fidelity; we can see him in his works, if we will take the trouble, " in his habit as he lived."

We are doing ourselves wrong, too, by pretending that Shakespeare "out-tops knowledge." He did not fill the world even in his own time: there was room beside him in the days of Elizabeth for Marlowe and Spenser, Ben Jonson and Bacon, and since then the spiritual outlook, like the material outlook, has widened to infinity. There is space in life now for a dozen ideals undreamed-of in the sixteenth century. Let us have done with this pretence of doglike humility; we, too, are men, and there is on earth no higher title, and in the universe nothing beyond our comprehending. It will be well for us to know Shakespeare and all his high qualities and do him reverence; it will be well for us, too, to see his limitations and his faults, for after all it is the human frailties in a man that call forth our sympathy and endear him to us, and without love there is no virtue in worship, no attraction in example.

The doubt as to the personality of Shakespeare, and the subsequent confusion and contradictions are in the main, I think, due to Coleridge. He was the first modern critic to have glimpses of the real Shakespeare, and the vision lent his words a singular authority. But Coleridge was a hero-worshipper by nature and carried reverence to lyric heights. He used all his powers to persuade men that Shakespeare was μυριόνους ἀνήρ—" the myriad-minded man"; a sort of demi-god who was every one and no one, a Proteus without individuality of his own. The theory has held the field for nearly a century, probably because it flatters our national vanity; for in itself it is fantastically absurd and leads to most ridiculous conclusions. For instance, when Coleridge had to deal with the fact that Shakespeare never drew a miser, instead of accepting the omission as characteristic, for it is confirmed by Ben Jonson's testimony that he was "of an open and free nature," Coleridge proceeded to argue that avarice is not a permanent passion in humanity, and that Shakespeare probably for that reason chose to leave it undescribed. This is an example of the ecstasy of hero-worship; it is begging the question to assume that whatever Shakespeare did was perfect; humanity cannot be penned up even in Shakespeare's brain. Like every other man of genius Shakespeare must have shown himself in his qualities and defects, in his preferences and prejudices; "a fallible being," as stout old Dr. Johnson knew, "will fail somewhere."

Even had Shakespeare tried to hide himself in his work, he could not have succeeded. Now that the print of a man's hand or foot or ear is enough to distinguish him from all other men, it is impossible to believe that the mask of his mind, the very imprint, form and pressure of his soul should be less distinctive. Just as Monsieur Bertillon's whorl-pictures of a thumb afford overwhelming proofs of a man's identity, so it is possible from Shakespeare's writings to establish beyond doubt the main features of his character and the chief incidents of his life. The time for random assertion about Shakespeare and unlimited eulogy of him has passed away for ever: the object of this inquiry is to show him as he lived and loved and suffered, and the proofs of this and of that trait shall be so heaped up as to stifle doubt and reach absolute conviction. For not only is the circumstantial evidence overwhelming and conclusive, but we have also the testimony of eye-witnesses with which to confirm it, and one of these witnesses, Ben Jonson, is of rare credibility and singularly well equipped.

Let us begin, then, by treating Shakespeare as we would treat any other writer, and ask simply how a dramatic author is most apt to reveal himself. A great dramatist may not paint himself for us at any time in his career with all his faults and vices; but when he goes deepest into human nature, we may be sure that self-knowledge is his guide; as Hamlet said, "To know a man well, were to know himself" (oneself), so far justifying the paradox that dramatic writing is merely a form of autobiography. We may take then as a guide this first criterion that, in his masterpiece of psychology, the dramatist will reveal most of his own nature.

If a dozen lovers of Shakespeare were asked to name the most profound and most complex character in all his dramas it is probable that everyone without hesitation would answer Hamlet. The current of cultivated opinion has long set in this direction. With the intuition of a kindred genius, Goethe was the first to put Hamlet on a pedestal: "the incomparable," he called him, and devoted pages to an analysis of the character. Coleridge followed with the confession whose truth we shall see later: "I have a smack of Hamlet myself, if I may say so." But even if it be admitted that Hamlet is the most complex and profound of Shakespeare's creations, and therefore probably the character in which Shakespeare revealed most of himself, the question of degree still remains to be determined. Is it possible to show certainly that even the broad outlines of Hamlet's character are those of the master-poet?

The Man Shakespeare

There are various ways in which this might be proved. For instance, if one could show that whenever Shakespeare fell out of a character he was drawing, he unconsciously dropped into the Hamlet vein, one's suspicion as to the identity of Hamlet and the poet would be enormously strengthened. There is another piece of evidence still more convincing. Suppose that Shakespeare in painting another character did nothing but paint Hamlet over again trait by trait—virtue by virtue, fault by fault—our assurance would be almost complete; for a dramatist only makes this mistake when he is speaking unconsciously in his proper person. But if both these kinds of proof were forthcoming, and not once but a dozen times, then surely our conviction as to the essential identity of Hamlet and Shakespeare would amount to practical certitude.

Of course it would be foolish, even in this event, to pretend that Hamlet exhausts Shakespeare; art does little more than embroider the fringe of the garment of life, and the most complex character in drama or even in fiction is simple indeed when compared with even the simplest of living men or women. Shakespeare included in himself Falstaff and Cleopatra, beside the author of the sonnets, and knowledge drawn from all these must be used to fill out and perhaps to modify the outlines given in Hamlet before one can feel sure that the portrait is a re-presentment of reality. But when this study is completed, it will be seen that, with many necessary limitations, Hamlet is indeed a revelation of some of the most characteristic traits of Shakespeare.

To come to the point quickly, I will take Hamlet's character as analyzed by Coleridge and Professor Dowden.

Hamlet: Romeo—Jaques

Coleridge says: " Hamlet's character is the prevalence of the abstracting and generalizing habit over the practical. He does not want courage, skill, will or opportunity; but every incident sets him thinking: and it is curious, and at the same time strictly natural, that Hamlet, who all the play seems reason itself, should be impelled at last by mere accident to effect his object." Again he says: " in Hamlet we see a great, an almost enormous intellectual activity and a proportionate aversion to real action consequent upon it."

Professor Dowden's analysis is more careful but hardly as complete. He calls Hamlet " the meditative son " of a strong-willed father, and adds, " he has slipped on into years of full manhood still a haunter of the university, a student of philosophies, an amateur in art, a ponderer on the things of life and death who has never formed a resolution or executed a deed. This long course of thinking apart from action has destroyed Hamlet's very capacity for belief. . . . In presence of the spirit he is himself ' a spirit,' and believes in the immortality of the soul. When left to his private thoughts he wavers uncertainly to and fro; death is a sleep; a sleep, it may be, troubled with dreams. . . . He is incapable of certitude. . . . After his fashion (that of one who relieves himself by speech rather than by deeds) he unpacks his heart in words."

Now what other personage is there in Shakespeare who shows these traits or some of them? He should be bookish and irresolute, a lover of thought and not of action, of melancholy temper too, and prone to unpack his heart with words. Almost every one who has followed the argument thus far will be inclined to think of Romeo.

Hazlitt declared that " Romeo is Hamlet in love. There is the same rich exuberance of passion and sentiment in the one, that there is of thought and sentiment in the other. Both are absent and self-involved; both live out of themselves in a world of imagination." Much of this is true and affords a noteworthy example of Hazlitt's occasional insight into character, yet for reasons that will appear later it is not possible to insist, as Hazlitt does, upon the identity of Romeo and Hamlet. The most that can be said is that Romeo is a younger brother of Hamlet, whose character is much less mature and less complex than that of the student-prince. Moreover, the characterization in Romeo —the mere drawing and painting—is very inferior to that put to use in Hamlet. Romeo is half hidden from us in the rose-mist of passion, and after he is banished from Juliet's arms we only see him for a moment as he rushes madly by into never-ending night, and all the while Shakespeare is thinking more of the poetry of the theme than of his hero's character. Romeo is crude and immature when compared with a profound psychological study like Hamlet. In " Hamlet " the action often stands still while incidents are invented for the mere purpose of displaying the peculiarities of the protagonist. " Hamlet," too, is the longest of Shakespeare's plays with the exception of " Antony and Cleopatra," and " the total length of Hamlet's speeches," says Dryasdust, " far exceeds that of those allotted by Shakespeare to any other of his characters." The important point, however, is that Romeo has a more than family likeness to Hamlet. Even in the heat and heyday of his passion Romeo plays thinker; Juliet says, " Good-night " and dis-

10

appears, but he finds time to give us the abstract truth:

" Love goes towards love, as schoolboys from their books,
But love from love, toward school with heavy looks."

Juliet appears again unexpectedly, and again Hamlet's generalizing habit asserts itself in Romeo:

" How silver-sweet sound lovers' tongues by night,
Like softest music to attending ears."

We may be certain that Juliet would have preferred more pointed praise. He is indeed so lost in his ill-timed reverie that Juliet has to call him again and again by name before he attends to her.

Romeo has Hamlet's peculiar habit of talking to himself. He falls into a soliloquy on his way to Juliet in Capulet's orchard, when his heart must have been beating so loudly that it would have prevented him from hearing himself talk, and into another when hurrying to the apothecary. In this latter monologue, too, when all his thoughts must have been of Juliet and their star-crossed fates, and love-devouring Death, he is able to picture for us the apothecary and his shop with a wealth of detail that says more for Shakespeare's painstaking and memory than for his insight into character. The fault, however, is not so grave as it would be if Romeo were a different kind of man; but like Hamlet he is always ready to unpack his heart with words, and if they are not the best words sometimes, sometimes even very inappropriate words, it only shows that in his first tragedy Shakespeare was not the master of his art that he afterwards became.

In the churchyard scene of the fifth act Romeo's likeness to Hamlet comes into clearest light.

Hamlet says to Laertes:

> " I pr'ythee, take thy fingers from my throat;
> For though I am not splenitive and rash
> Yet have I something in me dangerous
> Which let thy wisdom fear."

In precisely the same temper, Romeo says to Paris:

> " Good, gentle youth, tempt not a desperate man;
> Fly hence and leave me; think upon these gone,
> Let them affright thee."

This magnanimity is so rare that its existence would almost of itself be sufficient to establish a close relationship between Romeo and Hamlet. Romeo's last speech, too, is characteristic of Hamlet: on the very threshold of death he generalizes:

> " How oft when men are at the point of death,
> Have they been merry? which their keepers call
> A lightening before death."

There is in Romeo, too, that peculiar mixture of pensive sadness and loving sympathy which is the very vesture of Hamlet's soul; he says to " Noble County Paris ":

> " O, give me thy hand,
> One writ with me in sour misfortune's book."

And finally Shakespeare's supreme lyrical gift is used by Romeo as unconstrainedly as by Hamlet himself. The beauty in the last soliloquy is of passion rather than of intellect, but in sheer triumphant beauty some lines of it have never been surpassed:

> "Here, here will I remain
> With worms that are thy chambermaids; O, here
> Will I set up my everlasting rest
> And shake the yoke of inauspicious stars
> From this world-wearied flesh."

The whole soliloquy and especially the superb epithet "world-wearied" are at least as suitable to Hamlet as to Romeo. Passion, it is true, is more accentuated in Romeo, just as there is greater irresolution combined with intenser self-consciousness in Hamlet, yet all the qualities of the youthful lover are to be found in the student-prince. Hamlet is evidently the later finished picture of which Romeo was merely the charming sketch.

Hamlet says he is revengeful and ambitious, although he is nothing of the kind, and in much the same way Romeo says:

> "I'll be a candle-holder and look on,"

whereas he plays the chief part and a very active part in the drama. If he were more of a "candle-holder" and onlooker, he would more resemble Hamlet. Then too, though he generalizes, he does not search the darkness with aching eyeballs as Hamlet does; the problems of life do not as yet lie heavy on his soul; he is too young to have felt their mystery and terror; he is only just within the shadow of that melancholy which to Hamlet discolours the world.

Seven or eight years after writing "Romeo and Juliet," Shakespeare growing conscious of these changes in his own temperament embodied them in another character, the melancholy "Jaques" in

13

" As You Like It." Everyone knows that Jaques is Shakespeare's creation; he is not to be found in Lodge's " Rosalynde," whence Shakespeare took the story and most of the characters of his play. Jaques is only sketched in with light strokes, but all his traits are peculiarly Hamlet's traits. For Jaques is a melancholy student of life as Hamlet is, with lightning-quick intelligence and heavy heart, and these are the Hamlet qualities which were not brought into prominence in the youthful Romeo. Passages taken at haphazard will suffice to establish my contention. " Motley's the only wear," says Jaques, as if longing to assume the cap and bells, and Hamlet plays the fool's part with little better reason. Jaques exclaims:

> " Give me leave
> To speak my mind, and I will through and through
> Cleanse the foul body of the infected world,
> If they will patiently receive my medicine."

And Hamlet cries:

> " The Time is out of joint; O cursèd spite
> That ever I was born to set it right."

The famous speech of Jaques, " All the world's a stage," might have been said by Hamlet, indeed belongs of right to the person who gave the exquisite counsel to the players. Jaques' confession of melancholy, too, both in manner and matter is characteristic of Hamlet. How often Shakespeare must have thought it over before he was able to bring the peculiar nature of his own malady into such relief:

" I have neither the scholar's melancholy, which is emulation; nor the musician's, which is fantastical; nor the courtier's, which is proud; nor the soldier's,

which is ambitious; nor the lawyer's, which is politic;
nor the lady's, which is nice; nor the lover's, which
is all these; but it is a melancholy of mine own,
compounded of many simples, extracted from many
objects, and indeed, the sundry contemplation of
my travels; which, by often rumination, wraps me
in a most humourous sadness."

This "humourous sadness," the child of contemplation, was indeed Shakespeare's most constant
mood. Jaques, too, loves solitude and the country
as Hamlet loved them—and above all the last trait
recorded of Jaques, his eagerness to see the reformed
Duke and learn from the convert, is a perfect example of that intellectual curiosity which is one of
Hamlet's most attaching characteristics. Yet another trait is attributed to Jaques, which we must on
no account forget. The Duke accuses him of lewdness though lewdness seems out of place in Jaques'
character, and is certainly not shown in the course
of the action. If we combine the characters of
Romeo, the poet-lover, and Jaques, the pensive-sad
philosopher, we have almost the complete Hamlet.

It is conceivable that even a fair-minded reader
of the plays will admit all I have urged about the
likeness of Romeo and Jaques to Hamlet without
concluding that these preliminary studies, so to
speak, for the great portrait render it at all certain
that the masterpiece of portraiture is a likeness of
Shakespeare himself. The impartial critic will
probably say, "You have raised a suspicion in my
mind; a strong suspicion it may be, but still a suspicion that is far from certitude." Fortunately the
evidence still to be offered is a thousand times more
convincing than any inferences that can properly
be drawn from Romeo or from Jaques, or even from
both together.

CHAPTER II

THERE is a later drama of Shakespeare's, a drama which comes between " Othello " and " Lear," and belongs, therefore, to the topmost height of the poet's achievement, whose principal character is Hamlet, Hamlet over again, with every peculiarity and every fault; a Hamlet, too, entangled in an action which is utterly unsuited to his nature. Surely if this statement can be proved, it will be admitted by all competent judges that the identity of Hamlet and his creator has been established. For Shakespeare must have painted this second Hamlet unconsciously. Think of it. In totally new circumstances the poet speaks with Hamlet's voice in Hamlet's words. The only possible explanation is that he is speaking from his own heart, and for that reason is unaware of the mistake. The drama I refer to is " Macbeth."

No one, so far as I know, has yet thought of showing that there is any likeness between the character of Hamlet and that of Macbeth, much less identity; nevertheless, it seems to me easy to prove that Macbeth, " the rugged Macbeth," as Hazlitt and Brandes call him, is merely our gentle, irresolute, humanist, philosopher Hamlet masquerading in gallygaskins as a Scottish thane.

Let us take the first appearance of Macbeth, and we are forced to remark at once that he acts and speaks exactly as Hamlet in like circumstances would act and speak. The honest but slow Banquo

16

is amazed when Macbeth starts and seems to fear
the fair promises of the witches; he does not see
what the nimble Hamlet-intellect has seen in a flash
—the dread means by which alone the promises can
be brought to fulfilment. As soon as Macbeth is
hailed " Thane of Cawdor " Banquo warns him,
but Macbeth, in spite of the presence of others,
falls at once, as Hamlet surely would have fallen,
into a soliloquy: a thing, considering the circumstances, most false to general human nature, for
what he says must excite Banquo's suspicion, and
is only true to the Hamlet-mind, that in and out of
season loses itself in meditation. The soliloquy,
too, is startlingly characteristic of Hamlet. After
giving expression to the merely natural uplifting
of his hope, Macbeth begins to weigh the for and
against like a student-thinker:

" This supernatural soliciting
  Cannot be ill; cannot be good; if ill,
  Why hath it given me earnest of success,
  Commencing in a truth? I am thane of Cawdor:
  If good, why do I yield to that suggestion
  Whose horrid image . . . . .
              . . . . . function
  Is smothered in surmise and nothing is
  But what is not,——"

When Banquo draws attention to him as " rapt,"
Macbeth still goes on talking to himself, for at
length he has found arguments against action:

" If chance will have me King, why chance may crown
    me,
  Without my stir,"—

all in the true Hamlet vein. At the end of the
17

act, Macbeth when excusing himself to his companions becomes the student of Wittenberg in proper person. The courteous kindliness of the words is almost as characteristic as the bookish illustration:

> " Kind gentlemen, your pains
> Are registered where every day I turn
> The leaf to read them."

If this is not Hamlet's very tone, manner and phrase, then individuality of nature has no peculiar voice.

I have laid such stress upon this, the first scene in which Macbeth appears, because the first appearance is by far the most important for the purpose of establishing the main outlines of a character; first impressions in a drama being exceedingly difficult to modify and almost impossible to change.

Macbeth, however, acts Hamlet from one end of the play to the other; and Lady Macbeth's first appearance (a personage almost as important to the drama as Macbeth himself) is used by Shakespeare to confirm this view of Macbeth's character. After reading her husband's letter almost her first words are:

> " Yet do I fear thy nature.
> It is too full o' the milk of human kindness
> To catch the nearest way."

What is this but a more perfect expression of Hamlet's nature than Hamlet himself gives? Hamlet declares bitterly that he is " pigeon livered," and lacks " gall to make oppression bitter "; he says to Laertes, " I loved you ever," and to his mother:

"I must be cruel only to be kind,"

and she tells the King that he wept for Polonius' death. But the best phrase for his gentle-heartedness is what Lady Macbeth gives here: he is "too full o' the milk of human kindness." The words are as true of the Scottish chieftain as of the Wittenberg student; in heart they are one and the same person.

Though excited to action by his wife, Macbeth's last words in this scene are to postpone decision. "We will speak further," he says, whereupon the woman takes the lead, warns him to dissemble, and adds, "leave all the rest to me." Macbeth's doubting, irresolution, and dislike of action could hardly be more forcibly portrayed.

The seventh scene of the first act begins with another long soliloquy by Macbeth, and this soliloquy shows us not only Hamlet's irresolution and untimely love of meditation, but also the peculiar pendulum-swing of Hamlet's thought:

> "If it were done when 't is done, then 't were well
> It were done quickly: if the assassination
> Could trammel up the consequence, and catch
> With his surcease success: that but this blow
> Might be the be-all and the end-all; here,
> But here upon this bank and shoal of time
> We'd jump the life to come. . . . . ."

Is not this the same soul which also in a soliloquy questions fate?—"Whether 'tis better in the mind. . . ."

Macbeth, too, has Hamlet's peculiar and exquisite intellectual fairness—a quality, be it remarked in passing, seldom found in a ruthless murderer. He sees even the King's good points:

. . . . . " this Duncan
Hath borne his faculties so meek, hath been
So clear in his great office, that his virtues
Will plead like angels, trumpet-tongued, against
The deep damnation of his taking off."

Is it not like Hamlet to be able to condemn himself in this way beforehand? Macbeth ends this soliloquy with words which come from the inmost of Hamlet's heart:

" I have no spur
To prick the sides of my intent, but only
Vaulting ambition, which o'erleaps itself,
And falls on the other."

Hamlet, too, has no spur to prick the sides of his intent, and Hamlet, too, would be sure to see how apt ambition is to overleap itself, and so would blunt the sting of that desire. This monologue alone should have been sufficient to reveal to all critics the essential identity of Hamlet and Macbeth. Lady Macbeth, too, tells us that Macbeth left the supper table where he was entertaining the King, in order to indulge himself in this long monologue, and when he hears that his absence has excited comment, that he has been asked for even by the King, he does not attempt to excuse his strange conduct, he merely says, "We will proceed no further in this business," showing in true Hamlet fashion how resolution has been " sicklied o'er with the pale cast of thought." In fact, as his wife says to him, he lets " ' I dare not ' wait upon ' I would ' like the poor cat i' the adage." Even when whipped to action by Lady Macbeth's preternatural eagerness, he asks:

" If we should fail? "

whereupon she tells him to screw his courage to the sticking place, and describes the deed itself. Infected by her masculine resolution, Macbeth at length consents to what he calls the " terrible feat." The word " terrible " here is surely more characteristic of the humane poet-thinker than of the chieftain-murderer. Even at this crisis, too, of his fate Macbeth cannot cheat himself ; like Hamlet he is compelled to see himself as he is :

" False face must hide what the false heart doth know."

I have now considered nearly every word used by Macbeth in this first act : I have neither picked passages nor omitted anything that might make against my argument ; yet every impartial reader must acknowledge that Hamlet is far more clearly sketched in this first act of " Macbeth " than in the first act of " Hamlet." Macbeth appears in it as an irresolute dreamer, courteous, and gentle-hearted, of perfect intellectual fairness and bookish phrase ; and in especial his love of thought and dislike of action are insisted upon again and again.

In spite of the fact that the second act is one chiefly of incident, filled indeed with the murder and its discovery, Shakespeare uses Macbeth as the mouthpiece of his marvellous lyrical faculty as freely as he uses Hamlet. A greater singer even than Romeo, Hamlet is a poet by nature, and turns every possible occasion to account, charming the ear with subtle harmonies. With a father's murder to avenge, he postpones action and sings to himself of life and death and the undiscovered country in words of such magical spirit-beauty that they can be compared to nothing in the world's literature save perhaps to the last chapter of Ecclesiastes. From the beginning to the end of the drama Hamlet is a great lyric poet, and this supreme personal gift is so natural to him that it is hardly mentioned by the critics. This gift, however, is possessed by Macbeth in at least equal degree and excites just as little notice. It is credible that Shakespeare used the drama sometimes as a means of reaching the highest lyrical utterance.

Without pressing this point further let us now take up the second act of the play. Banquo and Fleance enter; Macbeth has a few words with them; they depart, and after giving a servant an order, Macbeth begins another long soliloquy. He thinks he sees a dagger before him, and immediately falls to philosophizing:

> "Come, let me clutch thee:—
> I have thee not and yet I see thee still.
> Art thou not, fatal vision, sensible
> To feeling as to sight, or art thou but
> A dagger of the mind, a false creation
> Proceeding from the heat-oppressed brain?
> I see thee yet in form as palpable
> As that which now I draw. . . . .
>
> . . . . . .
>
> Mine eyes are made the fools o' the other senses.
> Or else worth all the rest: I see thee still;
> And on thy blade and dudgeon gouts of blood
> Which was not so before.—There's no such thing."

What is all this but an illustration of Hamlet's assertion:

> "There is nothing either good or bad
> But thinking makes it so."

Just too as Hamlet swings on his mental balance, so that it is still a debated question among academic critics whether his madness was feigned

22

or real, so here Shakespeare shows us how Macbeth loses his foothold on reality and falls into the void.

The lyrical effusion that follows is not very successful, and probably on that account Macbeth breaks off abruptly:

> "Whiles I threat he lives,
> Words to the heat of deeds too cold breath gives,"

which is, of course, precisely Hamlet's complaint:

> "This is most brave;
> That I, the son of a dear father murdered,
> Prompted to my revenge by heaven and hell,
> Must, like a whore, unpack my heart with words."

After this Lady Macbeth enters, and the murder is committed, and now wrought to the highest tension Macbeth must speak from the depths of his nature with perfect sincerity. Will he exult, as the ambitious man would, at having taken successfully the longest step towards his goal? Or will he, like a prudent man, do his utmost to hide the traces of his crime, and hatch plans to cast suspicion on others? It is Lady Macbeth who plays this part; she tells Macbeth to " get some water,"

> "And wash this filthy witness from your hand,"

while he, brainsick, rehearses past fears and shows himself the sensitive poet-dreamer inclined to piety: here is the incredible scene:

> "*Lady M.* There are two lodged together.
> *Macb.* One cried, 'God bless us!' and 'Amen' the other,
> As they had seen me with these hangman's hands.

Listening their fear, I could not say ' Amen,'
When they did say ' God bless us.'
    Lady M.   Consider it not so deeply.
    Macb. But wherefore could not I pronounce ' Amen '?
I had most need of blessing, and 'Amen '
Stuck in my throat."

This religious tinge colouring the weakness of
self-pity is to be found again and again in " Hamlet "; Hamlet, too, is religious-minded; he begs
Ophelia to remember his sins in her orisons. When
he first sees his father's ghost he cries:

    " Angels and ministers of grace defend us,"

and when the ghost leaves him his word is, " I'll go
pray." This new trait, most intimate and distinctive, is therefore the most conclusive proof of the
identity of the two characters. The whole passage
in the mouth of a murderer is utterly unexpected
and out of place; no wonder Lady Macbeth exclaims:
    " These deeds must not be thought
After these ways: so, it will make us mad."

But nothing can restrain Macbeth; he gives rein
to his poetic imagination, and breaks out in an exquisite lyric, a lyric which has hardly any closer
relation to the circumstances than its truth to
Shakespeare's nature:

" Methought I heard a voice cry, ' Sleep no more!
  Macbeth does murder sleep,'—the innocent sleep:
  Sleep, that knits up the ravelled sleave of care,"

and so forth—the poet in love with his own imagin-
ings.

Again Lady Macbeth tries to bring him back to a sense of reality; tells him his thinking unbends his strength, and finally urges him to take the daggers back and

<blockquote>
" smear
The sleepy grooms with the blood."
</blockquote>

But Macbeth's nerve is gone; he is physically broken now as well as mentally o'erwrought; he cries:

<blockquote>
" I'll go no more;
I am afraid to think what I have done.
Look on't again I dare not."
</blockquote>

All this is exquisitely characteristic of the nervous student who has been screwed up to a feat beyond his strength, " a terrible feat," and who has broken down over it, but the words are altogether absurd in the mouth of an ambitious, half-barbarous chieftain.

His wife chides him as fanciful, childish—" infirm of purpose,"—she'll put the daggers back herself; but nothing can hearten Macbeth; every household noise sets his heart thumping:

<blockquote>
" Whence is that knocking?
How is't with me when every noise appals me? "
</blockquote>

His mind rocks; he even imagines he is being tortured:

<blockquote>
" What hands are here? Ha!
They pluck out my eyes."
</blockquote>

And then he swings into another incomparable lyric:

<blockquote>
" Will all great Neptune's ocean wash this blood
Clean from my hand? No, this my hand will rather
</blockquote>

The multitudinous seas incarnadine,
Making the green one red."

There is a great deal of the poet-neuropath and
very little of the murderer for ambition's sake in
this lyrical hysteria. No wonder Lady Macbeth
declares she would be ashamed " to wear a heart so
white." It is all Hamlet over again, Hamlet wrought
up to a higher pitch of intensity. And here it
should be remembered that " Macbeth " was written
three years after " Hamlet " and probably just before " Lear "; one would therefore expect a greater
intensity and a deeper pessimism in Macbeth than
in Hamlet.

The character-drawing in the next scene is necessarily slight. The discovery of the murder impels
every one save the protagonist to action, but Macbeth finds time even at the climax of excitement
to coin Hamlet-words that can never be forgotten:

" There's nothing serious in mortality; "

and the description of Duncan:

" His silver skin laced with his golden blood "

—as sugar'd sweet as any line in the sonnets, and
here completely out of place.

In these first two acts the character of Macbeth
is outlined so firmly that no after-touches can efface
the impression.

Now comes a period in the drama in which deed
follows so fast upon deed, that there is scarcely
any opportunity for characterization. To the
casual view Macbeth seems almost to change his
nature, passing from murder to murder quickly if
not easily. He not only arranges for Banquo's as-

sassination, but leaves Lady Macbeth innocent of the knowledge. The explanation of this seeming change of character is at hand. Shakespeare took the history of Macbeth from Holinshed's Chronicle, and there it is recorded that Macbeth murdered Banquo and many others, as well as Macduff's wife and children. Holinshed makes Duncan have "too much of clemencie," and Macbeth "too much of crueltie." Macbeth's actions correspond with his nature in Holinshed; but Shakespeare first made Macbeth in his own image—gentle, bookish and irresolute—and then found himself fettered by the historical fact that Macbeth murdered Banquo and the rest. He was therefore forced to explain in some way or other why his Macbeth strode from crime to crime. It must be noted as most characteristic of gentle Shakespeare that even when confronted with this difficulty he did not think of lending Macbeth any tinge of cruelty, harshness, or ambition. His Macbeth commits murder for the same reason that the timorous deer fights—out of fear.

> "To be thus is nothing;
> But to be safely thus. Our fears in Banquo
> Stick deep, and in his royalty of nature
> Reigns that which would be feared":

And again:

> "There is none but he
> Whose being I do fear": . . . .

This proves, as nothing else could prove, the all-pervading, attaching kindness of Shakespeare's nature. Again and again Lady Macbeth saves the situation and tries to shame her husband into stern resolve, but in vain; he 's "quite unmann'd in folly."

Had Macbeth been made ambitious, as the com-

mentators assume, there would have been a sufficient motive for his later actions.   But ambition is
foreign to the Shakespeare-Hamlet nature, so the
poet does not employ it.   Again and again he
returns to the explanation that the timid grow
dangerous when " frighted out of fear."   Macbeth
says:

" But let the frame of things disjoint, both the worlds
        suffer
    Ere we will eat our meal in fear, and sleep
    In the affliction of these terrible dreams
    That shake us nightly."

In passing I may remark that Hamlet, too, complains of " bad dreams."
In deep Hamlet melancholy, Macbeth now begins
to contrast his state with Duncan's:

    " After life's fitful fever he sleeps well.
    Treason has done his worst: nor steel nor poison,
    Malice domestic, foreign levy, nothing,
    Can touch him further."

Lady Macbeth begs him to sleek o'er his rugged
looks, be bright and jovial.   He promises obedience;
but soon falls into the dark mood again and predicts " a deed of dreadful note."   Naturally his wife
questions him, and he replies:

" Be innocent of the knowledge, dearest chuck,
    Till thou applaud the deed.   Come, seeling night,
    Scarf up the tender eye of pityful day,
    And with thy bloody and invisible hand
    Cancel and tear to pieces that great bond
    Which keeps me pale."

Hamlet—Macbeth

No other motive for murder is possible to Shakespeare-Macbeth but fear.

Banquo is murdered, but still Macbeth cries:

> " I am cabined, cribbed, confined, bound in
> To saucy doubts and fears."

The scene with the ghost of Banquo follows, wherein Macbeth again shows the nervous imaginative Hamlet nature. His next speech is mere reflection, and again Hamlet might have framed it:

> " the time has been
> That when the brains were out the man would die
> And there an end ": . . .

But while fear may be an adequate motive for Banquo's murder, it can hardly explain the murder of Macduff's wife and children. Shakespeare feels this, too, and therefore finds other reasons natural enough; but the first of these reasons, " his own good," is not especially characteristic of Macbeth, and the second, while perhaps characteristic, is absurdly inadequate: men don't murder out of tediousness:

> " For mine own good
> All causes shall give way: I am in blood [1]
> Stepped in so far, that, should I wade no more,
> Returning were as tedious as go o'er."

[1] It seems to me probable that Shakespeare, unable to find an adequate motive for murder, borrowed this one from " Richard III." Richard says:

> " But I am in
> So far in blood that sin will pluck on sin "—

This is an explanation following the fact rather than a cause producing it—an explanation, moreover, which may be true in the case of a fiend like Richard, but is not true of a Macbeth.

Take it all in all, this latter reason is as poor a motive for cold-blooded murder as was ever given, and Shakespeare again feels this, for he brings in the witches once more to predict safety to Macbeth and adjure him to be " bloody, bold and resolute." When they have thus screwed his courage to the sticking place as his wife did before, Macbeth resolves on Macduff's murder, but he immediately recurs to the old explanation; he does not do it for " his own good " nor because " returning is tedious "; he does it

> " That I may tell pale-hearted fear it lies,
> And sleep in spite of thunder."

It is fair to say that Shakespeare's Macbeth is so gentle-kind, that he can find no motive in himself for murder, save fear. The words Shakespeare puts into Hubert's mouth in " King John " are really his own confession:

> "Within this bosom never enter'd yet
> The dreadful motion of a murderous thought."

The murders take place and the silly scenes in England between Malcolm and Macduff follow, and then come Lady Macbeth's illness, and the characteristic end. The servant tells Macbeth of the approach of the English force, and he begins the wonderful monologue:

> "my May of life
> Is fall'n into the sere, the yellow leaf;
> And that which should accompany old age,
> As honour, love, obedience, troops of friends,
> I must not look to have; but in their stead
> Curses, not loud, but deep, mouth-honour, breath
> Which the poor heart would fain deny, and dare not."

Hamlet—Macbeth

Truly this is a strange murderer who longs for
" troops of friends," and who at the last push of
fate can find in himself kindness enough towards
others to sympathize with the " poor heart." All
this is pure Hamlet; one might better say, pure
Shakespeare.

We are next led into the field with Malcolm and
Macduff, and immediately back to the castle again.
While the women break into cries, Macbeth solilo-
quizes in the very spirit of bookish Hamlet:

> " I have almost forgot the taste of fears,
> The time has been, my senses would have cooled
> To hear a night-shriek; and my fell of hair
> Would at a dismal treatise rouse and stir
> As life were in't."

The whole passage, and especially the " dismal
treatise," recalls the Wittenberg student with a
magic of representment.

The death of the Queen is announced, and
wrings from Macbeth a speech full of despairing
pessimism, a bitterer mood than ever Hamlet
knew; a speech, moreover, that shows the student
as well as the incomparable lyric poet:

> " She should have died hereafter:
> There would have been a time for such a word.—
> To-morrow, and to-morrow, and to-morrow,
> Creeps in this petty pace from day to day,
> To the last syllable of recorded time;
> And all our yesterdays have lighted fools
> The way to dusty death. Out, out, brief candle!
> Life's but a walking shadow; a poor player,
> That struts and frets his hour upon the stage,
> And then is heard no more: it is a tale
> Told by an idiot, full of sound and fury,
> Signifying nothing."

Macbeth's philosophy, like Hamlet's, ends in utter doubt, in a passion of contempt for life, deeper than anything in Dante. The word " syllable " in this lyric outburst is as characteristic as the " dismal treatise " in the previous one, and more characteristic still of Hamlet is the likening of life to " a poor player."

The messenger tells Macbeth that Birnam Wood has begun to move, and he sees that the witches have cheated him. He can only say, as Hamlet might have said:

> " I 'gin to be aweary of the sun,
> And wish the estate o' the world were now undone.—
> Ring the alarum bell! Blow wind! Come, wrack!
> At least we'll die with harness on our back."

And later he cries:

> " They have tied me to a stake; I cannot fly,
> But bear-like I must fight the course."

This seems to me intensely characteristic of Hamlet; the brutal side of action was never more contemptuously described, and Macbeth's next soliloquy makes the identity apparent to every one; it is in the true thinker-sceptic vein:

> " Why should I play the Roman [1] fool and die
> On mine own sword? "

Macbeth then meets Macduff, and there follows

---

[1] About the year 1600 Shakespeare seems to have steeped himself in Plutarch. For the next five or six years, whenever he thinks of suicide, the Roman way of looking at it occurs to him. Having made up his mind to kill himself, Laertes cries:

> " I am more an antique Roman than a Dane,"

and, in like case, Cleopatra talks of dying " after the high Roman fashion."

the confession of pity and remorse, which must be compared to the gentle-kindness with which Hamlet treats Laertes and Romeo treats Paris. Macbeth says to Macduff:

> " Of all men else I have avoided thee:
>   But get thee back, my soul is too much charged
>   With blood of thine already."

Then comes the " something desperate " in him that Hamlet boasted of—and the end.

Here we have every characteristic of Hamlet without exception. The crying difference of situation only brings out the essential identity of the two characters. The two portraits are of the same person and finished to the finger-tips. The slight shades of difference between Macbeth and Hamlet only strengthen our contention that both are portraits of the poet; for the differences are manifestly changes in the same character, and changes due merely to age. Just as Romeo is younger than Hamlet, showing passion where Hamlet shows thought, so Macbeth is older than Hamlet; in Macbeth the melancholy has grown deeper, the tone more pessimistic, and the heart gentler.[1] I venture, therefore, to as-

---

[1] Immediately after the publication of these first two essays, Sir Henry Irving seized the opportunity and lectured before a distinguished audience on the character of Macbeth. He gave it as his opinion that " Shakespeare has presented Macbeth as one of the most blood-thirsty, most hypocritical villains in his long gallery of men, instinct with the virtues and vices of their kind (*sic*)." Sir Henry Irving also took the occasion to praise the simile of pity:

> " And pity, like a naked new-born babe,
>   Striding the blast."

This ridiculous fustian seemed to him " very beautiful." All this was perfectly gratuitous: no one needed to be informed that a man might have merit as an actor and yet be without any understanding of psychology or any taste in letters.

sert that the portrait we find in Romeo and Jaques first, and then in Hamlet, and afterwards in Macbeth, is the portrait of Shakespeare himself, and we can trace his personal development through these three stages.

CHAPTER III

IT may be well to add here a couple of portraits of Shakespeare in later life in order to establish beyond question the chief features of his character. With this purpose in mind I shall take a portrait that is a mere sketch of him, Duke Vincentio in "Measure for Measure," and a portrait that is minutely finished and perfect, though consciously idealized, Posthumus, in "Cymbeline." And the reason I take this careless, wavering sketch, and contrast it with a highly-finished portrait, is that, though the sketch is here and there hardly recognizable, the outline being all too thin and hesitating, yet now and then a characteristic trait is over-emphasized, as we should expect in careless work. And this sketch in lines now faint, now all too heavy, is curiously convincing when put side by side with a careful and elaborate portrait in which the same traits are reproduced, but harmoniously, and with a perfect sense of the relative value of each feature. No critic, so far as I am aware, not Hazlitt, not Brandes, not even Coleridge, has yet thought of identifying either Duke Vincentio or Posthumus with Hamlet, much less with Shakespeare himself. The two plays are very unlike each other in tone and temper; "Measure for Measure" being a sort of tract for the times, while "Cymbeline" is a purely romantic drama. Moreover, "Measure for Measure" was probably written a couple of years after

"Hamlet," towards the end of 1603, while "Cymbeline" belongs to the last period of the poet's activity, and could hardly have been completed before 1610 or 1611. The dissimilarity of the plays only accentuates the likeness of the two protagonists.

"Measure for Measure" is one of the best examples of Shakespeare's contempt for stagecraft. Not only is the mechanism of the play, as we shall see later, astonishingly slipshod, but the ostensible purpose of the play, which is to make the laws respected in Vienna, is not only not attained, but seems at the end to be rather despised than forgotten. This indifference to logical consistency is characteristic of Shakespeare; Hamlet speaks of "the undiscovered country from whose bourne no traveller returns" just after he has been talking with his dead father; the poetic dreamer cannot take the trouble to tie up the loose ends of a story. The real purpose of "Measure for Measure," which is the confusion of the pretended ascetic Angelo, is fulfilled, and that is sufficient for the thinker, who has thus shown what "our seemers be." It is no less characteristic of Shakespeare that Duke Vincentio, his *alter ego*, should order another to punish loose livers—a task which his kindly nature found too disagreeable. But, leaving these general considerations, let us come to the first scene of the first act: the second long speech of the Duke should have awakened the suspicion that Vincentio is but another mask for Shakespeare. The whole speech proclaims the poet; the Duke begins:

Angelo

There is a kind of character in thy life:"

Hamlet says to Rosencrantz and Guildenstern in what is supposed to be prose:

Duke Vincentio—Posthumus

"There is a kind of confession in your looks."

A little later the line:

"Spirits are not finely touched
But to fine issues,"

is so characteristic of Hamlet-Shakespeare that it
should have put every reader on the track.

The speeches of the Duke in the fourth scene of
the first act are also characteristic of Shakespeare.
But the four lines,

"My holy sir, none better knows than you
How I have ever loved the life removed,
And held in idle price to haunt assemblies,
Where youth and cost and witless bravery keep,"

are to me an intimate, personal confession; a fuller
rendering indeed of Hamlet's "Man delights not
me; no, nor woman neither." In any case it will be
admitted that a dislike of assemblies and cost and
witless bravery is peculiar in a reigning monarch, so
peculiar indeed that it reminds me of the exiled Duke
in "As You Like It," or of Duke Prospero in "The
Tempest" (two other incarnations of Shakespeare),
rather than of any one in real life. A love of solitude; a keen contempt for shows and the "witless
bravery" of court-life were, as we shall see, characteristics of Shakespeare from youth to old age.

In the first scene of the third act the Duke as a
friar speaks to the condemned Claudio. He argues
as Hamlet would argue, but with, I think, a more
convinced hopelessness. The deepening scepticism
would of itself force us to place "Measure for Measure" a little later than "Hamlet":

37

The Man Shakespeare

> " Reason thus with life:—
> If I do lose thee, I do lose a thing
> That none but fools would keep; a breath thou art,
>
> .   .   .   .   .
>
>   The best of rest is sleep,
> And that thou oft provok'st, yet grossly fear'st
> Thy death which is no more. Thou'rt not thyself;
> For thou exist'st on many a thousand grains
> That issue out of dust. Happy thou art not;
> For what thou hast not, still thou striv'st to get,
> And what thou hast, forgett'st.
>
> .   .   .   .   .
>
>   What's in this,
> That bears the name of life? Yet in this life
> Lie hid more thousand deaths; yet death we fear,
> That makes these odds all even."

That this scepticism of Vincentio is Shakespeare's scepticism appears from the fact that the whole speech is worse than out of place when addressed to a person under sentence of death. Were we to take it seriously, it would show the Duke to be curiously callous to the sufferings of the condemned Claudio; but callous the Duke is not, he is merely a pensive poet-philosopher talking in order to lighten his own heart. Claudio makes unconscious fun of the Duke's argument:

> " To sue to live, I find I seek to die,
> And seeking death, find life: let it come on."

This scepticism of Shakespeare which shows itself out of place in Angelo and again most naturally in Claudio's famous speech, is one of the salient traits of his character which is altogether over-emphasized in this play. It is a trait, moreover, which finds expression in almost everything he wrote. Like nearly all the great spirits of the Renaissance, Shakespeare was perpetually occupied with the heavy problems of man's life and man's destiny. Was there any meaning or purpose in life, any result of the striving? was Death to be feared or a Hereafter to be desired?—incessantly he beat straining wings in the void. But even in early manhood he never sought to deceive himself. His Richard II. had sounded the shallow vanity of man's desires, the futility of man's hopes; he knew that man

" With nothing shall be pleased, till he be eased
  With being nothing."

And this sad knowledge darkened all Shakespeare's later thinking. Naturally, when youth passed from him and disillusionment put an end to dreaming, his melancholy deepened, his sadness became despairing; we can see the shadows thickening round him into night. Brutus takes an " everlasting farewell " of his friend, and goes willingly to his rest. Hamlet dreads " the undiscovered country "; but unsentient death is to him " a consummation devoutly to be wished." Vincentio's mood is half-contemptuous, but the melancholy persists; death is no " more than sleep," he says, and life a series of deceptions; while Claudio in this same play shudders away from death as from annihilation, or worse, in words which one cannot help regarding as Shakespeare's:

" *Claud.* Ay, but to die, and go we know not where;
  To lie in cold obstruction and to rot. . . ."

A little later and Macbeth's soul cries to us from the outer darkness: " there's nothing serious in mortality "; life's

The Man Shakespeare

" a tale
Told by an idiot, full of sound and fury,
Signifying nothing."

And from this despairing gloom come Lear's shrieks
of pain and pitiful ravings, and in the heavy inter
vals the gibberings of the fool. Even when the
calmer mood of age came upon Shakespeare and
took away the bitterness, he never recanted; Posthumus speaks of life and death in almost the words
used by Vincentio, and Prospero has nothing to add
save that " our little life is rounded with a sleep."

It is noteworthy that Shakespeare always gives
these philosophic questionings to those characters
whom I regard as his impersonations,[1] and when he
breaks this rule, he breaks it in favour of some
Claudio who is not a character at all, but the mere
mouthpiece of one of his moods.

I now come to a point in the drama which at once
demands and defies explanation. In the first scene
of the third act the Duke, after listening to the terrible discussion between Isabella and Claudio, first of
all tells Claudio that " Angelo had never the purpose to corrupt " Isabella, and then assures Claudio

---

[1] One of my correspondents, Mr. Theodore Watts-Dunton,
has been kind enough to send me an article contributed to
" Colbourn's Magazine " in 1873, in which he declares that
" Shakespeare seems to have kept a sort of Hamlet note-
book, full of Hamlet thoughts, of which ' To be or not to be '
may be taken as the type. These he was burdened with.
These did he cram into Hamlet as far as he could, and then
he tossed the others indiscriminately into other plays, tragedies and histories, perfectly regardless of the character who
uttered them." Though Mr. Watts-Dunton sees that some of
these " Hamlet thoughts " are to be found in Macbeth and
Prospero and Claudio, he evidently lacks the key to Shakespeare's personality, or he would never have said that Shakespeare tossed these reflections "indiscriminately into other
plays." Nevertheless the statement itself is interesting, and
deserves more notice than has been accorded to it.

that to-morrow he must die. The explanation of
these two falsehoods would be far to seek, unless we
take it that they were invented simply in order to
prolong our interest in the drama. But this assumption, though probable, does not increase our sympathy with the protagonist—the lies seem to be too
carelessly uttered to be even characteristic—nor yet
our admiration of the structure of a play that needs
to be supported by such flimsy buttresses. Still this
very carelessness of fact, as I have said, is Shakespearean; the philosophic dreamer paid little attention to the mere incidents of the story.

The talk between the Duke and Isabella follows.
The form of the Duke's speech, with its touch of
euphuistic conceit, is one which Hamlet-Shakespeare
affects:

" The hand that hath made you fair hath made you
good: the goodness that is cheap in beauty makes
beauty brief in goodness; but grace, being the soul of
your complexion, shall keep the body of it ever fair."

This Duke plays philosopher, too, in and out of
season as Hamlet did: he says to Isabella:

"Virtue is bold, and goodness never fearful,"

generalizing his praise even to a woman.

Again, when Pompey is arrested, he passes from
the individual to the general, exclaiming:

" That we were all as some would seem to be,
Free from our faults, as from faults seeming free! "

Then follows the interesting talk with Lucio, who
awakens the slightly pompous Duke to natural life
with his contempt. When Lucio tells the Duke, who

is disguised as a friar, that he (the Duke) was a
notorious loose-liver—" he had some feeling of the
sport; he knew the service "—the Duke merely de-
nies the soft impeachment; but when Lucio tells him
that the Duke is not wise, but " a very superficial,
ignorant, unweighing fellow," the Duke bursts out,
" either this is envy in you, folly, or mistaking:
. . . Let him but be testimonied in his own bring-
ings-forth, and he shall appear to the envious a
scholar, a statesman, and a soldier," which recalls
Hamlet's " Friends, scholars, and soldiers," and
Ophelia's praise of Hamlet as " courtier, soldier,
scholar." Lucio goes off, and the Duke " moralizes "
the incident in Hamlet's very accent:

" No might nor greatness in mortality
   Can censure 'scape; backwounding calumny
   The whitest virtue strikes. What king so strong
   Can tie the gall up in the slanderous tongue? "

Hamlet says to Ophelia:

" Be thou as chaste as ice, as pure as snow, thou shalt
not escape calumny."

And Laertes says that " virtue itself " cannot escape
calumny.

The reflection is manifestly Shakespeare's own,
and here the form, too, is characteristic. It may be
as well to recall now that Shakespeare himself was
calumniated in his lifetime; the fact is admitted in
Sonnet 36, where he fears his " guilt " will " shame "
his friend.

In his talk with Escalus the Duke's speech becomes
almost obscure from excessive condensation of
thought—a habit which grew upon Shakespeare.

Duke Vincentio—Posthumus

Escalus asks:

" What news abroad in the world? "

The Duke answers:

" None, but that there is so great a fever on goodness, that the dissolution of it must cure it: novelty
is only in request. . . . There is scarce truth enough
alive to make societies secure, but security enough to
make fellowships accursed."

Escalus then tells us of the Duke's temperament
in words which would fit Hamlet perfectly; for,
curiously enough, they furnish us with the best description of Shakespeare's melancholy:

" Rather rejoicing to see another merry, than merry
at anything which professed to make him rejoice."

And, lastly, the curious rhymed soliloquy of Vincentio which closes this third act, must be compared
with the epilogue to " The Tempest ":

> " He who the sword of Heaven will bear
> Should be as holy as severe;
> Pattern in himself to know,
> Grace to stand and virtue go;
>
> Shame to him whose cruel striking
> Kills for faults of his own liking!
> Twice treble shame on Angelo,
> To weed my vice and let his grow! "

In the fifth act the Duke, freed from making plots
and plans, speaks without constraint and reveals his
nature ingenuously. He uses words to Angelo that
recall the sonnets:

"O, your desert speaks loud; and I should wrong it,
To lock it in the wards of covered bosom,
When it deserves, with characters of brass,
A forted residence 'gainst the tooth of time
And razure of oblivion." [1]

Again, the Duke argues in gentle Shakespeare's
fashion for Angelo and against Isabella:

"If he had so offended,
He would have weighed thy brother by himself
And not have cut him off."

It seems impossible for Shakespeare to believe
that the sinner can punish sin. It reminds one of
the sacred "He that is without sin among you let
him first cast a stone." The detections and for-
givings of the last act follow.

It will be admitted, I think, on all hands that
Duke Vincentio speaks throughout the play with
Shakespeare's voice. From the point of view of
literary art his character is very far from being as
complex or as deeply realized as that of Hamlet
or Macbeth, or even as that of Romeo or of Jaques,
and yet one other trait besides that of sceptical
brooding is so over-accentuated that it can never
be forgotten. In the last scene the Duke orders
Barnardine to the block and the next moment re-
spites him; he condemns

"An Angelo for Claudio; death for death,"

then pardons Angelo, and at once begins to chat
with him in kindly intimacy; he asserts that he
cannot forgive Lucio, Lucio who has traduced him,

[1] Cf. Sonnet 122 with its "full character'd" and "razed
oblivion."

shall be whipped and hanged, and in the same breath he remits the heavy penalty. Truly he is " an unhurtful opposite " [1] whose anger has no steadfastness; but the gentle forgivingness of disposition that is so marked in Vincentio is a trait we found emphasized in Romeo, and again in Hamlet and again in Macbeth. It is, indeed, one of the most permanent characteristics of Shakespeare. From the beginning to the end of the play, Duke Vincentio is weakly-kind in act and swayed by fitful impulses; his assumed austerity of conduct is the thin varnish of vanity that will not take on such soft material. The Hamlet weakness is so exaggerated in him, and so unmotived, that I am inclined to think Shakespeare was even more irresolute and indisposed to action than Hamlet himself.

In the character of Posthumus, the hero of " Cymbeline," Shakespeare has painted himself with extraordinary care; has, in fact, given us as deliberate

---

[1] The critics are at variance over this ending, and, indeed, over the whole play. Coleridge says that " our feelings of justice are grossly wounded in Angelo's escape"; for " cruelty with lust and damnable baseness cannot be forgiven." Mr. Swinburne, too, regrets the miscarriage of justice; the play to him is a tragedy, and should end tragically with the punishment of the " autotype of the huge national vice of England." Perhaps, however, Puritan hypocrisy was not so widespread or so powerful in the time of Shakespeare as it is nowadays; perhaps, too, Shakespeare was not so good a hater as Mr. Swinburne, nor so strenuous a moralist as Coleridge was, at least in theory. In any case it is evident that Shakespeare found it harder to forgive Lucio, who had hurt his vanity, than Angelo, who pushed lust to outrage and murder, which strange, yet characteristic, fact I leave to the mercy of future commentators. Mr. Sidney Lee regards " Measure for Measure " as " one of Shakespeare's greatest plays." Coleridge, however, thought it " a hateful work "; it is also a poor work, badly constructed, and for the most part carelessly written. In essence it is a mere tract against Puritanism, and in form a sort of Arabian Nights' Entertainment in which the hero plays the part of Haroun-al-Raschid.

and almost as complete a picture of himself as he did in Hamlet. Unluckily his hand had grown weaker in the ten years' interval, and he gave such loose rein to his idealizing habit that the portrait is neither so veracious nor so lifelike. The explanation of all this will be given later; it is enough for the moment to state that as Posthumus is perhaps the completest portrait of him that we have after his mental shipwreck, we must note the traits of it carefully, and see what manner of man Shakespeare took himself to be towards the end of his career.

It is difficult to understand how the commentators have been able to read " Cymbeline " without seeing the likeness between Posthumus and Hamlet. The wager which is the theme of the play may have hindered them a little, but as they found it easy to excuse its coarseness by attributing lewdness to the time, there seems to have been no reason for not recognizing Posthumus. Posthumus is simply a staider Hamlet considerably idealized. I am not at all sure that the subject of the play was void of offence in the time of Elizabeth; all finer spirits must even then have found it puerile and coarse. What would Spenser have said about it? Shakespeare used the wager because of the opportunities it gave him of painting himself and an ideal woman. His view of it is just indicated; Iachimo says:

" I make my wager rather against your confidence than her reputation: and, to bar your offence herein too, I durst attempt it against any lady in the world."

But in spite of the fact that Iachimo makes his insult general, Posthumus warns him that:

" If she remain unseduced . . . for your ill opinion,

and the assault you have made to her chastity, you shall
answer me with your sword."

From this it appears that the bet was distasteful to
Posthumus; it is not so offenceful to him as it should
have been according to our modern temper, but this
shortcoming, an unconscious shortcoming, is the
only fault which Shakespeare will allow in his hero.
In the first scene of the first act Posthumus is praised
as men never praise the absent without a personal
motive; the First Gentleman says of him:

> " I do not think
> So fair an outward and such stuff within
> Endows a man but he."

The Second Gentleman replies:

> " You speak him far; "

and the First Gentleman continues:

> "I do extend him, sir, within himself;
> Crush him together, rather than unfold
> His measure duly."

And as if this were not enough, this gentleman-
eulogist goes on to tell us that Posthumus has sucked
in " all the learnings " of his time " as we do air,"
and further:

> "He lived in court—
> Which rare it is to do—most praised, most loved;
> A sample to the young'st, to the more mature
> A glass that feated them; and to the graver
> A child that guided dotards."

This gross praise is ridiculously unnatural, and
outrages our knowledge of life; men are much more

47

apt to criticize than to praise the absent; but it shows a prepossession on Shakespeare's part in favour of Posthumus which can only be explained by the fact that in Posthumus he was depicting himself. Every word is significant to us, for Shakespeare evidently tells us here what he thought about himself, or rather what he wished to think, towards the end of his life. It is impossible to believe that he was "most praised, most loved"; men do not love or praise their superiors in looks, or intellect.

The first words which Posthumus in this same scene addresses to Imogen, shows the gentle Shakespeare nature:

> "O lady, weep no more, lest I give cause
> To be suspected of more tenderness
> Than doth become a man."

And when Imogen gives him the ring and tells him to wear it till he woos another wife, he talks to her exactly as Romeo would have talked:

> "How! how! another?—
> You gentle gods, give me but this I have,
> And sear up my embracements from a next
> With bonds of death!   [*Putting on the ring.*
> Remain, remain thou here
> While sense can keep it on."

And he concludes as self-depreciating Hamlet would have concluded:

> "And sweetest, fairest,
> As I my poor self did exchange for you,
> To your so infinite loss, so in our trifles
> I still win of you; for my sake wear this:
> It is a manacle of love; I'll place it
> Upon this fairest prisoner.
> [*Putting a bracelet on her arm.*]"

In his fight with Cloten he is depicted as a rare swordsman of wonderful magnanimity. Pisanio says:

> " My master rather played than fought,
> And had no help of anger."

I call this gentle kindness which Posthumus displays, the birthmark of Shakespeare; he had " no help of anger." As the play goes on we find Shakespeare's other peculiarities, or Hamlet's. Iachimo represents Posthumus as " merry," " gamesome," " the Briton reveller "; but curiously enough Imogen answers as Ophelia might have answered about Hamlet:

> " When he was here,
> He did incline to sadness; and ofttimes
> Not knowing why."

This uncaused melancholy that distinguishes Romeo, Jaques, Hamlet, Macbeth, and Vincentio is not more characteristic of the Hamlet-Shakespeare nature than the way Posthumus behaves when Iachimo tries to make him believe that he has won the wager. Posthumus is convinced almost at once; jumps to the conclusion, indeed, with the heedless rapidity of the naïve, sensitive, quick-thinking man who has cultivated his emotions and thoughts by writing in solitude, and not the suspicions and distrust of others which are developed in the market-place. One is reminded of Goethe's famous couplet:

> "Es bildet ein Talent sich in der Stille,
> Sich ein Charakter in dem Strom der Welt."

Posthumus is all in fitful extremes; not satisfied with believing the lie, he gives Iachimo Imogen's ring as well, and bursts into a diatribe:

> "Let there be no honour
Where there's beauty; truth, where semblance; love,
Where there's another man,"

and so forth. Even Philario, who has no stake in
the matter, is infinitely harder to convince:

> "Have patience, sir,
And take your ring again; 'tis not yet won:
It may be probable she lost it."

Then this "unstable opposite," Posthumus, demands
his ring back again, but as soon as Iachimo swears
that he had the bracelet from her arm, Posthumus
swings round again to belief from sheer rapidity of
thought. Again Philario will not be convinced. He
says:

> "Sir, be patient,
This is not strong enough to be believed
Of one persuaded well of—"

But Posthumus will not await the proof for which
he has asked. He is convinced upon suspicion, as
Othello was, and the very nimbleness of his Hamlet-
intellect, seeing that probabilities are against him,
entangles him in the snare. Even his servant
Pisanio will not believe in Imogen's guilt though
his master assures him of it. Shakespeare does not
notice this peculiar imprudent haste of his hero, as
he notices, for example, the hasty speech of Hotspur
by letting Harry of England imitate it, simply because the quick-thinking was his own; while the hurried stuttering speech was foreign to him. Posthumus goes on to rave against women as Hamlet
did; as all men do who do not understand them:

> "For even to vice
They are not constant, but are changing still."

And Posthumus betrays as clearly as ever Hamlet
did that he is merely Shakespeare masquerading:

> " I'll write against them,
> Detest them, curse them—yet 'tis greater skill
> In a true hate, to pray they have their will:
> The very devils cannot plague them better."

" Write against them " indeed! This is the same
threat which Shakespeare uses against his dark mistress in Sonnet 140, and every one will admit that
it is more in the character of the poet and man of
letters than in that of the warrior son-in-law of a
half-barbarous king. The last line here, because it
is a little superfluous, a little emphatic, seems to me
likely to have a personal application. When Shakespeare's mistress had her will, did she fall to misery,
I wonder?

I may be allowed to notice here how intensely
characteristic all this play is of Shakespeare. In
the third scene of the third act, life in the country
is contrasted to its advantage with life at Court;
and then gold is treated as dirt by the princely
brothers—both these, the love of country life, and
the contempt of gold, are, as we shall see later,
abiding peculiarities of Shakespeare.

When we come to Posthumus again almost at the
end of the play we find that his anger with Imogen
has burned itself out. He is angry now with Pisanio
for having executed his order and murdered her; he
should have " saved the noble Imogen to repent."
Surely the poet Shakespeare and not the outraged
lover speaks in this epithet, " noble."

Posthumus describes the battle in which he took
so gallant a part in Shakespeare's usual manner.
He falls into rhyme; he shows the cheap modesty of

the conventional hero; he tells of what others did,
and nothing of his own feats; Belarius and the two
striplings, he says:

" With their own nobleness . . . gilded pale looks."

Unfortunately one is reminded of the exquisite sonnet line:

" Gilding pale streams with heavenly alchemy."

" Gild " is one of Shakespeare's favourite words;
he uses it very often, sometimes indeed as in this
case, ineffectively.

But the scene which reveals the character of Posthumus beyond all doubt is the prison scene in the
fifth act. His soliloquy which begins:

" Most welcome, bondage, for thou art a way,
   I think, to liberty "—

is all pure Shakespeare. When he determines to
give up life, he says:

"O Imogen!
I'll speak to thee in silence,"

and Hamlet at his death comes to the self-same
word:

" The rest is silence."

The scene with the gaoler is from Hamlet's soul;
Posthumus jests with his keeper as Hamlet with the
gravedigger:

" So, if I prove a good repast to the spectators, the
ship pays the shot; "

and the Hamlet melancholy:

Duke Vincentio—Posthumus

"I am merrier to die than thou art to live;"

and the Hamlet riddle still unsolved:

"I tell thee, fellow, there are none want eyes to direct them the way I am going; but such as wink, and will not use them."

When the messenger comes to bring him to the king, Posthumus cries:

"Thou bringest good news, I am called to be made free,"

for there are "no bolts for the dead."

Those who wish to see how Shakespeare's mind worked will compare Posthumus' speech to Iachimo, when he has learned the truth, with Othello's words when he is convinced of his own fatal error and of Desdemona's chastity. The two speeches are twins; though the persons uttering them should be of totally different characters. The explanation of this astounding similarity will be given when we come to "Othello."

It is characteristic of Posthumus that he should strike Imogen in her page's dress, not recognizing her; he is ever too quick—a mere creature of impulse. More characteristic still is the way he forgives Iachimo, just as Vincentio forgave Angelo:

"Kneel not to me:
The power that I have on you, is to spare you,
The malice towards you, to forgive you. Live
And deal with others better."

In judging his fellow-men this is Shakespeare's harshest word. Posthumus, then, is presented to us

in the beginning of the play as perfect, a model to
young and old, of irreproachable virtue and of all
wonderful qualities. In the course of the play, however, he shows himself very nimble-witted, credulous,
and impulsive, quick to anger and quicker still to
forgive; with thoughts all turned to sadness and to
musing; a poet—ever in extremes; now hating his
own rash errors to the point of demanding the
heaviest punishment for them; now swearing that he
will revenge himself on women by writing against
them; a philosopher—he jests with his gaoler and
consoles himself with despairing speculation in the
very presence of the Arch-Fear. All these are manifestly characteristics of Hamlet, and Posthumus
possesses no others.

So far, then, from finding that Shakespeare never
revealed himself in his dramas, I have shown that he
pictured himself as the hero [1] of six plays written
at widely different times; in fact that, like Rembrandt, he painted his own portrait in all the critical
periods of life: as a sensuous youth given over to
love and poetry in Romeo; a few years later as a
melancholy onlooker at life's pageant in Jaques; in
middle age as the passionate, melancholy, aesthete-
philosopher of kindliest nature in Hamlet and Macbeth; as the fitful Duke incapable of severity in
" Measure for Measure," and finally, when standing
within the shadow, as Posthumus, an idealized yet
feebler *replica* of Hamlet.

[1] A hypercritic might contend that Jaques was not the hero
of " As You Like It "; but the objection really strengthens
my argument. Shakespeare makes of Jaques, who is merely
a secondary character without influence on the action, the
principal person in the play simply because in Jaques he satisfied his own need of self-revealing.

CHAPTER IV

SHAKESPEARE'S MEN OF ACTION: THE BASTARD, ARTHUR, AND KING RICHARD II.

IT is time now, I think, to test my theory by considering the converse of it. In any case, the attempt to see the other side, is pretty sure to make for enlightenment, and may thus justify itself. In the mirror which Shakespeare held up to human nature, we not only see Romeo, and Jaques, Hamlet, Macbeth and Posthumus; but also the leonine, frank face of the Bastard, the fiery, lean, impatient mask of Hotspur, and the cynical, bold eyes of Richard III. Even if it were admitted that Shakespeare preferred the type of the poet-philosopher, he was certainly able, one would say, to depict the man of action with extraordinary vigour and success. He himself then must have possessed a certain strength of character, certain qualities of decision and courage; he must have had, at least, " a good stroke in him," as Carlyle phrased it. This is the universal belief, a belief sanctioned by Coleridge and Goethe, and founded apparently on plain facts, and yet, I think, it is mistaken, demonstrably untrue. It might even be put more plausibly than any of its defenders has put it. One might point out that Shakespeare's men of action are nearly all to be found in the historical plays which he wrote in early manhood, while the portrait of the philosopher-poet is the favourite study of his riper years. It would then be possible to suggest that Shakespeare grew from a bold, roistering youth into a melancholy, thoughtful old age, touching both extremes of manhood in his own development. But even this comforting explanation will not stand: his earliest impersonations are all thinkers.

Let us consider, again, how preference in a writer is established. Everyone feels that Sophocles prefers Antigone to Ismene; Ismene is a mere sketch of gentle feminine weakness; while Antigone is a great portrait of the *revoltée*, the first appearance indeed in literature of the " new woman," and the place she fills in the drama, and the ideal qualities attributed to her girlhood—alike betray the personal admiration of the poet. In the same way Shakespeare's men of action are mere sketches in comparison with the intimate detailed portrait of the aesthete-philosopher-poet with his sensuous, gentle, melancholy temperament. Moreover, and this should be decisive, Shakespeare's men of action are all taken from history, or tradition, or story, and not from imagination, and their characteristics were supplied by the chroniclers and not invented by the dramatist. To see how far this is true I must examine Shakespeare's historical plays at some length. Such an examination did not form a part of my original purpose. It is very difficult, not to say impossible, to ascertain exactly how far history and verbal tradition helped Shakespeare in his historical portraits of English worthies. Jaques, for instance, is his own creation from top to toe; every word given to him therefore deserves careful study; but how much of Hotspur is Shakespeare's, and how much of the Bastard? Without pretending, however, to define exactly the sources or the limits of the master's inspiration, there are certain indications in the historical plays which throw a flood of light on

the poet's nature, and certain plain inferences from
his methods which it would be folly not to draw.

Let us begin with " King John," as one of the
easiest and most helpful to us at this stage, and remembering that Shakespeare's drama was evidently
founded on the old play entitled " The Troublesome
Raigne of King John," let us from our knowledge
of Shakespeare's character forecast what his part
in the work must have been.   A believer in the theory
I have set forth would guess at once that the strong,
manly character of the Bastard was vigorously
sketched even in the old play, and just as surely one
would attribute the gentle, feminine, pathetic character of Arthur to Shakespeare.   And this is precisely what we find: Philip Fauconbridge is excellently depicted in the old play; he is called:

" A hardy wildehead, tough and venturous,"

and he talks and acts the character to the life.   In
" The Troublesome Raigne," as in " King John,"
he is proud of his true father, the lion-hearted Richard, and careless of the stain of his illegitimate
birth; he cries:

" The world's in my debt,
There's something owing to Plantaginet.
I, marrie Sir, let me alone for game
Ile act some wonders now I know my name;
By blessed Marie Ile not sell that pride
For England's wealth and all the world beside."

Who does not feel the leaping courage and hardihood of the Bastard in these lines?   Shakespeare
seizes the spirit of the character and renders it, but
his emendations are all by way of emphasis: he does
not add a new quality; his Bastard is the Bastard

of " The Troublesome Raigne." But the gentle, pathetic character of Arthur is all Shakespeare's. In the old play Arthur is presented as a prematurely wise youth who now urges the claims of his descent and speaks boldly for his rights, and now begs his vixenish mother to

> " Wisely winke at all
> Least further harmes ensue our hasty speech."

Again, he consoles her with the same prudence:

> " Seasons will change and so our present griefe
> May change with them and all to our reliefe."

This Arthur is certainly nothing like Shakespeare's Arthur. Shakespeare, who had just lost his only son Hamnet,[1] in his twelfth year, turns Arthur from a young man into a child, and draws all the pathos possible from his weakness and suffering; Arthur's first words are of " his powerless hand," and his advice to his mother reaches the very fount of tears:

> " Good my mother, peace!
> I would that I were low laid in my grave;
> I am not worth this coil that's made for me."

When taken prisoner his thought is not of himself:

> " O, this will make my mother die with grief."

He is a woman-child in unselfish sympathy.

The whole of the exquisitely pathetic scene be-

---

[1] Some months before writing " King John " Shakespeare had visited Stratford for the first time after ten years' absence and had then perhaps learned to know and love young Hamnet.

tween Hubert and Arthur belongs, as one might
have guessed, to Shakespeare, that is, the whole
pathos of it belongs to him.

In the old play Arthur thanks Hubert for his
care, calls him " curteous keeper," and, in fact, behaves as the conventional prince. He has no words
of such affecting appeal as Shakespeare puts into
Arthur's mouth:

> " I would to heaven
> I were your son, so you would love me, Hubert."

This love and longing for love is the characteristic
of Shakespeare's Arthur; he goes on:

> " Are you sick, Hubert?   You look pale to-day.
> In sooth, I would you were a little sick,
> That I might sit all night and watch with you:
> I warrant, I love you more than you do me."

A girl could not be more tender, more anxious for
love's assurance.   In " The Troublesome Raigne,"
when Hubert tells Arthur that he has bad news for
him, tidings of " more hate than death," Arthur
faces the unknown with a man's courage; he asks:

> " What is it, man? if needes be don.
> Act it, and end it, that the paine were gon."

It might be the Bastard speaking, so hardy-reck-
less are the words.   When this Arthur pleads for his
eyesight, he does it in this way:

> " I speake not only for eyes priviledge,
> The chiefe exterior that I would enjoy:
> But for thy perill, farre beyond my paine,
> Thy sweete soules losse more than my eyes vaine lack."

Again at the end he says:

> " Delay not, Hubert, my orisons are ended,
>   Begin I pray thee, reave me of my sight."

And when Hubert relents because his " conscience bids him desist," Arthur says:

> " Hubert, if ever Arthur be in state
>   Looke for amends of this received gift."

In all this there is neither realization of character nor even sincere emotion. But Shakespeare's Arthur is a masterpiece of soul-revealing, and moves us to pity at every word:

> " Will you put out mine eyes?
>   These eyes that never did, nor never shall,
>   So much as frown on you? "

And then the child's imaginative horror of being bound:

> " For heaven's sake, Hubert, let me not be bound.
>   Nay, hear me, Hubert: drive these men away,
>   And I will sit as quiet as a lamb;
>   I will not stir, nor wince, nor speak a word."

When Hubert relents, Shakespeare's Arthur does not promise reward, he simply breathes a sigh of exquisite affection:

> " O, now you look like Hubert: all this while
>   You were disguised."

And finally, when Hubert promises never to hurt him, his words are:

> " O heaven! I thank you, Hubert."

Arthur's character we owe entirely to Shake-

speare, there is no hint of his weakness and tenderness in the original, no hint either of the pathos of
his appeal—these are the inventions of gentle Shakespeare, who has manifestly revealed his own exceed-
ing tenderness and sweetness of heart in the person
of the child Prince. Of course, there are faults in
the work; faults of affectation and word-conceit
hardly to be endured. When Hubert says he will
burn out his eyes with hot irons, Arthur replies:

> " Ah, none, but in this iron age, would do it!
>   The iron of itself, though heat red-hot,"

and so forth. . . . Nor does this passage of tinsel
stand alone. When the iron cools and Hubert says
he can revive it, Arthur replies with pinchbeck conceits:

> "And if you do you will but make it blush,
>   And glow with shame at your proceedings,"

and so forth. The faults are bad enough; but the
heavenly virtues carry them all off triumphantly.
There is no creation like Arthur in the whole realm
of poetry; he is all angelic love and gentleness, and
yet neither mawkish nor unnatural; his fears make
him real to us, and the horror of his situation allows
us to accept his exquisite pleading as possible. We
need only think of Tennyson's May Queen, or of
his unspeakable Arthur, or of Thackeray's prig
Esmond, in order to understand how difficult it is
in literature to make goodness attractive or even
credible. Yet Shakespeare's art triumphs where no
one else save Balzac and Tourgenief has achieved
even a half-success.

I cannot leave this play without noticing that

Shakespeare has shown in it a hatred of murder just
as emphatically as he has revealed his love of gentleness and pity in the creation of Arthur. In spite of
the loyalty which the English nobles avow in the
second scene of the fourth act, which is a quality
that always commends itself to Shakespeare, Pembroke is merely their mouthpiece in requesting the
King to " enfranchise Arthur." As soon as John
tells them that Arthur is dead they throw off their
allegiance and insult the monarch to his face. Even
John is startled by their indignation, and brought
as near remorse as is possible for him:

> " I repent;
> There is no sure foundation set on blood;
> No certain life achieved by others' death—"

—which reads like a reflection of Shakespeare himself. When the Bastard asks the nobles to return
to their allegiance, Salisbury finds an astonishing
phrase to express their loathing of the crime:

> " The King hath dispossess'd himself of us;
> We will not line his thin bestained cloak
> With our pure honours, *nor attend the foot*
> *That leaves the print of blood where'er it walks.*"

In all literature there is no more terrible image:
Shakespeare's horror of bloodshed has more than
Aeschylean intensity. When the dead body of
Arthur is found each of the nobles in turn expresses
his abhorrence of the deed, and all join in vowing
instant revenge. Even the Bastard calls it

> " A damned and bloody work,
> The graceless action of a heavy hand,"

and a little later the thought of the crime brings even this tough adventurer to weakness:

> " I am amazed, methinks, and lose my way
> Among the thorns and dangers of this world."

—a phrase that suits the weakness of Richard II. or Henry VI. or Shakespeare himself better than it suits the hardy Bastard. Even as a young man Shakespeare hated the cruelty of ambition and the savagery of war as much as he loved all the ceremonies of chivalry and observances of gentle courtesy.

Very similar inferences are to be drawn from a study of Shakespeare's " King Richard II.," which in some respects is his most important historical creation. Coleridge says: " I know of no character drawn by our great poet with such unequalled skill as that of Richard II." Such praise is extravagant; but it would have been true to say that up to 1593 or 1594, when Shakespeare wrote " King Richard II." he had given us no character so complex and so interesting as this Richard. Coleridge overpraised the character-drawing probably because the study of Richard's weakness and irresolution, and the pathos resulting from such helplessness, must have seemed very like an analysis of his own nature.

Let us now examine " Richard II.," and see what light it casts on Shakespeare's qualities. There was an old play of the same title, a play which is now lost, but we can form some idea of what it was like from the description in Forman's Diary. Like most of the old history-plays it ranged over twenty years of Richard's reign, whereas Shakespeare's tragedy is confined to the last year of Richard's life.

It is probable that the old play presented King
Richard as more wicked and more deceitful than
Shakespeare imagines him. We know that in the
" Confessio Amantis," Gower, the poet, cast off his
allegiance to Richard; for he cancelled the dedication of the poem to Richard, and dedicated it instead to Henry. William Langland, too, the
author of the " Vision of Piers Plowman," turned
from Richard at the last, and used his deposition as
a warning to ill-advised youth. It may be assumed,
then, that tradition pictured Richard as a vile
creature in whom weakness nourished crime. Shakespeare took his story partly from Holinshed's narrative, and partly either from the old play or from the
traditional view of Richard's character. When he
began to write the play he evidently intended to
portray Richard as even more detestable than history and tradition had presented him. In Holinshed
Richard is not accused of the murder of Gloster,
whereas Shakespeare directly charges him with it,
or rather makes Gaunt do so, and the accusation is
not denied, much less disproved. At the close of the
first act we are astonished by the revelation of
Richard's devilish heartlessness. The King hearing
that his uncle, John of Gaunt, is " grievous sick,"
cries out:

> " Now, put it, God, in his physician's mind,
> To help him to his grave immediately!
> The lining of his coffers shall make coats
> To deck our soldiers for these Irish wars.
> Come, gentlemen, let's all go visit him:
> Pray God we may make haste and come too late."

This mixture of greed and cold cruelty decked out
with blasphemous phrase is viler, I think, than anything attributed by Shakespeare to the worst of his

villains. But surely some hint of Richard's incredible vileness should have come earlier in the play, should have preceded at least his banishment of Bolingbroke, if Shakespeare had really meant to present him to us in this light.

In the first scene of the second act, when Gaunt reproves him, Richard turns on him in a rage, threatening. In the very same scene York reproves Richard for seizing Gaunt's money and land, and Richard retorts:

" Think what you will: we seize into our hands
His plate, his goods, his money, and his lands."

But when York blames him to his face and predicts that evil will befall him and leaves him, Richard in spite of this at once creates:

" Our uncle York, Lord Governor of England;
For he is just, and always loved us well."

This Richard of Shakespeare is so far, I submit, almost incomprehensible. When reproved by Gaunt and warned, Richard rages and threatens; when blamed by York much more severely, Richard rewards York; the two scenes contradict each other. Moreover, though his callous selfishness, greed and cruelty are apparently established, in the very next scene of this act our sympathy with Richard is called forth by the praise his queen gives him. She says:

" I know no cause
Why I should welcome such a guest as grief,
Save bidding farewell to so sweet a guest
As my sweet Richard."

And from this scene to the end of the play Shakespeare enlists all our sympathy for Richard. Now, what is the reason of this right-about-face on the part of the poet?

It appears to me that Shakespeare began the play intending to present the vile and cruel Richard of tradition. But midway in the play he saw that there was no emotion, no pathos, to be got out of the traditional view. If Richard were a vile, scheming, heartless murderer, the loss of his crown and life would merely satisfy our sense of justice, but this outcome did not satisfy Shakespeare's desire for emotion, and particularly his desire for pathos,[1] and accordingly he veers round, says nothing more of Richard's vileness, lays stress upon his weakness and sufferings, discovers, too, all manner of amiable qualities in him, and so draws pity from us for his dethronement and murder.

The curious thing is that while Shakespeare is depicting Richard's heartlessness, he does his work badly; the traits, as I have shown, are crudely extravagant and even contradictory; but when he paints Richard's gentleness and amiability, he works like a master, every touch is infallible: he is painting himself.

It was natural for Shakespeare to sympathize deeply with Richard; he was still young when he wrote the play, young enough to remember vividly how he himself had been led astray by loose companions, and this formed a bond between them. At this time of his life this was Shakespeare's favourite subject: he treated it again in " Henry IV.," which is at once the epilogue to " Richard II.," and a com-

[1] In the last scene of the last act of " Lear," Albany says:

" This judgement of the heavens, that makes us tremble
Touches us not with pity.'"

panion picture to it; for the theme of both plays
is the same—youth yielding to unworthy companions—though the treatment in the earlier play is
incomparably feebler than it became in "King
Henry IV." Bushy, Bagot, and Green, the favourites of Richard, are not painted as Shakespeare
afterwards painted Falstaff and his followers. But
partly because he had not yet attained to such objective treatment of character, Shakespeare identified himself peculiarly with Richard; and his painting of Richard is more intimate, more subtle, more
self-revealing and pathetic than anything in
"Henry IV."

As I have already said, from the time when Richard appoints York as Regent, and leaves England,
Shakespeare begins to think of himself as Richard,
and from this moment to the end no one can help
sympathizing with the unhappy King. At this point,
too, the character-drawing becomes, of a sudden,
excellent. When Richard lands in England, he is
given speech after speech, and all he says and does
afterwards throws light, it seems to me, on Shakespeare's own nature. Let us mark each trait. First
of all Richard is intensely, frankly emotional: he
"weeps for joy" to be in England again; "weeping, smiling," he greets the earth of England, and
is full of hope. "The thief, the traitor," Bolingbroke, will not dare to face the light of the sun;
for "every man that Bolingbroke has in his pay,"
he cries exultantly, God hath given Richard a
"glorious angel; . . . . Heaven still guards the
right." A moment later he hears from Salisbury
that the Welshmen whom he had relied upon as allies
are dispersed and fled. At once he becomes "pale
and dead." From the height of pride and confidence he falls to utter hopelessness.

> " All souls that will be safe fly from my side;
> For time hath set a blot upon my pride."

Aumerle asks him to remember who he is, and at once he springs from dejection to confidence again. He cries:

> " Awake, thou sluggard majesty! thou sleepest.
> Is not the king's name forty thousand names?"

The next moment Scroop speaks of cares, and forthwith fitful Richard is in the dumps once more. But this time his weakness is turned to resignation and sadness, and the pathos of this is brought out by the poet:

> " Strives Bolingbroke to be as great as we?
> Greater he shall not be; if he serve God
> We'll serve him, too, and be his fellow so.
> Revolt our subjects? that we cannot mend;
> They break their faith to God, as well as us.
> Cry woe, destruction, ruin, loss, decay;
> The worst is death, and death will have his day."

Who does not hear Hamlet speaking in this memorable last line? Like Hamlet, too, this Richard is quick to suspect even his friends' loyalty. He guesses that Bagot, Bushy, and Green have made peace with Bolingbroke, and when Scroop seems to admit this, Richard is as quick as Hamlet to unpack his heart with words:

> "O villains, vipers, damned without redemption!
> Dogs, easily won to fawn on any man!
> Snakes,"

and so forth.

But as soon as he learns that his friends are dead

he breaks out in a long lament for them which
ranges over everything from worms to kings, and in
its melancholy pessimism is the prototype of those
meditations which Shakespeare has put in the mouth
of nearly all his favourite characters. Who is not
reminded of Hamlet's great monologue when he
reads:

" For within the hollow crown,
That rounds the mortal temples of a king,
Keeps Death his court: and there the antic sits,
Scoffing his state, and grinning at his pomp;
Allowing him a breath, a little scene
To monarchize, be fear'd and kill with looks;
Infusing him with self and vain conceit,
As if this flesh, which walls about our life,
Were brass impregnable; and, humour'd thus,
Comes at the last, and with a little pin [1]
Bores through his castle wall, and—farewell, King! "

Let us take another two lines of this soliloquy:

" For God's sake, let us sit upon the ground
And tell sad stories of the death of kings."

In the second scene of the third act of " Titus
Andronicus " we find Titus saying to his daughter:

" I'll to thy closet; and go read with thee
Sad stories chancèd in the times of old."

Again, in the " Comedy of Errors," Ægeon tells us
that his life was prolonged:

" To tell sad stories of my own mishaps."

The similarity of these passages shows that in the
very spring of life and heyday of the blood Shake-

[1] In Hamlet's famous soliloquy the pin is a " bodkin."

speare had in him a certain romantic melancholy which was developed later by the disappointments of life into the despairing of Macbeth and Lear.

When the Bishop calls upon Richard to act, the King's weathercock mind veers round again, and he cries:

> "This ague fit of fear is over-blown,
> An easy task it is to win our own."

But when Scroop tells him that York has joined with Bolingbroke, he believes him at once, gives up hope finally, and turns as if for comfort to his own melancholy fate:

> "Beshrew thee, cousin, which didst lead me forth
> Of that sweet way I was in to despair!"

That "sweet way" of despair is Romeo's way, Hamlet's, Macbeth's and Shakespeare's way.

In the next scene Richard meets his foes, and at first plays the king. Shakespeare tells us that he looks like a king, that his eyes are as "bright as an eagle's"; and this poetic admiration of state and place seems to have got into Richard's blood, for at first he declares that Bolingbroke is guilty of treason, and asserts that:

> "My master, God omnipotent,
> Is mustering in his clouds, on our behalf,
> Armies of pestilence."

Of course, he gives in with fair words the next moment, and the next rages against Bolingbroke; and then comes the great speech in which the poet reveals himself so ingenuously that at the end of it the King he pretends to be, has to admit that he has talked but idly. I cannot help transcribing the

The Bastard, Arthur, and King Richard II.

whole of the passage, for it shows how easily Shake-speare falls out of this King's character into his own:

" What must the King do now? Must he submit?
The King shall do it. Must he be depos'd?
The King shall be contented: must he lose
The name of king? O! God's name, let it go:
I'll give my jewels for a set of beads;
My gorgeous palace for a hermitage;
My gay apparel for an alms-man's gown;
My figur'd goblets for a dish of wood;
My sceptre for a palmer's walking staff;
My subjects for a pair of carved saints;
And my large kingdom for a little grave,
A little, little grave, an obscure grave:—
Or I'll be buried in the King's highway,
Some way of common trade, where subjects' feet
May hourly trample on their sovereign's head:
For on my heart they tread, now whilst I live;
And, buried once, why not upon my head?—
Aumerle, thou weep'st; my tender-hearted cousin!—
We'll make foul weather with despised tears;
Our sighs, and they, shall lodge the summer corn,
And make a dearth in this revolting land.
Or shall we play the wantons with our woes,
And make some pretty match with shedding tears?
As thus:—To drop them still upon one place,
Till they have fretted us a pair of graves
Within the earth; and, therein laid,—There lies
Two kinsmen digg'd their graves with weeping eyes.
Would not this ill do well?—Well, well, I see
I talk but idly, and you mock at me.—
Most mighty prince, my lord Northumberland,
What says King Bolingbroke? will his majesty
Give Richard leave to live till Richard die?
You make a leg, and Bolingbroke says ay."

Every one will admit that the poet himself speaks

here, at least, from the words " I'll give my jewels "
to the words " Would not this ill do well? "   But
the melancholy mood, the pathetic acceptance of
the inevitable, the tender poetic embroidery now
suit the King who is fashioned in the poet's likeness.

The next moment Richard revolts once more
against his fate:

> " Base court, where kings grow base,
> To come at traitors' calls, and do them grace."

And when Bolingbroke kneels to him he plays
upon words, as Gaunt did a little earlier in the play,
misery making sport to mock itself.   He says:

> "Up, cousin, up; your heart is up, I know,
> Thus high at least, although your knee be low "—

and then he abandons himself to do " what force will
have us do."

The Queen's wretchedness is next used to heighten
our sympathy with Richard, and immediately afterwards we have that curious scene between the gardener and his servant which is merely youthful Shakespeare, for such a gardener and such a servant never
yet existed.   The scene [1] shows the extravagance of
Shakespeare's love of hierarchy, and shows also that

---

[1] Coleridge gives this scene as an instance of Shakespeare's
" wonderful judgement "; the introduction of the gardener,
he says, " realizes the thing," and, indeed, the introduction of
a gardener would have this tendency, but not the introduction
of this pompous, priggish philosopher togged out in old
Adam's likeness.   Here is the way this gardener criticises the
King:
> " All superfluous branches
> We lop away, that bearing boughs may live;
> Had he done so, himself had borne the crown,
> Which waste of idle hours hath quite thrown down."

his power of realizing character is as yet but slight. The abdication follows, when Richard in exquisite speech after speech unpacks his heavy heart. To the very last his irresolution comes to show as often as his melancholy. Bolingbroke is sharply practical:

"Are you contented to resign the crown?"

Richard answers:

"Ay, no; no, ay;—for I must nothing be;
Therefore, no, no, for I resign to thee."

When he is asked to confess his sins in public, he moves us all to pity:

"Must I do so? and must I ravel out
My weaved up follies? Gentle Northumberland,
If thy offences were upon record,
Would it not shame thee, in so fair a troop,
To read a lecture of them?"

His eyes are too full of tears to read his own faults, and sympathy brings tears to our eyes also. Richard calls for a glass wherein to see his sins, and we are reminded of Hamlet, who advises the players to hold the mirror up to nature. He jests with his grief, too, in quick-witted retort, as Hamlet jests:

"*Rich.* Say that again.
The shadow of my sorrow? Ha! let's see:—
'Tis very true, my grief lies all within;
And these external manners of lament
Are merely shadows to the unseen grief,
That swells with silence in the tortur'd soul."

Hamlet touches the self-same note:

" 'Tis not alone my inky cloak, good mother,
Nor customary suits of solemn black,

.　　.　　.　　.　　.

But I have that within which passeth show;
These but the trappings and the suits of woe."

In the fifth act the scene between the Queen and
Richard is used simply to move our pity.　She
says he is "most beauteous," but all too mild, and
he answers her:

" I am sworn brother, sweet,
To grim necessity; and he and I
Will keep a league till death."

He bids her take,

"As from my death-bed, my last living leave,"

and for her consolation he turns again to the telling of romantic melancholy stories:

"In winter's tedious nights, sit by the fire
With good old folks; and let them tell thee tales
Of woeful ages long ago betid:
And, ere thou bid good night, to quit their grief,
Tell thou the lamentable fall of me,
And send the hearers weeping to their beds,
For why; the senseless brands will sympathize
The heavy accent of thy moving tongue."

I cannot copy this passage without drawing attention to the haunting music of the third line.

The scene in which York betrays his son to Bolingbroke and prays the king not to pardon but
" cut off " the offending member, is merely proof,
if proof were wanted, of Shakespeare's admiration
of kingship and loyalty, which in youth, at least,
often led him to silliest extravagance.

The Bastard, Arthur, and King Richard II.

The dungeon scene and Richard's monologue in it are as characteristic of Shakespeare as the similar scene in " Cymbeline " and the soliloquy of Posthumus:

> " *K. Rich.* I have been studying how I may compare
> This prison where I live unto the world:
> And for because the world is populous,
> And here is not a creature but myself,
> I cannot do it; yet I'll hammer it out,
> My brain I'll prove the female to my soul,
> My soul the father; and these two beget
> A generation of still breeding thoughts,
> And these same thoughts people this little world,
> In humours like the people of this world,
> For no thought is contented. . . . . "

Here we have the philosopher playing with his own thoughts; but soon the Hamlet-melancholy comes to tune the meditation to sadness, and Shakespeare speaks to us directly:

> " Thus play I in one person many people,
> And none contented: sometimes am I king;
> Then treasons make me wish myself a beggar,
> And so I am: then crushing penury
> Persuades me I was better when a king;
> Then am I king'd again; and by and by
> Think, that I am unking'd by Bolingbroke,
> And straight am nothing; but whate'er I be,
> Nor I nor any man that but man is
> With nothing shall be pleased, till he be eased
> With being nothing."

Later one hears Kent's lament for Lear in Richard's words:

> " How these vain weak nails
> May tear a passage through the flinty ribs
> Of this hard world, my ragged prison walls."

75

To Richard music is "sweet music," as it is to all the characters that are merely Shakespeare's masks, and the scene in which Hamlet asks Guildenstern to "play upon the pipe" is prefigured for us in Richard's self-reproach:

> "And here have I the daintiness of ear,
> To check time broke in a disordered string;
> But for the concord of my state and time,
> Had not an ear to hear my true time broke."

In the last three lines of this monologue which I am now about to quote, I can hear Shakespeare speaking as plainly as he spoke in Arthur's appeals; the feminine longing for love is the unmistakable note:

> "Yet blessing on his heart that gives it me!
> For 'tis a sign of love; and love to Richard
> Is a strange brooch in this all-hating world."

And at the last, by killing the servant who assaults him, this Richard shows that he has the "something desperate" in him of which Hamlet boasted.

The murderer's praise that this irresolute-weak and loving Richard is "as full of valour as of royal blood" is nothing more than an excellent instance of Shakespeare's self-illusion. He comes nearer the fact in "Measure for Measure," where the Duke, his other self, is shown to be "an unhurtful opposite" too gentle-kind to remember an injury or punish the offender, and he rings the bell at truth's centre, when, in "Julius Caesar," his mask Brutus admits that he

> ". . . . carries anger, as the flint bears fire
> Who much enforcèd shows a hasty spark
> And straight is cold again."

The Bastard, Arthur, and King Richard II.

If a hasty blow were proof of valour then Walter Scott's Eachin in " The Fair Maid of Perth " would be called brave. But courage to be worth the name must be founded on stubborn resolution, and all Shakespeare's incarnations, and in especial this Richard, are as unstable as water.

The whole play is summed up in York's pathetic description of Richard's entrance into London:

> " No man cried, God save him;
> No joyful tongue gave him his welcome home:
> But dust was thrown upon his sacred head;
> Which with such gentle sorrow he shook off—
> His face still combating with tears and smiles,
> The badges of his grief and patience—
> That had not God, for some strong purpose, steel'd
> The hearts of men, they must perforce have melted,
> And barbarism itself have pitied him."

This passage it seems to me both in manner and matter is as truly characteristic of Shakespeare as any that can be found in all his works: his loving pity for the fallen, his passionate sympathy with " gentle sorrow " were never more perfectly expressed.

Pity, indeed, is the note of the tragedy, as it was in the Arthur-scenes in " King John," but the knowledge of Shakespeare derived from " King John " is greatly widened by the study of " King Richard II." In the Arthur of " King John " we found Shakespeare's exquisite pity for weakness, his sympathy with suffering, and, more than all, his girlish-tender love and desire of love. In " Richard II.," the weakness Shakespeare pities is not physical weakness, but mental irresolution and incapacity for action, and these Hamlet-weaknesses are accompanied by a habit of philosophic thought, and are

77.

enlivened by a nimble wit and great lyrical power. In Arthur Shakespeare is bent on revealing his qualities of heart, and in " Richard II." his qualities of mind, and that these two are but parts of the same nature is proved by the fact that Arthur shows great quickness of apprehension and felicity of speech, while Richard once or twice at least displays a tenderness of heart and longing for love worthy of Arthur.

It appears then that Shakespeare's nature even in hot, reckless youth was most feminine and affectionate, and that even when dealing with histories and men of action he preferred to picture irresolution and weakness rather than strength, and felt more sympathy with failure than with success.

CHAPTER V

SHAKESPEARE'S MEN OF ACTION (*continued*):
HOTSPUR, HENRY V.

THE conclusions we have already reached will
be borne out and strengthened in unexpected
ways by the study of Hotspur—Shakespeare's mas-
terpicture of the man of action. The setting sun of
chivalry falling on certain figures threw gigantic
shadows across Shakespeare's path, and of these
figures no one deserved immortality better than
Harry Percy. Though he is not introduced in
" The Famous Victories of Henry V.," the old play
which gave Shakespeare his roistering Prince and
the first faint hint of Falstaff, Harry Percy lived
in story and in oral tradition. His nickname itself
is sufficient evidence of the impression he had made
on the popular fancy. And both Prince Henry when
mocking him, and his wife when praising him, bear
witness to what were, no doubt, the accepted peculiarities of his character. Hotspur lived in the
memory of men, we may be sure, with thick, hasty
speech, and hot, impatient temper, and it is easy, I
think, even at this late date, to distinguish Shakespeare's touches on the traditional portrait. It is
for the reader to say whether Shakespeare blurred
the picture, or bettered it.

Hotspur's first words to the King in the first act
are admirable; they bring the brusque, passionate
soldier vividly before us; but I am sure Shakespeare
had the fact from history or tradition.

"My liege, I did deny no prisoners.
But, I remember, when the fight was done,
When I was dry with rage and extreme toil,
Breathless and faint, leaning upon my sword,
Came there a certain lord, neat, trimly dressed,
Fresh as a bridegroom."

Hotspur's picture of this "popinjay" with
pouncet-box in hand, and "perfuméd like a milli-
ner," is splendid self-revelation:

"he made me mad,
To see him shine so brisk and smell so sweet,
And talk so like a waiting gentlewoman."

But immediately afterwards Hotspur's defence of
Mortimer shows the poet Shakespeare rather than
the rude soldier who hates nothing more than "mincing poetry." The beginning is fairly good:

"*Hot.*   Revolted Mortimer!
He never did fall off, my sovereign liege,
But by the chance of war; to prove that true,
Needs no more but one tongue for all those wounds,
Those mouthéd wounds which valiantly he took,
When on the gentle Severn's sedgy bank." . . .

This "gentle Severn's sedgy bank" is too poetical
for Hotspur; but what shall be said of his description of the river?

"Who then, affrighted with their bloody looks,
Ran fearfully among the trembling reeds,
And hid his crisp head in the hollow bank
Blood-stainéd with these valiant combatants."

Shakespeare was still too young, too much in
love with poetry to confine himself within the nature
80

of Hotspur. But the character of Hotspur was so
well known that Shakespeare could not long remain
outside it. When the King cuts short the audience
with the command to send back the prisoners, we
find the passionate Hotspur again:

> "And if the devil come and roar for them,
> I will not send them.—I will after straight,
> And tell him so: for I will ease my heart,
> Although it be with hazard of my head."

The last line strikes a false note; such a reflection
throws cold water on the heat of passion, and that
is not intended, for though reproved by his father
Hotspur storms on:

> "Speak of Mortimer!
> 'Zounds! I will speak of him; and let my soul
> Want mercy, if I do not join with him. . . ."

The next long speech of Hotspur is mere poetic
slush; he begins:

> "Nay, then, I cannot blame his cousin king,
> That wish'd him on the barren mountains starve. . . ."

and goes on for thirty lines to reprove the conspirators for having put down "Richard, that sweet
lovely rose," and planted "this thorn, Bolingbroke."
This long speech retards the action, obscures the
character of Hotspur, and only shows Shakespeare
poetising without a flash of inspiration. Then
comes Hotspur's famous speech about honour:

> "By heaven, methinks it were an easy leap,
> To pluck bright honour from the pale-faced moon:
> Or dive into the bottom of the deep . . ."

And immediately afterwards a speech in which

his uncontrollable impatience and the childishness
which always lurks in anger, find perfect expression. To soothe him, Worcester says he shall keep
his prisoners; Hotspur bursts out:

> "Nay, I will: that's flat.
> He said, he would not ransom Mortimer;
> Forbad my tongue to speak of Mortimer;
> But I will find him when he lies asleep,
> And in his ear I'll holla—'Mortimer!' Nay,
> I'll have a starling shall be taught to speak
> Nothing but 'Mortimer,' and give it him,
> To keep his anger still in motion."

No wonder Lord Worcester reproves him, and his
father chides him as " a wasp-stung and impatient
fool," who will only talk and not listen. But again
Hotspur breaks forth, and again his anger paints
him to the life:

> " Why, look you, I am whipped and scourged with rods,
> Nettled and stung with pismires, when I hear
> Of this vile politician, Bolingbroke.
> In Richard's time,—what do you call the place?—
> A plague upon 't—it is in Glostershire;—
> 'Twas where the madcap duke his uncle kept,— . . ."

The very ecstasy of impatience and of puerile passionate temper has never been better rendered.

His soliloquy, too, in the beginning of scene iii,
when he reads the letter which throws the cold light
of reason on his enterprise, is excellent, though it
repeats qualities we already knew in Hotspur, and
does not reveal new ones:

> " 'The purpose you undertake is dangerous';—why
> that's certain: 'tis dangerous to take a cold, to sleep, to
> drink; but I tell you, my lord fool, out of this nettle

danger, we pluck this flower safety. . . . What a frosty-spirited rogue is this! . . . O, I could divide myself and go to buffets, for moving such a dish of skimmed milk with so honourable an action! Hang him! Let him tell the King: we are prepared. I will set forward to-night."

But the topmost height of self-revealing is reached in the scene with his wife which immediately follows this. Lady Percy enters, and Hotspur greets her:

"How now, Kate? I must leave you within these two hours."

The lady's reply is too long and too poetical. Hotspur interrupts her by calling the servant and giving him orders. Then Lady Percy questions, and Hotspur avoids a direct answer, and little by little Shakespeare works himself into the characters till even Lady Percy lives for us:

> "*Lady*. Come, come, you paraquito, answer me
> Directly unto this question that I ask.
> In faith, I'll break thy little finger, Harry,
> An if thou wilt not tell me true.
>   *Hot*.   Away,
> Away, you trifler!—Love?—I love thee not,
> I care not for thee, Kate; this is no world
> To play with mammets and to tilt with lips. . . ."

It shows a certain immaturity of art that Hotspur should introduce the theme of "love," and not Lady Percy; but, of course, Lady Percy seizes on the word:

> "*Lady*. Do you not love me? do you not indeed?
> Well, do not then; for since you love me not,

I will not love myself. Do you not love me?
Nay, tell me, if you speak in jest or no?
    Hot. Come, wilt thou see me ride?
And when I am o' horseback, I will swear
I love thee infinitely. . . ."

All this is superb; Hotspur's coarse contempt of
love deepens our sense of his soldier-like nature and
eagerness for action; but though the qualities are
rendered magically the qualities themselves are few:
Shakespeare still harps upon Hotspur's impatience;
but even a soldier is something more than hasty
temper, and disdain of love's dalliance. But the
portrait is not finished yet. The first scene in the
third act between Hotspur and Glendower is on
this same highest level; Hotspur's impatience of
Glendower's bragging at length finds an unforget-
able phrase:

" *Glend.* I can call spirits from the vasty deep.
    Hot. Why, so can I, or so can any man;
But will they come when you do call for them? "

Then Hotspur disputes over the division of England; he wants a larger share than that allotted
to him; the trait is typical, excellent; but the next
moment Shakespeare effaces it. As soon as Glendower yields, Hotspur cries:

" I do not care; I'll give thrice so much land
    Away to any well-deserving friend;
    But in the way of bargain, mark ye me,
    I'll cavil on the ninth part of a hair. . . ."

This large generosity is a trait of Shakespeare
and not of Hotspur; the poet cannot bear to lend
his hero a tinge of meanness, or of avarice, and yet

84

the character needs a heavy shadow or two, and
no shadow could be more appropriate than this, for
greed of land has always been a characteristic of
the soldier-aristocrat.

Shakespeare is perfectly willing to depict Hotspur as scorning the arts. When Glendower praises
poetry, Hotspur vows he'd " rather be a kitten and
cry mew . . . than a metre ballad-monger. . . ."
Nothing sets his teeth on edge " so much as mincing poetry ": and a little later he prefers the howl-
ing of a dog to music. When he is reproved by
Lord Worcester for " defect of manners, want of
government, . . . pride, haughtiness, disdain," his
reply is most characteristic:

> " Well, I am schooled: good manners be your speed,
>   Here come our wives, and let us take our leave."

He is too old to learn, and his self-assurance is not
to be shaken; but though he hates schooling he
will school his wife:

> " Swear me, Kate, like a lady as thou art,
>   A good mouth-filling oath; and leave, ' in sooth,'
>   And such protest of pepper-gingerbread
>   To velvet guards and Sunday citizens."

This is merely a repetition of the trait shown in
his first speech when he sneered at the popinjay-lord
for talking in " holiday and lady terms." But
not only does Shakespeare repeat well-known traits
in Hotspur, he also uses him as a mere mouthpiece
again and again, as he used him at the beginning
in the poetic description of the Severn. The fourth
act opens with a speech of Hotspur to Douglas,
which is curiously illustrative of this fault:

" *Hot.* Well said, my noble Scot, if speaking truth
In this fine age were not thought flattery,
Such attribution should the Douglas have,
As not a soldier of this season's stamp
Should go so general current through the world.
By God, I cannot flatter; I defy
The tongues of soothers; but a braver place
In my heart's love hath no man than yourself.
Nay, task me to my word; approve me, lord."

In the first five lines of this skimble-skamble stuff
I hear Shakespeare speaking in his cheapest way;
with the oath, however, he tries to get into the
character again, and succeeds indifferently.

Immediately afterwards Hotspur is shocked by
the news that his father is sick and has not even sent
the promised assistance; struck to the heart by the
betrayal, the hot soldier should now reveal his true
character; one expects him to curse his father and
rising to the danger, to cry that he is stronger
without traitors and faint-heart friends. But
Shakespeare the philosopher is chiefly concerned with
the effect of such news upon a rebel camp, and again
he speaks through Hotspur:

" Sick now! droop now! this sickness doth infect
The very life-blood of our enterprise;
'Tis catching hither, even to our camp."

Then Shakespeare pulls himself up and tries to get
into Hotspur's character again by representing to
himself the circumstance:

"He writes me here, that inward sickness—
And that his friends by deputation could not
So soon be drawn; nor did he think it meet—"

and so forth to the question: ". . . What say you
to it? "

86

Hotspur, Prince Henry, and Henry V.

"*Wor.* Your father's sickness is a maim to us.
Hot. A perilous gash, a very limb lopped off:—"

Shakespeare sees that he cannot go on exaggerating the injury—that is not Hotspur's line, is indeed utterly false to Hotspur's nature; and so he tries to stop himself and think of Hotspur:

"And yet, in faith, it's not; his present want
   Seems more than we shall find it: were it good
   To set the exact wealth of all our states
   All at one cast? to set so rich a main
   On the nice hazard of one doubtful hour?
   It were not good; for therein should we read
   The very bottom and the soul of hope,
   The very list, the very utmost bound
   Of all our fortunes."

After the first two lines, which Hotspur might have spoken, we have the sophistry of the thinker poetically expressed, and not one word from the hot, high-couraged soldier. Indeed, in the last four lines from the bookish "we read" to the end, we have the gentle poet in love with desperate extremities. The passage must be compared with Othello's—

"Here is my journey's end, here is my butt,
And very sea-mark of my utmost sail."

But at length when Worcester adds fear to danger Hotspur half finds himself:

"*Hot.*   You strain too far.
I rather of his absence make this use:—
It lends a lustre, and more great opinion,
A larger dare to our great enterprise,
Than if the earl were here; for men must think,
If we, without his help can make a head

87

> To push against the kingdom; with his help
> We shall o'erturn it topsy-turvy down.—
> Yet all goes well, yet all our joints are whole."

And this is all. The scene is designed, the situation constructed to show us Hotspur's courage. here, if anywhere, the hot blood should surprise us and make of danger the springboard of leaping hardihood. But this is the best Shakespeare can reach—this fainting, palefaced " Yet all goes well, yet all our joints are whole." The inadequacy, the feebleness of the whole thing is astounding. Milton had not the courage of the soldier, but he had more than this: he found better words for his Satan after defeat than Shakespeare found for Hotspur before the battle:

> " What though the field be lost?
> All is not lost; the unconquerable will,
> And study of revenge, immortal hate,
> And courage never to submit or yield,
> And what is else not to be overcome;
> That glory never shall his wrath or might
> Extort from me."

When Shakespeare has to render Hotspur's impatience he does it superbly, when he has to render Hotspur's courage he fails lamentably.

In the third scene of this fourth act we have another striking instance of Shakespeare's shortcoming. Sir Walter Blount meets the rebels " with gracious offers from the King," whereupon Hotspur abuses the King through forty lines; this is the kind of stuff:

> " My father and my uncle and myself
> Did give him that same royalty he wears;

> And when he was not six and twenty strong,
> Sick in the world's regard, wretched and low,
> A poor unminded outlaw sneaking home,
> My father gave him welcome to the shore; . . ."

and so on and on, like Hamlet, he unpacks his heart
with words, till Blount cries:

> " Tut, I came not to hear this."

Hotspur admits the reproof, but immediately starts
off again:

> " *Hot.*   Then to the point.
> In short time after he deposed the king;
> Soon after that, deprived him of his life,"

and so forth for twenty lines more, till Blount pulls
him up again with the shrewd question:

> " Shall I return this answer to the king?"

Hotspur replies:

> " Not so, Sir Walter; we'll withdraw awhile.
> Go to the king.   .   .   .   .
> And in the morning early shall mine uncle
> Bring him our purposes; and so farewell."

And yet this Hotspur who talks interminably when
he would do much better to keep quiet, assures us
a little later that he has not well " the gift of
tongue," and again declares he's glad a messenger
has cut him short, for " I profess not talking."

The truth is the real Hotspur did not talk much,
but Shakespeare had the gift of the gab, if ever a
man had, and Hotspur was a mouthpiece.   It is
worth noting that though the dramatist usually

works himself into a character gradually, Hotspur is best presented in the earlier scenes: Shakespeare began the work with the Hotspur of history and tradition clear in his mind, but as he wrote he grew interested in Hotspur and identified himself too much with his hero and so almost spoiled the portrait. This is well seen in Hotspur's end; Prince Henry has said he'd crop his budding honours and make a garland for himself out of them, and this is how the dying Hotspur answers him:

" O Harry, thou hast robbed me of my youth!
I better brook the loss of brittle life
Than those proud titles thou hast won of me;
They wound my thoughts worse than thy sword my
    flesh:—
But thought's the slave of life, and life time's fool,
And time, that takes survey of all the world,
Must have a stop. O, I could prophesy,
But that the earthly and cold hand of death
Lies on my tongue:—no, Percy, thou art dust,
And food for —— "

Of course, Prince Henry concludes the phrase, and continues the Hamlet-like philosophic soliloquy:

"*P. Henry.* For worms, brave Percy; fare thee well,
    great heart!—
Ill-weaved ambition, how much art thou shrunk!
When that this body did contain a spirit,
A kingdom for it was too small a bound;
But now two paces of the vilest earth
Is room enough: . . . ."

I have tried to do justice to this portrait of Hotspur, for Shakespeare never did a better picture of a man of action, indeed, as we shall soon see, he never did as well again. But take away from Hot-

spur the qualities given to him by history and tradition, the hasty temper, and thick stuttering
speech, and contempt of women, and it will be seen
how little Shakespeare added. He makes Hotspur
hate " mincing poetry," and then puts long poetic
descriptions in his mouth; he paints the soldier de-
spising " the gift of tongue " and forces him to talk
history and poetic slush in and out of season; he
makes the aristocrat greedy and sets him quarrel-
ling with his associates for more land, and the next
moment, when the land is given him, Hotspur abandons it without further thought; he frames an occasion calculated to show off Hotspur's courage, and
then allows him to talk faint-heartedly, and finally,
when Hotspur should die mutely, or with a short
curse, biting to the last, Shakespeare's Hotspur
loses himself in mistimed philosophic reflection and
poetic prediction. Yet such is Shakespeare's magic
of expression that when he is revealing the qualities
which Hotspur really did possess, he makes him
live for us with such intensity of life that no number of false strokes can obliterate the impression.
It is only the critic working *sine ira et studio* who
will find this portrait blurred by the intrusion of
the poet's personality.

It is the companion picture of Prince Henry
that shows as in a glass Shakespeare's poverty
of conception when he is dealing with the distinc-
tively manly qualities. In order to judge the matter fairly we must remember that Shakespeare did
not create Prince Henry any more than he created
Hotspur. In the old play entitled " The Famous
Victories of Henry V.," and in the popular mouth,
Shakespeare found roistering Prince Hal; the madcap Prince, like Harry Percy, was a creature of
popular sympathy; his high spirits and extrava-

gances, the vigorous way in which he had sown his wild oats, had taken the English fancy, the historic personage had been warmed to vivid life by the popular emotion.

Shakespeare was personally interested in this princely hero. As we have seen, he dims Hotspur's portrait by intrusion of his own peculiarities; and in the case of Prince Henry this temptation will be stronger.

The subject of the play, a young man of noble gifts led astray by loose companions, was a favourite subject with Shakespeare at this time; he had treated it already in " Richard II."; and he handled it here again with such zest that we are almost forced to believe in the tradition that Shakespeare himself in early youth had sown wild oats in unworthy company. Helped by a superb model, and in full sympathy with his theme, Shakespeare might be expected to paint a magnificent picture. But Prince Henry is anything but a great portrait; he is at first hardly more than a prig, and later a feeble and colourless replica of Hotspur. It is very curious that even in the comedy scenes with Falstaff Shakespeare has never taken the trouble to realize the Prince: he often lends him his own word-wit, and now and then his own high intelligence, but he never for a moment discovers to us the soul of his hero. He does not even tell us what pleasure Henry finds in living and carousing with Falstaff. Did the Prince choose his companions out of vanity, seeking in the Eastcheap tavern a court where he might throne it? Or was it the infinite humour of Falstaff which attracted him? Or did he break bounds merely out of high spirits, when bored by the foolish formalities of the palace? Shakespeare, one would have thought, would have given us the key to the mystery in the very first scene. But this scene, which paints Falstaff to the soul, tells us nothing of the Prince; but rather blurs a figure which everyone imagines he knows at least in outline. Prince Henry's first speech is excellent as description; Falstaff asks him the time of day; he replies:

"Thou art so fat-witted, with drinking of old sack, and unbuttoning thee after supper, and sleeping upon benches after noon, that thou hast forgotten to demand that truly which thou wouldst truly know . . ."

This helps to depict Falstaff, but does not show us the Prince, for good-humoured contempt of Falstaff is universal; it has nothing individual and peculiar in it.

Then comes the speech in which the Prince talks of himself in Falstaff's strain as one of " the moon's men," who " resolutely snatch a purse of gold on Monday night," and " most dissolutely spend it on Tuesday morning." A little later he plays with Falstaff by asking: " Where shall we take a purse to-morrow, Jack? " It looks as if the Prince were ripe for worse than mischief. But when Falstaff wants to know if he will make one of the band to rob on Gadshill, he cries out, as if indignant and surprised:

"*P. Hen.* Who, I rob? I a thief? Not I, by my faith.
Fal. There's neither honesty, manhood, nor good fellowship in thee, nor thou camest not of the blood royal, if thou darest not stand for ten shillings.
P. Hen. Well then, once in my days I'll be a madcap.
Fal. Why, that's well said.
P. Hen. Well, come what will, I'll tarry at home."

He is only persuaded at length by Poins's proposal
to rob the robbers. It may be said that these changes
of the Prince are natural in the situation: but they
are too sudden and unmotived; they are like the
nodding of the mandarin's head—they have no
meaning; and surely, after the Prince talks of himself as one of " the moon's men," it would be more
natural of him, when the direct proposal to rob is
made, not to show indignant surprise, which seems
forced or feigned; but to talk as if repenting a previous folly. The scene, in so far as the Prince is
concerned, is badly conducted. When he yields to
Poins and agrees to rob Falstaff, his words are:
" Yea, but I doubt they will be too hard for us,"—
a phrase which hardly shows wild spirits or high
courage, or even the faculty of judging men, and
the soliloquy which ends the scene lamely enough
is not the Prince's, but Shakespeare's, and unfortunately Shakespeare the poet, and not Shakespeare
the dramatist:

> " *P. Hen.* I know you all and will awhile uphold
> The unyoked humour of your idleness.
> Yet herein will I imitate the sun,
> Who doth permit the base contagious clouds
> To smother up his beauty from the world,
> That, when he please again to be himself,
> Being wanted, he may be more wondered at,
> By breaking through the foul and ugly mists
> Of vapours, that did seem to strangle him. . . ."

If we could accept this stuff we should take Prince
Henry for the prince of prigs; but it is impossible
to accept it, and so we shrug our shoulders with
the regret that the madcap Prince of history is not
illuminated for us by Shakespeare's genius. In this
" First Part of Henry IV.," when the Prince is not

calling names with Falstaff, or playing prig, he
either shows us a quality of Harry Percy or of
Shakespeare himself. Everyone remembers the
scene when Falstaff, carrying Percy's corpse, meets
the Princes, and tells them he has killed Percy:

> " *P. John.* This is the strangest tale that e'er I heard.
> *P. Hen.* This is the strangest fellow, brother John.—
> Come, bring your luggage nobly on your back:
> For my part, if a lie may do thee grace,
> I'll gild it with the happiest terms I have."

Both in manner and in matter these last two lines
are pure Shakespeare, and Shakespeare speaks to
us, too, when Prince Henry gives up Douglas to
his pleasure " ransomless and free." But not only
does the poet lend the soldier his own sentiments and
lilt of phrase, he also presents him to us as a shadowy replica of Hotspur, even during Hotspur's lifetime. We have already noticed Hotspur's admirable answer when Glendower brags that he can call
spirits from the vasty deep:

> " *Hot.* Why, so can I, or so can any man;
> But will they come, when you do call for them? "

The same love of truth is given to Prince Henry
in the previous act:

> " *Fal.* Owen, Owen,—the same;—and his son-in-law,
> Mortimer; and old Northumberland; and that sprightly
> Scot of Scots, Douglas, that runs o' horseback up a hill
> perpendicular,—
> *P. Hen.* He that rides at high speed, and with his
> pistol kills a sparrow flying.
> *Fal.* You have hit it.
> *P. Hen.* So did he never the sparrow."

But this frank contempt of lying is not the only or the chief characteristic possessed by Hotspur and Harry Percy in common. Hotspur disdains the Prince:

> " *Hot.*   Where is his son,
> The nimble-footed mad-cap Prince of Wales,
> And his comrádes that daffed the world aside
> And bid it pass? "

and the Prince mimics and makes fun of Hotspur:

> " *P. Hen.* He that kills me some six or seven dozen of Scots at a breakfast, washes his hands and says to his wife, ' Fie upon this quiet life! I want work.' "

Then Hotspur brags of what he will do when he meets his rival:

> " *Hot.*   Once ere night
> I will embrace him with a soldier's arm,
> That he shall shrink under my courtesy."

And in precisely the same strain Prince Henry talks to his father:

> " *P. Hen.*   The time will come
> That I shall make this northern youth exchange
> His glorious deeds for my indignities."

It is true that Prince Henry on more than one occasion praises Hotspur, while Hotspur is content to praise himself, but the differentiation is too slight to be significant: such as it is, it is well seen when the two heroes meet.

> " *Hot.* My name is Harry Percy.
> *P. Hen.*   Why, then I see
> A very valiant rebel of that name."

Hotspur, Prince Henry, and Henry V.

But Prince Henry immediately doffs this kingly mood to imitate Hotspur. He goes on:

> " I am the Prince of Wales, and think not, Percy,
> To share with me in glory any more;
> Two stars keep not their motion in one sphere,
> Nor can our England brook a double reign
> Of Harry Percy and the Prince of Wales . . ."

And so the bombast rolls, and one brags against the other like systole and diastole which balance each other in the same heart. But the worst of the matter is, that Prince Henry and Hotspur, as we have already noticed, have both the same soul and the same inspiring motive in love of honour. They both avow this again and again, though Hotspur finds the finer expressions for it when he cries that he will " pluck bright honour from the pale-faced moon."

To the student of the play it really looks as if Shakespeare could not imagine any other incentive to noble or heroic deeds but this love of glory: for nearly all the other serious characters in the play sing of honour in the same key. King Henry IV. envies Northumberland

> " A son who is the theme of honour's tongue,"

and declares that Percy hath got " never-dying honour against renownéd Douglas." The Douglas, too, can find no other word with which to praise Hotspur—" thou art the king of honour ": even Vernon, a mere secondary character, has the same mainspring: he says to Douglas:

> " If well-respected honour bid me on,
> I hold as little counsel with weak fear
> As you or any Scot that this day lives."

Falstaff himself declares that nothing " pricks him on but honour," and bragging Pistol admits that " honour is cudgelled " from his weary limbs. The French, too, when they are beaten by Henry V., all bemoan their shame and loss of honour, and have no word of sorrow for their ruined homesteads and outraged women and children. The Dauphin cries:

> " Reproach and everlasting shame
> Sits mocking in our plumes."

And Bourbon echoes him:

> " Shame and eternal shame, nothing but shame."

It is curious that Bourbon falls upon the same thought which animated Hotspur. Just before the decisive battle Hotspur cries:

> " O, gentlemen! the time of life is short;
> To spend that shortness basely were too long."

And when the battle turns against the French, Bourbon exclaims:

> " The devil take order now! I'll to the throng:
> Let life be short; else shame will be too long."

As Jaques in " As You Like It " says of the soldier: they are " jealous in honour " and all seek " the bubble reputation, even in the cannon's mouth."

It is only in Shakespeare that men have no other motive for brave deeds but love of honour, no other fear but that of shame with which to overcome the dread of death. We shall see later that the desire of fame was the inspiring motive of his own youth.

Hotspur, Prince Henry, and Henry V.

In the " Second Part of King Henry IV." there is very little told us of Prince Henry; he only appears in the second act, and in the fourth and fifth; and in all he is the mouthpiece of Shakespeare and not the roistering Prince: yet on his first appearance there are traces of characterization, as when he declares that his " appetite is not princely," for he remembers " the poor creature, small beer," whereas in the last act he is merely the poetic prig. Let us give the best scene first:

" *P. Hen.* Shall I tell thee one thing, Poins?

.   .   .   .   .

P. Hen. Marry, I tell thee,—it is not meet that I should be sad, now my father is sick; albeit I could tell to thee—as to one it pleases me, for fault of a better, to call my friend—I could be sad, and sad, indeed, too.

Poins. Very hardly upon such a subject.

P. Hen. By this hand, thou think'st me as far in the devil's book as thou and Falstaff for obduracy and persistency: let the end try the man. But I tell thee, my heart bleeds inwardly that my father is so sick; and keeping such vile company as thou art hath in reason taken from me all ostentation of sorrow.

Poins. The reason?

P. Hen. What would'st thou think of me if I should weep?

Poins. I would think thee a most princely hypocrite.

P. Hen. It would be every man's thought; and thou art a blessed fellow to think as every man thinks; never a man's thought in the world keeps the roadway better than thine: every man would think me an hypocrite indeed. And what accites your most worshipful thought to think so?

Poins. Why, because you have been so lewd, and so much engraffed to Falstaff."

By far the best thing in this page—the contempt

for every man's thought as certain to be mistaken—
is, I need hardly say, pure Shakespeare. Exactly
the same reflection finds a place in " Hamlet "; the
student-thinker tells us of a play which in his opinion, and in the opinion of the best judges, was excellent, but which was only acted once, for it
" pleased not the million; 'twas caviare to the general." Very early in life Shakespeare made the discovery, which all men of brains make sooner or
later, that the thoughts of the million are worthless,
and the judgement and taste of the million are
execrable.

There is nothing worthy to be called character-
drawing in this scene; but there's just a hint of it
in the last remark of Poins. According to his favourite companion the Prince was very " lewd," and
yet Shakespeare never shows us his lewdness in
action; does not " moralize " it as Jaques or Hamlet would have been tempted to do. It is just mentioned and passed over lightly. It is curious, too,
that Shakespeare's *alter ego*, Jaques, was also accused of lewdness by the exiled Duke; Vincentio, too,
another incarnation of Shakespeare, was charged
with lechery by Lucio; but in none of these cases
does Shakespeare dwell on the failing. Shakespeare
seems to have thought reticence the better part in
regard to certain sins of the flesh. But it must be
remarked that it is only when his heroes come into
question that he practises this restraint: he is content to tell us casually that Prince Henry was a
sensualist; but he shows us Falstaff and Doll Tearsheet engaged at lips' length. To put it briefly,
Shakespeare attributes lewdness to his impersonation, but will not emphasize the fault by instances.
Nor will Shakespeare allow his " madcap Prince "
even to play " drawer " with hearty goodwill. While

consenting to spy on Falstaff in the tavern, the
Prince tells Poins that " from a Prince to a prentice "
is " a low transformation," and scarcely has the fun
commenced when he is called to the wars and takes
his leave in these terms:

> "*P. Hen.* By Heaven, Poins, I feel me much to
> blame,
> So idly to profane the precious time
> When tempest of commotion, like the south
> Borne with black vapour, doth begin to melt
> And drop upon our bare, unarmèd heads."

The first two lines are priggish, and the last three
mere poetic balderdash. But it is in the fourth act,
when Prince Henry is watching by the bedside of his
dying father, that Shakespeare speaks through him
without disguise:

> "Why doth the crown lie there upon his pillow
> Being so troublesome a bedfellow?
> O polished perturbation! golden care!
> That keep'st the ports of slumber open wide
> To many a watchful night!—Sleep with it now,
> Yet not so sound and half so deeply sweet
> As he whose brow with homely biggin bound
> Snores out the watch of night."

In the third act we have King Henry talking in
precisely the same way:

> "O sleep, O gentle sleep,
> Nature's soft nurse, how have I frighted thee? . . .
>
> .   .   .   .   .
>
> Wilt thou upon the high and giddy mast
> Seal up the ship-boy's eyes, and rock his brains
> In cradle of the rude imperious surge.   .   .   ."

The truth is that in both these passages, as in a

hundred similar ones, we find Shakespeare himself praising sleep as only those tormented by insomnia can praise it.

When his father reproaches him with " hunger for his empty chair," this is how Prince Henry answers:

> " O pardon me, my liege, but for my tears,
> The moist impediments unto my speech,
> I had forestalled this dear and deep rebuke.
> Ere you with grief had spoke and I had heard
> The course of it so far. . . ."

It might be Alfred Austin writing to Lord Salisbury—" the moist impediments," forsooth—and the daredevil young soldier goes on like this for forty lines.

The only memorable thing in the fifth act is the new king's contemptuous dismissal of Falstaff: I think it appalling at least in matter:

> " I know thee not, old man: fall to thy prayers;
> How ill white hairs become a fool and jester!
> I have long dreamed of such a kind of man,
> So surfeit-swelled, so old and so profane;
> But being awake I do despise my dream.
>
> . . . . .
>
> Reply not to me with a fool-born jest,
> Presume not that I am the thing I was;
>
> . . . . .
>
> Till then, I banish thee on pain of death,
> As I have done the rest of my misleaders,
> Not to come near our person by ten mile."

In the old play, " The Famous Victories," the sentence of banishment is pronounced; but this bitter contempt for the surfeit-swelled, profane old man is Shakespeare's. It is true that he mitigates the se-

verity of the sentence in characteristic generous
fashion: the King says:

> " For competence of life I will allow you
> That lack of means enforce you not to evil:
> And as we hear you do reform yourselves,
> We will, according to your strength and qualities,
> Give you advancement."

There is no mention in the old play of this " compe-
tence of life." But in spite of this generous fore-
thought the sentence is painfully severe, and Shakespeare meant every word of it, for immediately afterwards the Chief Justice orders Falstaff and his
company to the Fleet prison; and in " King Henry
V." we are told that the King's condemnation broke
Falstaff's heart and made the old jester's banishment eternal. To find Shakespeare more severe in
judgement than the majority of spectators and
readers is so astonishing, so singular a fact, that
it cries for explanation. I think there can be no
doubt that the tradition which tells us that Shakespeare in his youth played pranks in low company
finds further corroboration here. He seems to have
resented his own ignominy and the contemptuous
estimate put upon him by others somewhat extravagantly.

> " Presume not that I am the thing I was; "

—is a sentiment put again and again in Prince
Henry's mouth; he is perpetually assuring us of
the change in himself, and the great results which
must ensue from it. It is this distaste for his own
loose past and " his misleaders," which makes Shakespeare so singularly severe toward Falstaff. As we
have seen, he was the reverse of severe with Angelo

in " Measure for Measure," though in that case there was better ground for harshness. " Measure for Measure," it is true, was written six or seven years later than " Henry IV.," and the tragedy of Shakespeare's life separates the two plays. Shakespeare's ethical judgement was more inclined to severity in youth and early manhood than it was later when his own sufferings had deepened his sympathies, and he had been made " pregnant to good pity," to use his own words, " by the art of knowing and feeling sorrows." But he would never have treated old Jack Falstaff as harshly as he did had he not regretted the results, at least, of his own youthful errors. It looks as if Shakespeare, like other weak men, was filled with a desire to throw the blame on his " misleaders." He certainly exulted in their punishment.

It is difficult for me to write at length about the character of the King in " Henry V.," and fortunately it is not necessary. I have already pointed out the faults in the painting of Prince Henry with such fullness that I may be absolved from again dwelling on similar weakness where it is even more obvious than it was in the two parts of " Henry IV." But something I must say, for the critics in both Germany and England are agreed that " ' Henry V.' must certainly be regarded as Shakespeare's ideal of manhood in the sphere of practical achievement." Without an exception they have all buttered this drama with extravagant praise as one of Shakespeare's masterpieces, though in reality it is one of the worst pieces of work he ever did, almost as bad as " Titus Andronicus " or " Timon " or " The Taming of the Shrew." Unfortunately for the would-be judges, Coleridge did not guide their opinions of " Henry V."; he hardly mentioned

the play, and so they all write the absurdest non-
sense about it, praising because praise of Shakespeare has come to be the fashion, and also no
doubt because his bad work is more on the level of
their intelligence than his good work.

It can hardly be denied that Shakespeare identified himself as far as he could with Henry V. Before the King appears he is praised extravagantly,
as Posthumus was praised, but the eulogy befits
the poet better than the soldier. The Archbishop
of Canterbury says:

> . . . "When he speaks,
> The air, a charter'd libertine, is still,
> And the mute wonder lurketh in men's ears
> To steal his sweet and honey'd sentences."

the Bishop of Ely goes even further in excuse:

> . . . "The prince obscured his contemplation
> Under the veil of wildness."

And this is how the soldier-king himself talks:

> "My learned lord, we pray you to proceed
> And justly and religiously unfold
> Why the law Salique that they have in France
> Or should, or should not bar us in our claim;
> And God forbid, my dear and faithful lord,
> That you should fashion, wrest, or bow your read-
>   ing . . ."

All this is plainly Shakespeare and Shakespeare at
his very worst; and there are hundreds of lines like
these, jewelled here and there by an unforgettable
phrase, as when the Archbishop calls the bees:
" The singing masons building roofs of gold." The
reply made by the King when the Dauphin sends

him the tennis balls has been greatly praised for manliness and modesty; it begins:

> "We are glad the Dauphin is so pleasant with us;
> His present and your pains we thank you for:
> When we have match'd our rackets to these balls,
> We will, in France, by God's grace, play a set
> Shall strike his father's crown into the hazard."

The first line is most excellent, but Shakespeare found it in the old play, and the bragging which follows is hardly bettered by the pious imprecation.

Nor does the scene with the conspirators seem to me any better. The soldier-king would not have preached at them for sixty lines before condemning them. Nor would he have sentenced them with this extraordinary mixture of priggishness and pious pity:

> "*K. Hen.* God quit you in his mercy. Hear your sentence.
>
> .   .   .   .   .
>
> Touching our person seek we no revenge;
> But we our kingdom's safety must so tender,
> Whose ruin you have sought, that to her laws
> We do deliver you. Get you therefore hence,
> Poor miserable wretches, to your death,
> The task whereof, God of His mercy give
> You patience to endure, and true repentance
> Of all your dear offences!"

This "poor miserable wretches" would go better with a generous pardon, and such forgiving would be more in Shakespeare's nature. Throughout this play the necessity of speaking through the soldier-king embarrasses the poet, and the infusion of the poet's sympathy and emotion makes the puppet ridiculous. Henry's speech before Harfleur has been praised on all hands; not by the professors and critics merely, but by those who deserve attention. Carlyle finds deathless valour in the saying: " Ye, good yeomen, whose limbs were made in England," and not deathless valour merely, but " noble patriotism " as well; " a true English heart breathes, calm and strong through the whole business . . . this man (Shakespeare) too had a right stroke in him, had it come to that." I find no valour in it, deathless or otherwise; but the make-believe of valour, the completest proof that valour was absent. Here are the words:

> " *K. Hen.* Once more unto the breach, dear friends, once more;
> Or close the wall up with our English dead.
> In peace there's nothing so becomes a man
> As modest stillness and humility:
> But when the blast of war blows in our ears,
> Then imitate the action of the tiger;
> Stiffen the sinews, summon up the blood,
> Disguise fair nature with hard-favour'd rage;
> Then lend the eye a terrible aspect,
> Let it pry through the portage of the head
> Like the brass cannon; let the brow o'erwhelm it
> As fearfully as doth a galled rock
> O'erhang and jutty his confounded base. . . ."

And so on for another twenty lines. Now consider this stuff: first comes the reflection, more suitable to the philosopher than the man of action, " in peace there's nothing so becomes a man . . ."; then the soldier-king wishes his men to " imitate " the tiger's looks, to " disguise fair nature," and " lend the eye a terrible aspect." But the man who feels the tiger's rage tries to control the aspect of it: he does not put on the frown—that's Pistol's way.

107

The whole thing is mere poetic description of how an angry man looks and not of how a brave man feels, and that it should have deceived Carlyle, surprises me. The truth is that as soon as Shakespeare has to find, I will not say a magical expression for courage, but even an adequate and worthy expression, he fails absolutely. And is the patriotism in " Ye, good yeomen, whose limbs were made in England " a " noble patriotism "? or is it the simplest, the crudest, the least justifiable form of patriotism? There is a noble patriotism founded on the high and generous things done by men of one's own blood, just as there is the vain and empty self-glorification of " limbs made in England," as if English limbs were better than those made in Timbuctoo.

In the third scene of the fourth act, just before the battle, Henry talks at his best, or rather Shakespeare's best: and we catch the true accent of courage. Westmoreland wishes

> . . . " That we now had here
> But one ten thousand of those men in England
> That do no work to-day! "

but Henry lives on a higher plane:

> " No, my fair cousin:
> If we are marked to die, we are enow
> To do our country loss; and if to live,
> The fewer men the greater share of honour."

But this high-couraged sentiment is taken almost word for word from Holinshed. The rest of the speech shows us Shakespeare, as a splendid rhetorician, glorifying glory; and now and then the rhetoric is sublimated into poetry:

108

Hotspur, Prince Henry, and Henry V.

"We few, we happy few, we band of brothers,
For he to-day that sheds his blood with me
Shall be my brother; be he ne'er so vile,
This day shall gentle his condition."

Shakespeare's chief ambition about this time was
to get a coat of arms for his father, and so gentle
his condition. In all the play not one word of praise
for the common archers, who won the battle, no
mention save of the gentle.

Again and again in Henry V. the dissonance of
character between the poet and his soldier-puppet
jars upon the ears, and this dissonance is generally
characteristic. For example, in the third act Shakespeare, through King Henry, expressly charges his
soldiers that "there be nothing compelled from
the villages, nothing taken but paid for, none of
the French upbraided or abused in disdainful language; for when lenity and cruelty play for a kingdom, the gentler gamester is the soonest winner."
Wise words, not yet learned even by statesmen;
drops of wisdom's life-blood from the heart of gentle Shakespeare. But an act later, when the battle
is over, on the mere news that the French have
reinforced their scattered men, Henry V., with tears
in his eyes for the Duke of York's death, gives
orders to kill the prisoners:

"Then every soldier kill his prisoners;
Give the word through."

The puppet is not even human: mere wood!
In the fifth act King Henry takes on the voice
and nature of buried Hotspur. He woos Kath-
arine exactly as Hotspur talked to his wife: he
cannot "mince" it in love, he tells her, in Hotspur's
very words; but is forthright plain; like Hotspur

he despises verses and dancing; like Hotspur he can brag, too; finds it as "easy" to conquer kingdoms as to speak French; can "vault into his saddle with his armour on his back"; he is no carpet-soldier; he never "looks in his glass for love of anything he sees there," and to make the likeness complete he disdains those "fellows of infinite tongue, that can rhyme themselves into ladies' favours . . . a speaker is but a prater; a rhyme is but a ballad." But if Shakespeare had had any vital sympathy for soldiers and men of action he would not have degraded Henry V. in this fashion, into a feeble replica of the traditional Hotspur. In those narrow London streets by the river he must have rubbed shoulders with great adventurers; he knew Essex; had bowed to Raleigh at the Court; must have heard of Drake: inclination was lacking, not models. He might even have differentiated between Prince Henry and Hotspur without going outside his history-books; but a most curious point is that he preferred to smooth away their differences and accentuate the likeness. As a mere matter of fact Hotspur was very much older than Prince Henry, for he fought at Otterbourne in 1388, the year of the prince's birth; but Shakespeare purposely and explicitly makes them both youths. The King, speaking of Percy to Prince Henry, says:

"And being no more in debt to years than thou." . . .

It would have been wiser, I cannot but think, and more dramatic for Shakespeare to have left the hot-headed Percy as the older man who, in spite of years, is too impatient-quick to look before he leaps, while giving the youthful Prince the calm reflection and impersonal outlook which necessarily belong to a great winner of kingdoms. The dramatist could have further differentiated the rivals by making Percy greedy; he should not only have quarrelled with his associates over the division of the land, but insisted on obtaining the larger share, and even then have grumbled as if aggrieved; the soldier aristocrat has always regarded broad acres as his especial reward. On the other hand, Prince Henry should have been open-handed and carelessly-generous, as the patron of Falstaff was likely to be. Further, Hotspur might have been depicted as inordinately proud of his name and birth; the provincial aristocrat usually is, whereas Henry, the Prince, would surely have been too certain of his own qualities to need adventitious aids to pride. Percy might have been shown to us raging over imaginary slights; Worcester says he was " governed by a spleen "; while the Prince could have been given that high sense of honour and insatiate love of fame which were the poles of chivalry. Finally, the dramatist might have painted Hotspur, the soldier, as disdainful of women and the arts of music and poetry, while gracing Prince Henry with a wider culture and sympathy. If I draw attention to such obvious points it is only to show how incredibly careless Shakespeare was in making the conqueror a poor copy of the conquered. He was drawn to Hotspur a little by his quickness and impatience; but he was utterly out of sympathy with the fighter, and never took the trouble even to think of the qualities which a leader of men must possess.

CHAPTER VI

I THINK it hardly necessary to extend this review of Shakespeare's historical plays by subjecting the Three Parts of " King Henry VI." and " Richard III." to a detailed and minute criticism. Yet if I passed them over without mention it would probably be assumed that they made against my theory, or at least that I had some more pertinent reason for not considering them than their relative unimportance. In fact, however, they help to buttress my argument, and so at the risk of being tedious I shall deal with them, though as briefly as possible. Coleridge doubted whether Shakespeare had had anything to do with the " First Part of Henry VI.," but his fellow-actors, Heminge and Condell, placed the Three Parts of " King Henry VI." in the first collected edition of Shakespeare's plays, and our latest criticism finds good reasons to justify this contemporary judgement. Mr. Swinburne writes: " The last battle of Talbot seems to me as undeniably the master's work as the scene in the Temple Gardens, or the courtship of Margaret by Suffolk "; and it would be easy to prove that much of what the dying Mortimer says is just as certainly Shakespeare's work as any of the passages referred to by Mr. Swinburne. Like most of those who are destined to reach the heights, Shakespeare seems to have grown slowly, and even

at twenty-eight or thirty years of age his grasp
of character was so uncertain, his style so little
formed, so apt to waver from blank verse to rhyme,
that it is difficult to determine exactly what he did
write. We may take it, I think, as certain that he
wrote more than we who have his mature work in
mind are inclined to ascribe to him.

The "Second Part of King Henry VI." is a
poetic revision of the old play entitled "The First
Part of the Contention betwixt the Two Famous
Houses of Yorke and Lancaster," and so forth. It
is now generally agreed that Shakespeare's hand
can be traced in the old drama, and with especial
certainty in the comic scenes wherein Cade and his
followers play the chief parts. Notwithstanding
this, the revision was most thorough. Half the lines
in the "Second Part of Henry VI." are new, and
by far the greater number of these are now ascribed
to Shakespeare on good grounds. But some of the
changes are for the worse, and as my argument does
not stand in need of corroboration, I prefer to assume nothing, and shall therefore confine myself
to pointing out that whoever revised "The Contention" did it, in the main, as we should have expected our youthful Shakespeare to do it. For example, when Humphrey of Gloster is accused of de-
vising "strange torments for offenders," he answers
in the old play:

"Why, 'tis well known that whilst I was Protector,
  Pitie was all the fault that was in me,"

and the gentle reviser adds to this:

"For I should melt at an offender's tears,
  And lowly words were ransom for their fault."

113

Besides, the reviser adds a great deal to the part of the weak King with the evident object of making his helplessness pathetic. He gives Henry, too, his sweetest phrases, and when he makes him talk of bewailing Gloster's case "with sad unhelpful tears" we catch the very cadence of Shakespeare's voice. But he does not confine his emendations to the speeches of one personage: the sorrows of the lovers interest him as their affection interested him in the "First Part of Henry VI.," and the farewell words of Queen Margaret to Suffolk are especially characteristic of our gentle poet:

> "Oh, go not yet; even thus two friends condemned
> Embrace and kiss and take ten thousand leaves,
> Loather a hundred times to part than die.
> Yet now farewell; and farewell life with thee."

This reminds me almost irresistibly of Juliet's words when parting with Romeo, and of Imogen's words when Posthumus leaves her. Throughout the play Henry is the poet's favourite, and in the gentle King's lament for Gloster's death we find a peculiarity of Shakespeare's art. It was a part of the cunning of his exquisite sensibility to invent a new word whenever he was deeply moved, the intensity of feeling clothing itself aptly in a novel epithet or image. A hundred examples of this might be given, such as "The multitudinous seas incarnadine"; and so we find here "paly lips." The passage is:

> "Fain would I go to chafe his paly lips
> With twenty thousand kisses and to drain
> Upon his face an ocean of salt tears,
> To tell my love unto his dumb deaf trunk
> And with my finger feel his hand unfeeling."

King Henry VI., and Richard III.

It must be noticed, too, that in this "Second Part" the reviser begins to show himself as something more than the sweet lyric poet. He transposes scenes in order to intensify the interest, and where enemies meet, like Clifford and York, instead of making them rant in mere blind hatred, he allows them to show a generous admiration of each other's qualities; in sum, we find here the germs of that dramatic talent which was so soon to bear such marvellous fruit. No better example of Shakespeare's growth in dramatic power and humour could be found than the way he revises the scenes with Cade. It is very probable, as I have said, that the first sketch was his; when one of Cade's followers declares that Cade's "breath stinks," we are reminded that Coriolanus spoke in the same terms of the Roman rabble. But though it is his own work, Shakespeare evidently takes it up again with the keenest interest, for he adds inimitable touches. For instance, in the first scene, where the two rebels, George Bevis and John Holland, talk of Cade's rising and his intention to set a "new nap upon the commonwealth," George's remark:

"Oh, miserable age! virtue is not regarded in handicraftsmen"—

is an addition, and may be compared with Falstaff's:

"there is no virtue extant."

John answers:

"The nobility think scorn to go in leather aprons,"

which is in the first sketch. But George's reply—

115

"Nay, more; the King's Council are no good work-
men "—

is only to be found in the revised version. The
heightened humour of that "Oh, miserable age! virtue is not regarded in handicraftsmen," assures us
that the reviser was Shakespeare.

What is true of the "Second Part" is true in
the main of the "Third Part of King Henry VI."
Shakespeare's revisions are chiefly the revisions of
a lyric poet, and he scatters his emendations about
without much regard for character. In the Third
Part, as in the Second, however, he transposes scenes,
gives deeper life to the marionettes, and in various
ways quickens the dramatic interest. This Third
Part resembles "King John" in some respects and
a similar inference can be drawn from it. As in
"King John" we have the sharply contrasted figures of the Bastard and Arthur, so in this "Third
Part" there are two contrasted characters, Richard
Duke of Gloster and King Henry VI., the one a
wild beast whose life is action, and who knows
neither fear, love, pity, nor touch of any scruple;
the other, a saint-like King, whose worst fault is
gentle weakness. In "The True Tragedie of Richard," the old play on which this "Third Part"
was founded, the character of Richard is power-
fully sketched, even though the human outlines are
sometimes confused by his devilish malignity.
Shakespeare takes this character from the old play,
and alters it but very slightly. Indeed, the most
splendid piece of character-revealing in his Richard
is to be found in the old play:

"I had no father, I am like no father,
I have no brother, I am like no brother;

And this word *Love,* which greybeards call divine,
Be resident in men like one another,
And not in me:—I am myself alone."

The Satanic energy of this outburst declares its
author, Marlowe.[1] Shakespeare copies it word for
word, only omitting with admirable art the first line.
Indeed, though he alters the speeches of Richard and
improves them, he does nothing more; he adds no
new quality; his Richard is the Richard of " The
True Tragedie." But King Henry may be regarded
as Shakespeare's creation. In the old play the outlines of Henry's character are so feebly, faintly
sketched that he is scarcely recognizable, but with
two or three touches Shakespeare makes the saint a
living man. This King is happier in prison than
in his palace; this is how he speaks to his keeper,
the Lieutenant of the Tower:

" Nay, be thou sure, I'll well requite thy kindness,
For that it made my imprisonment a pleasure;
Ay, such a pleasure as encagèd birds
Conceive, when, after many moody thoughts,
At last by notes of household harmony
They quite forget their loss of liberty."

Just as the bird runs a little before he springs from
the earth and takes flight, so Shakespeare often
writes, as in this instance, an awkward weak line
or two before his song-wings move with freedom.
But the last four lines are peculiarly his; his the
thought; his, too, the sweetness of the words " encagèd birds " and " household harmony."

[1] Mr. Swinburne was the first, I believe, to attribute this
passage to Marlowe; he praises the verses, too, as they deserve; but as I had written the above before reading his work,
I let it stand.

117

Finally, Henry is not only shown to us as gentle and loving, but as a man who prefers quiet and the country to a King's Court and state. Even in eager, mounting youth this was Shakespeare's own choice: Prince Arthur in "King John" longs to be a shepherd: and this crowned saint has the same desire. From boyhood to old age Shakespeare preferred the "life removed."

> "O God, methinks it were a happy life
> To be no better than a homely swain;
> To sit upon a hill, as I do now,
> To carve out dials quaintly point by point,
> Thereby to see the minutes how they run;
> How many make the hour full complete;
> How many hours bring about the day;
> How many days will finish up the year;
> How many years a mortal man may live.
>
> . . . . .
>
> So minutes, hours, days, months, and years,
> Passed over to the end they were created,
> Would bring white hairs unto a quiet grave."

All this it seems to me is as finely characteristic of the gentle melancholy of Shakespeare's youth as Jaques' bitter words are of the deeper melancholy of his manhood:

> "And so from hour to hour we ripe and ripe,
> And then from hour to hour we rot and rot
> And thereby hangs a tale."

The "Third Part of Henry VI." leads one directly to "Richard III." It was Coleridge's opinion that Shakespeare "wrote hardly anything of this play except the character of Richard. He found the piece a stock play and re-wrote the parts which developed the hero's character; he certainly did not

write the scenes in which Lady Anne yielded to
the usurper's solicitations." In this instance Coleridge's positive opinion deserves to be weighed re-
spectfully. At the time when " Richard III." was
written Shakespeare was still rather a lyric than
a dramatic poet, and Coleridge was a good judge
of the peculiarities of his lyric style. Of course,
Professor Dowden, too, is in doubt whether " Richard III." should be ascribed to Shakespeare. He
says: " Its manner of conceiving and presenting
character has a certain resemblance, not elsewhere
to be found in Shakespeare's writings, to the ideal
manner of Marlowe. As in the plays of Marlowe,
there is here one dominant figure distinguished by
a few strongly marked and inordinately developed
qualities."

This faulty reasoning only shows how dangerous
it is for a professor to copy his teacher slavishly:
in " Coriolanus," too, we have the " one dominant
figure," and all the rest of it. The truth seems to
be that in the " Third Part of Henry VI." Shakespeare had been working with Marlowe, or, at least,
revising Marlowe's work; in either case he was so
steeped in Marlowe's spirit that he took, as we
have seen, the most splendid piece of Richard's self-
revealing directly from the older poet. Moreover,
the words of deepest characterization in Shakespeare's " Richard III.,"

" Richard loves Richard—that is, I am I,"

are manifestly a weak echo of the tremendous

" I am myself alone "

of Marlowe's Richard. At least to this extent, then,
Shakespeare used Marlowe in depicting Richard's

character. But this trait, important as it was, did not carry him far, and he was soon forced to draw on his own experience of life. Already he seems to have noticed that one characteristic of men of action is a blunt plainness of speech; their courage is shown in their frankness, and, besides, words stand for realities with them, and are, therefore, used with sincerity. Shakespeare's Richard III. uses plain speaking as a hypocritical mask, but already Shakespeare is a dramatist and in his clever hands Richard's plain speaking is so allied with his incisive intelligence that it appears to be now a mask, now native shamelessness, and thus the characterization wins in depth and mystery. Every now and then, too, this Richard sees things which no Englishman has been capable of seeing, except Shakespeare himself. The whole of Plato's " Gorgias " is comprised in the two lines:

" Conscience is but a word that cowards use,
   Devised at first to keep the strong in awe."

The declaration of the second murderer that conscience " makes a man a coward . . . it beggars any man that keeps it; it is turned out of all towns and cities for a dangerous thing; and every man that means to live well endeavours to trust to himself and to live without it," should be regarded as the complement of what Falstaff says of honour; in both the humour of Shakespeare's characteristic irony is not to be mistaken.

The whole play, I think, must be ascribed to Shakespeare; all the memorable words in it are indubitably his, and I cannot believe that any other hand drew for us that marvellous, masterful courtship of Anne which Coleridge, naturally enough, was unwilling to appreciate. The structure of the play, however, shows all the weakness of Marlowe's method: the interest is concentrated on the protagonist; there is not humour enough to relieve the gloomy intensity, and the scenes in which Richard does not figure are unattractive and feeble.

One has only to think of the two characters—Richard II. and Richard III.—and to recall their handling in order to get a deep impression of Shakespeare's nature. He cannot present the vile Richard II. at all; he has no interest in him; but as soon as he thinks of Richard's youth and remembers that he was led astray by others, he begins to identify himself with him, and at once Richard's weakness is made amiable and his sufferings affecting. In measure as Shakespeare lets himself go and paints himself more and more freely, his portraiture becomes astonishing, till at length the imprisoned Richard gives himself up to melancholy philosophic musing, without a tinge of bitterness or envy or hate, and every one with eyes to see, is forced to recognize in him a younger brother to Hamlet and Posthumus. "Richard III." was produced in a very different way. It was Marlowe's daemonic power and intensity that first interested Shakespeare in this Richard; under the spell of Marlowe's personality Shakespeare conceived the play, and especially the scene between Richard and Anne; but the original impulse exhausted itself quickly, and then Shakespeare fell back on his own experience and made Richard keen of insight and hypocritically blunt of speech—a sort of sketch of Iago. A little later Shakespeare either felt that the action was unsuitable to the development of such a character, or more probably he grew weary of the effort to depict a fiend; in any case, the play becomes less and less interesting, and even the character of Richard begins to waver. There is one astonishing instance of this towards the end of the drama. On the eve of the decisive battle Richard starts awake from his terrifying dreams, and now, if ever, one would expect from him perfect sincerity of utterance. This is what we find:

> " There is no creature loves me;
> And if I die no soul shall pity me;
> Nay, wherefore should they, since that I myself
> Find in myself no pity to myself? "

The first two lines bespeak a loving, gentle nature, Shakespeare's nature, the nature of a Henry VI. or an Arthur, a nature which Richard III. would certainly have despised, and the last two lines are merely an objective ethical judgement wholly out of place and very clumsily expressed.

To sum up, then, for this is not the place to consider Shakespeare's share in "Henry VIII.," I find that in the English historical plays the manly characters, Hotspur, Harry V., the great Bastard, and Richard III., are all taken from tradition or from old plays, and Shakespeare did nothing more than copy the traits which were given to him; on the other hand, the weak, irresolute, gentle, melancholy characters are his own, and he shows extraordinary resource in revealing the secret workings of their souls. Even in early manhood, and when handling histories and men of action, Shakespeare cannot conceal his want of sympathy for the practical leaders of men; he neither understands them deeply nor loves them; but in portraying the girlish Arthur and the Hamlet-like Richard II., and in drawing forth the pathos of their weakness, he is already without a rival or second in all literature.

King Henry VI., and Richard III.

I am anxious not to deform the truth by exaggeration; a caricature of Shakespeare would offend me as a sacrilege, even though the caricature were characteristic, and when I find him even in youth one-sided, a poet and dreamer, I am minded to tell less than the truth rather than more. He was extraordinarily sensitive, I say to myself, and lived in the stress of great deeds; he treated Henry V., a man of action if ever there was one, as an ideal, and lavished on him all his admiration, but it will not do: I cannot shut my eyes to the fact; the effort is worse than useless. He liked Henry V. because of his misled youth and his subsequent rise to highest honour, and not because of his practical genius. Where in his portrait gallery is the picture of a Drake, or even of a Raleigh? The adventurer was the characteristic product of that jostling time; but Shakespeare turned his head away; he was not interested in him. In spite of himself, however, he became passionately interested in the pitiful Richard II. and his untimely fate. Notwithstanding the praise of the critics, his King Henry V. is a wooden marionette; the intense life of the traditional madcap Prince has died out of him; but Prince Arthur lives deathlessly, and we still hear his childish treble telling Hubert of his love.

Those who disagree with me will have to account for the fact that, even in the historical plays written in early manhood, all his portraits of men of action are mere copies, while his genius shines in the portraits of a gentle saint like Henry VI., of a weakling like Richard II., or of a girlish youth like Arthur—all these favourite studies being alike in pathetic helplessness and tender affection.

It is curious that no one of the commentators has noticed this extraordinary one-sidedness of

Shakespeare. In spite of his miraculous faculty of expression, he never found wonderful phrases for the virile virtues or virile vices. For courage, revenge, self-assertion, and ambition we have finer words in English than any that Shakespeare coined. In this field Chapman, Milton, Byron, Carlyle, and even Bunyan are his masters.

Of course, as a man he had the instinct of courage, and an admiration of courage; his intellect, too, gave him some understanding of its range. Dr. Brandes declares that Shakespeare has only depicted physical courage, the courage of the swordsman; but that is beside the truth: Dr. Brandes has evidently forgotten the passage in " Antony and Cleopatra," when Caesar contemptuously refuses the duel with Antony and speaks of his antagonist as an " old ruffian." Enobarbus, too, sneers at Antony's proposed duel:

" Yes, like enough, high-battled Caesar will
　Unstate his happiness, and be staked to the show
　Against a sworder."

Unhelped by memory, Dr. Brandes might have guessed that Shakespeare would exhaust the obvious at first glance. But the soul of courage to Shakespeare is, as we have seen, a love of honour working on quick generous blood—a feminine rather than a masculine view of the matter.

Carlyle has a deeper sense of this aboriginal virtue. With the fanatic's trust in God his Luther will go to Worms, " though it rain devils "; and when in his own person Carlyle spoke of the small, honest minority desperately resolved to maintain their ideas though opposed by a huge hostile majority of fools and the insincere, he found one of the finest expressions for courage in all our literature. The vast

host shall be to us, he cried, as " stubble is to fire."
It may be objected that this is the voice of religious faith rather than of courage pure and simple,
and the objection is valid so far as it goes; but this
genesis of courage is peculiarly English, and the
courage so formed is of the highest. Every one remembers how Valiant-for-Truth fights in Bunyan's
allegory: " I fought till my sword did cleave to my
hand; and when they were joined together, as if a
sword grew out of my arm, and when the blood ran
through my fingers, then I fought with most courage." The mere expression gives us an understanding of the desperate resolution of Cromwell's Iron-
sides.

But if desperate courage is not in Shakespeare,
neither are its ancillary qualities—cruelty, hatred,
ambition, revenge. Whenever he talks on these
themes, he talks from the teeth outwards, as one
without experience of their violent delights. His
Gloucester rants about ambition without an illuminating or even a convincing word. Hatred and
revenge Shakespeare only studied superficially, and
cruelty he shudders from like a woman.

It is astounding how ill-endowed Shakespeare was
on the side of manliness. His intellect was so fine,
his power of expression so magical, the men about
him, his models, so brave—founders as they were
of the British empire and sea-tyranny—that he is
able to use his Hotspurs and Harrys to hide from
the general the poverty of his temperament. But
the truth will out: Shakespeare was the greatest of
poets, a miraculous artist, too, when he liked; but
he was not a hero, and manliness was not his *forte:*
he was by nature a neuropath and a lover.

He was a master of passion and pity, and it
astonishes one to notice how willingly he passed

always to that extreme of sympathy where nothing but his exquisite choice of words and images saved him from falling into the silly. For example, in "Titus Andronicus," with its crude, unmotived horrors, Titus calls Marcus a murderer, and when Marcus replies: "Alas, my lord, I have but killed a fly," Titus answers:

> "But how, if that fly had a father and mother?
> How would he hang his slender gilded wings,
> And buzz lamenting doings in the air?
> Poor harmless fly!
> That with his pretty buzzing melody,
> Came here to make us merry! and thou hast killed
>   him."

Even in his earliest plays in the noontide of lusty youth, when the heat of the blood makes most men cruel, or at least heedless of others' sorrows, Shakespeare was full of sympathy; his gentle soul wept with the stricken deer and suffered through the killing of a fly. Just as Ophelia turned "thought and affliction, passion, hell itself" to "favour and to prettiness," so Shakespeare's genius turned the afflictions and passions of man to pathos and to pity.

CHAPTER VII

SHAKESPEARE began the work of life as a lyric poet. It was to be expected therefore that when he took up playwriting he would use the play from time to time as an opportunity for a lyric, and in fact this was his constant habit. From the beginning to the end of his career he was as much a lyric poet as a dramatist. His first comedies are feeble and thin in character-drawing and the lyrical sweetness is everywhere predominant. His apprenticeship period may be said to have closed with his first tragedy, " Romeo and Juliet." I am usually content to follow Mr. Furnival's " Trial Table of the order of Shakespeare's Plays," in which " Richard II.," " Richard III.," and " King John " are all placed later than " Romeo and Juliet," and yet included in the first period that stretches from 1585 to 1595. But " Romeo and Juliet " seems to me to be far more characteristic of the poet's genius than any of these histories; it is not only a finer work of art than any of them, and therefore of higher promise, but in its lyrical sweetness far more truly representative of Shakespeare's youth than any of the early comedies or historical plays. Whatever their form may be, nearly all Shakespeare's early works are love-songs, " Venus and Adonis," " Lucrece," " Love's Labour's Lost," " The Two Gentlemen of Verona," and he may be said to have ended his apprenticeship with the imperishable tragedy of first love, " Romeo and Juliet."

127

In the years from 1585 to 1595 Shakespeare brought the lyric element into something like due subordination and managed to free himself almost completely from his early habit of rhyming. Mr. Swinburne has written of Shakespeare's use of rhymed verse with a fullness of knowledge and sympathy that leaves little to be desired. He compares it aptly to the use of the left hand instead of the right, and doubts cogently whether Shakespeare ever attained such mastery of rhyme as Marlowe in "Hero and Leander." But I like to think that Shakespeare's singing quickly became too sincere in its emotion and too complex in its harmonies to tolerate the definite limits set by rhyme. In any case by 1595 Shakespeare had learned to prefer blank verse to rhyme, at least for play-writing; he thus made the first great step towards a superb knowledge of his instrument.

The period of Shakespeare's maturity defines itself sharply; it stretches from 1595 to 1608 and falls naturally into two parts; the first part includes the trilogy "Henry IV." and "Henry V." and his golden comedies; the second, from 1600 to 1608, is entirely filled with his great tragedies. The characteristic of this period, so far as regards the instrument, is that Shakespeare has come to understand the proper function of prose. He sees first that it is the only language suited to broad comedy, and goes on to use it in moments of sudden excitement, or when dramatic truth to character seems to him all important. At his best he uses blank verse when some emotion sings itself to him, and prose as the ordinary language of life, the language of surprise, laughter, strife, and of all the commoner feelings. During these twelve or fourteen years the lyric note is not obtrusive;

it is usually subordinated to character and suited to action.

His third and last period begins with " Pericles " and ends with " The Tempest "; it is characterized, as we shall see later, by bodily weakness and by a certain contempt for the dramatic fiction. But the knowledge of the instrument once acquired never left Shakespeare. It is true that the lyric note becomes increasingly clear in his late comedies; but prose too is used by him with the same mastery that he showed in his maturity.

In the first period Shakespeare was often unable to give his puppets individual life; in maturity he was interested in the puppets themselves and used them with considerable artistry; in the third period he had grown a little weary of them and in " The Tempest " showed himself inclined, just as Goethe in later life was inclined, to turn his characters into symbols or types.

The place of " Twelfth Night " is as clearly marked in Shakespeare's works as " Romeo and Juliet " or " The Tempest." It stands on the dividing line between his light, joyous comedies and the great tragedies; it was all done at the topmost height of happy hours, but there are hints in it which we shall have to notice later, which show that when writing it Shakespeare had already looked into the valley of disillusion which he was about to tread. But " Twelfth Night " is written in the spirit of " As You Like It " or " Much Ado," only it is still more personal-ingenuous and less dramatic than these; it is, indeed, a lyric of love and the joy of living.

There is no intenser delight to a lover of letters than to find Shakespeare singing, with happy unconcern, of the things he loved best—not the Shakespeare of Hamlet or Macbeth, whose intellect speaks in critical judgements of men and of life, and whose heart we are fain to divine from slight indications; nor Shakespeare the dramatist, who tried now and again to give life to puppets like Coriolanus and Iago, with whom he had little sympathy; but Shakespeare the poet, Shakespeare the lover, Shakespeare whom Ben Jonson called "the gentle," Shakespeare the sweet-hearted singer, as he lived and suffered and enjoyed. If I were asked to complete the portrait given to us by Shakespeare of himself in Hamlet-Macbeth with one single passage, I should certainly choose the first words of the Duke in "Twelfth Night." I must transcribe the poem, though it will be in every reader's remembrance; for it contains the completest, the most characteristic, confession of Shakespeare's feelings ever given in a few lines:

> "If music be the food of love, play on;
> Give me excess of it, that surfeiting
> The appetite may sicken, and so die.
> That strain again;—it had a dying fall:
> Oh, it came o'er my ear like the sweet south
> That breathes upon a bank of violets,
> Stealing and giving odour.—Enough! no more;
> 'Tis not so sweet now as it was before."

Every one will notice that Shakespeare as we know him in Romeo is here depicted again with insistence on a few salient traits; here, too, we have the poet of the Sonnets masquerading as a Duke and the protagonist of yet another play. There is still less art used in characterizing this Duke than there is in characterizing Macbeth; Shakespeare merely lets himself go and sings his feelings in the most beautiful words. This is his philosophy of music and of love:

> "Give me excess of it, that surfeiting,
> The appetite may sicken, and so die;"

and then:

> "Enough, no more;
> 'Tis not so sweet now as it was before."

—the quick revulsion of the delicate artist-voluptuary who wishes to keep unblunted in memory the most exquisite pang of pleasure.

Speech after speech discovers the same happy freedom and absolute abandonment to the "sense of beauty." Curio proposes hunting the hart, and at once the Duke breaks out:

> "Why, so I do, the noblest that I have.
> O, when mine eyes did see Olivia first,
> Methought she purged the air of pestilence.
> That instant was I turned into a hart,
> And my desires, like fell and cruel hounds,
> E'er since pursue me."—

Valentine then comes to tell him that Olivia is still mourning for her brother, and the Duke seizes the opportunity for another lyric:

> "O, she that hath a heart of that fine frame
> To pay this debt of love but to a brother,
> How will she love, when the rich golden shaft
> Hath killed the flock of all affections else
> That live in her; when liver, brain, and heart,
> These sovereign thrones, are all supplied and filled—
> Her sweet perfections—with one self King!—
> Away before me to sweet beds of flowers,
> Love-thoughts lie rich when canopied with bowers."

The last two lines show clearly enough that Shakespeare was not troubled with any thought of reality as he wrote: he was transported by Fancy into that enchanted country of romance where beds of flowers are couches and bowers, canopies of love. But what a sensuality there is in him!

> " When liver, brain, and heart,
> These sovereign thrones, are all supplied and filled—
> Her sweet perfections—with one self King!——"

Of course, too, this Duke is inconstant, and swings from persistent pursuit of Olivia to love of Viola without any other reason than the discovery of Viola's sex. In the same way Romeo turns from Rosaline to Juliet at first sight. This trait has been praised by Coleridge and others as showing singular knowledge of a young man's character, but I should rather say that inconstancy was a characteristic of sensuality and belonged to Shakespeare himself, for Orsino, like Romeo, has no reason to change his love; and the curious part of the matter is that Shakespeare does not seem to think that the quick change in Orsino requires any explanation at all. Moreover, the love of Duke Orsino for Olivia is merely the desire of her bodily beauty—the counterpart of the sensual jealousy of Othello. Speaking from Shakespeare's very heart, the Duke says:

> " Tell her, my love, more noble than the world,
> Prizes not quantity of dirty lands;
> The parts that Fortune hath bestowed upon her,
> Tell her, I hold as giddily as Fortune;
> But 'tis that miracle and queen of gems
> That nature pranks her in attracts my soul."

So the body wins the soul according to this Orsino, who is, I repeat again, Shakespeare in his most ingenuous and frankest mood; the contempt of wealth—" dirty lands "—and the sensuality—" that miracle and queen of gems "—are alike characteristic.

A few more touches and the portrait of this Duke will be complete; he says to the pretended Cesario when sending him as ambassador to Olivia:

> " Cesario,
> Thou knowest no less but all; I have unclasped
> To thee the book even of my secret soul;
> Therefore, good youth,"—

and so forth.

It is a matter of course that this Duke should tell everything to his friend; a matter of course, too, that he should love books and bookish metaphors. Without being told, one knows that he delights in all beautiful things—pictures with their faërie false presentment of forms and life; the flesh-firm outline of marble, the warmth of ivory and the sea-green patine of bronze—was not the poop of the vessel beaten gold, the sails purple, the oars silver, and the very water amorous?

This Duke shows us Shakespeare's most intimate traits even when the action does not suggest the self-revelation. When sending Viola to woo Olivia for him he adds:

> " Some four or five, attend him;
> All if you will; for I myself am best
> When least in company."

Like Vincentio, that other mask of Shakespeare, this Duke too loves solitude and " the life removed "; he is " best when least in company."

If there is any one who still doubts the essential identity of Duke Orsino and Shakespeare, let him

consider the likeness in thought and form between
the Duke's lyric effusions and the Sonnets, and if
that does not convince him I might use a hitherto
untried argument.   When a dramatist creates a
man's character he is apt to make him, as the French
say, too much of a piece—too logical.   But, in this
instance, though Shakespeare has given the Duke
only a short part, he has made him contradict himself with the charming ease that belongs peculiarly
to self-revealing.   The Duke tells us:

" For such as I am all true lovers are,—
  Unstaid and skittish in all motions else,
  Save in the constant image of the creature
  That is beloved."

The next moment he repeats this:

" For, boy, however we do praise ourselves,
  Our fancies are more giddy and unfirm,
  More longing, wavering, sooner lost and won,
  Than women's are."

And the moment after he asserts:

" There is no woman's sides
  Can bide the beating of so strong a passion
  As love doth give my heart; no woman's heart
  So big, to hold so much; they lack retention.
  Alas! their love may be called appetite,
  No motion of the liver, but the palate,
  That suffers surfeit, cloyment, and revolt!"

Hamlet contradicts himself, too: at one moment
he declares that his soul is immortal, and at the
next is full of despair.   But Hamlet is so elaborate
a portrait, built up of so many minute touches, that
self-contradiction is a part, and a necessary part,
of his many-sided complexity.   But the Duke in
134

" Twelfth Night " reveals himself as it were acci-
dentally; we know little more of him than that he
loves music and love, books and flowers, and that he
despises wealth and company; accordingly, when
he contradicts himself, we may suspect that Shakespeare is letting himself speak freely without much
care for the coherence of characterization. And the
result of this frankness is that he has given a more
intimate, a more confidential, sketch of himself in
Duke Orsino of " Twelfth Night " than he has given
us in any play except perhaps " Hamlet " and
" Macbeth."

I hardly need to prove that Shakespeare in his
earliest plays, as in his latest, in his Sonnets as in
his darkest tragedy, loved flowers and music. In
almost every play he speaks of flowers with affection and delight. One only needs to recall the song
in " A Midsummer Night's Dream," " I know a
bank," or Perdita's exquisite words:

> " Daffodils,
> That come before the swallow dares, and take
> The wind of March with beauty; violets dim,
> But sweeter than the lids of Juno's eyes
> Or Cytherea's breath; pale primroses,
> That die unmarried ere they can behold
> Bright Phoebus in his strength, a malady
> Most incident to maids; bold oxlips, and
> The crown-imperial; lilies of all kinds,
> The flower-de-luce being one ";

or Arviragus' praise of Imogen:

> " Thou shalt not lack
> The flower that's like thy face, pale primrose, nor
> The azured harebell like thy veins; no, nor
> The leaf of eglantine, whom not to slander
> Outsweetened not thy breath."

Shakespeare praises music so frequently and so enthusiastically that we must regard the trait as characteristic of his deepest nature. Take this play which we are handling now. Not only the Duke, but both the heroines, Viola and Olivia, love music. Viola can sing " in many sorts of music," and Olivia admits that she would rather hear Viola solicit love than " music from the spheres." Romeo almost confounds music with love, as does Duke Orsino:

> " How silver-sweet sound lovers' tongues by night,
> Like softest music to attending ears!"

And again:
> " And let rich music's tongue
> Unfold the imagin'd happiness that both
> Receive in either by this dear encounter."

It is a curious and characteristic fact that Shakespeare gives almost the same words to Ferdinand in " The Tempest " that he gave ten years earlier to the Duke in " Twelfth Night." In both passages music goes with passion to allay its madness:

> " This music crept by me upon the waters,
> Allaying both their fury and my passion
> With its sweet air "

and Duke Orsino says:

> " That old and antique song we heard last night,
> Methought it did relieve my passion much."

This confession is so peculiar; shows, too, so exquisitely fine a sensibility, that its repetition makes me regard it as Shakespeare's. The most splendid lyric on music is given to Lorenzo in " The Merchant of Venice," and it may be remarked in passing that

136

Twelfth Night

Lorenzo is not a character, but, like Claudio, a mere
name and a mouthpiece of Shakespeare's feeling.
Shakespeare was almost as well content, it appears,
to play the lover as to play the Duke. I cannot help
transcribing the magical verses, though they must
be familiar to every lover of our English tongue:

> " How sweet the moonlight sleeps upon this bank!
> Here will we sit, and let the sounds of music
> Creep in our ears; soft stillness and the night
> Become the touches of sweet harmony.
> Sit, Jessica: Look how the floor of heaven
> Is thick inlaid with patines of bright gold.
> There's not the smallest orb which thou behold'st
> But in his motion like an angel sings,
> Still quiring to the young-eyed cherubims.
> Such harmony is in immortal souls;
> But, whilst this muddy vesture of decay
> Doth grossly close it in, we cannot hear it."

The first lines of this poem are conceived in the
very spirit of the poems of " Twelfth Night," and
in the last lines Shakespeare puts to use that
divine imagination which lifts all his best verse into
the higher air of life, and reaches its noblest in
Prospero's solemn-sad lyric.

Shakespeare's love of music is so much a part of
himself that he condemns those who do not share
it; this argument, too, is given to Lorenzo:

> " The man that hath no music to himself,
> Nor is not moved with concord of sweet sounds,
> Is fit for treasons, stratagems, and spoils;
> The motions of his spirit are dull as night,
> And his affections dark as Erebus:
> Let no such man be trusted."

That this view was not merely the expression of

a passing mood is shown by the fact that Shakespeare lends no music to his villains; but Timon gives welcome to his friends with music, just as Hamlet welcomes the players with music and Portia calls for music while her suitors make their eventful choice. Titania and Oberon both seek the aid of music to help them in their loves, and the war-worn and time-worn Henry IV. prays for music to bring some rest to his "weary spirit"; in much the same mood Prospero desires music when he breaks his wand and resigns his magical powers.

Here, again, in "Twelfth Night" in full manhood Shakespeare shows himself to us as Romeo, in love with flowers and music and passion. True, this Orsino is a little less occupied with verbal quips, a little more frankly sensual, too, than Romeo; but then Romeo would have been more frankly sensual had he lived from twenty-five to thirty-five. As an older man, too, Orsino has naturally more of Hamlet-Shakespeare's peculiar traits than Romeo showed; the contempt of wealth and love of solitude are qualities hardly indicated in Romeo, while in Orsino as in the mature Shakespeare they are salient characteristics. To sum up: Hamlet-Macbeth gives us Shakespeare's mind; but in Romeo-Orsino he has discovered his heart and poetic temperament to us as ingenuously, though not, perhaps, so completely, as he does in the Sonnets.

CHAPTER VIII

SHAKESPEARE'S portraits of himself are not to be mistaken; the changes in him caused by age bring into clearer light the indestructible individuality, and no difference of circumstance or position has any effect upon this distinctive character: whether he is the lover, Romeo; the murderer, Macbeth; the courtier, Hamlet; or the warrior, Posthumus; he is always the same—a gentle yet impulsive nature, sensuous at once and meditative; half poet, half philosopher, preferring nature and his own reveries to action and the life of courts; a man physically fastidious to disgust, as is a delicate woman, with dirt and smells and common things; an idealist daintily sensitive to all courtesies, chivalries, and distinctions. The portrait is not yet complete—far from it, indeed; but already it is manifest that Shakespeare's nature was so complex, so tremulously poised between world-wide poles of poetry and philosophy, of what is individual and concrete on the one hand and what is abstract and general on the other, that the task of revealing himself was singularly difficult. It is not easy even to describe him as he painted himself: it may be that, wishing to avoid a mere catalogue of disparate qualities, I have brought into too great prominence the gentle passionate side of Shakespeare's nature; though that would be difficult and in any case no bad fault; for this is the side which has hitherto been neglected or rather overlooked by the critics.

My view of Shakespeare can be made clearer by examples. I began by taking Hamlet the philosopher as Shakespeare's most profound and complex study, and went on to prove that Hamlet is the most complete portrait which Shakespeare has given of himself, other portraits being as it were sides of Hamlet or less successful *replicas* of him; and finally I tried to complete the Hamlet by uniting him with Duke Orsino, Orsino the poet-lover being, so to speak, Shakespeare's easiest and most natural portrait. In Hamlet, if one may dare to say so, Shakespeare has discovered too much of himself: Hamlet is at one and the same time philosopher and poet, critic and courtier, lover and cynic—the extremes that Shakespeare's intellect could cover— and he fills every part so easily that he might almost be a bookish Admirable Crichton, a type of perfection rather than an individual man, were it not for his feminine gentleness and forgivingness of nature, and particularly for the brooding melancholy and disbelief which darkened Shakespeare's outlook at the time. But though the melancholy scepticism was an abiding characteristic of Shakespeare, to be found in his Richard II. as in his Prospero, it did not overshadow all his being as it does Hamlet's. There was a summer-time, too, in Shakespeare's life, and in his nature a capacity for sunny gaiety and a delight in life and love which came to full expression in the golden comedies, " Much Ado," " As You Like It " and " Twelfth Night." The complement to Hamlet, the sad philosopher-sceptic, is the sensuous happy poet-lover Orsino, and when we take these seeming antitheses and unite them we have a good portrait of Shakespeare. But these two, Hamlet and Orsino, are in reality one; every quality of Orsino is to be found or divined in Hamlet, and therefore the easiest and surest way to get at Shakespeare is to take Hamlet and deepen those peculiarities in him which we find in Orsino.

Some critics are sure to say that I have now given a portrait of Coleridge rather than a portrait of Shakespeare. This is not altogether the fact, though I for one see no shame in acknowledging the likeness. Coleridge had a " smack of Hamlet " in him, as he himself saw; indeed, in his rich endowment as poet and philosopher, and in his gentleness and sweetness of disposition, he was more like Shakespeare than any other Englishman whom I can think of; but in Coleridge the poet soon disappeared, and a little later the philosopher in him faded into the visionary and sophist; he became an upholder of the English Church and found reasons in the immutable constitution of the universe for aprons and shovel-hats. Shakespeare, on the other hand, though similarly endowed, was far more richly endowed: he had stronger passions and greater depth of feeling; the sensuousness of Keats was in him; and this richness of nature not only made him a greater lyric poet than Coleridge and a far saner thinker, but carried him in spite of a constitutional dislike of resolve and action to his astounding achievement.

But even when we thus compare Shakespeare with Coleridge, as we compare trees of the same species, showing that as the roots of the one go deeper and take a firmer hold of earth, so in exact measure the crest rises into higher air, still there is something lacking to our comparison. Even when we hold Hamlet-Orsino before us as the best likeness of the master-poet, our impression of him is still incomplete.

There remains a host of creations from Launce to Autolycus, and from Dame Quickly to Maria, which proves that Shakespeare was something more than the gentle lover-thinker-poet whom we have shown. It is Shakespeare's humour that differentiates him, not only from Coleridge and Keats, but also from the world-poets, Goethe, Dante, and Homer. It is this unique endowment that brings him into vital touch with reality and common life, and hinders us from feeling his all-pervading ideality as disproportioned or one-sided. Strip him of his humour and he would have been seen long ago in his true proportions. His sympathies are not more broad and generous than Balzac's; his nature is too delicate, too sensitive, too sensuous; but his humour blinds us to the truth. Of course his comic characters, like his captains and men of action, are due originally to his faculty of observation; but while his observation of the fighting men is always superficial and at times indifferent, his humorous observation is so intensely interested and sympathetic that its creations are only inferior in artistic value to his portraits of the poet-philosopher-lover.

The intellect in him had little or nothing to go upon in the case of the man of action; he never loved the Captain or watched him at work; it is his mind and second-hand knowledge that made Henry V. and Richard III.; and how slight and shallow are these portraits in comparison with the portrait of a Parolles or a Sir Toby Belch, or the ever-famous Nurse, where the same intellect has played about the humorous trait and heightened the effect of loving observation. The critics who have ignorantly praised his Hotspur and Bastard as if he had been a man of deeds as well as a man of words have only obscured the truth that Shakespeare the poet-philosopher, the lover *quand même*, only reached a sane balance of nature through his overflowing humour. He whose intellect and sensibilities inspired him with nothing but contempt and loathing for the mass of mankind, the aristocrat who in a dozen plays sneers at the greasy caps and foul breaths of the multitude, fell in love with Dogberry, and Bottom, Quickly and Tearsheet, clod and clown, pimp and prostitute, for the laughter they afforded. His humour is rarely sardonic; it is almost purged of contempt; a product not of hate but of love; full of sympathy; summer-lightning humour, harmless and beautiful.

Sometimes the sympathy fails and the laughter grows grim, and these lapses are characteristic. He hates false friends and timeservers, the whole tribe of the ungrateful, the lords of Timon's acquaintance and his artists; he loathes Shylock, whose god is greed and who battens on others' misfortunes; he laughs at the self-righteous Malvolio and not with him, and takes pleasure in unmasking the pretended ascetic and Puritan Angelo; but for the frailties of the flesh he has an ever-ready forgiveness. Like the greatest of ethical teachers, he can take the publican and the sinner to his heart, but not the hypocrite or the Pharisee or the money-lender.

It does not come within the scope of this essay to attempt a detailed criticism of Shakespeare's comic characters; it will be enough for my purpose to show that even in his masterpiece of humour, the incomparable Falstaff, he betrays himself more than once: more than once we shall find Shakespeare, the poet, or Shakespeare, the thinker, speaking through Falstaff's mouth. Yet to criticize Falstaff is difficult, and if easy, it would still be an offence to those capable of gratitude. I would as soon find fault with Ariel's most exquisite lyric, or the impeccable loveliness of the " Dove Sono," as weigh the rich words of the Lord of Comedy in small balances of reason. But such considerations must not divert me from my purpose; I have undertaken to discover the very soul of Shakespeare, and I must, therefore, trace him in Falstaff as in Hamlet.

Falstaff enters and asks the Prince the time. The Prince answers that unless " hours were cups of sack and so forth, he can't understand why Falstaff should care about anything so superfluous as time." Falstaff replies: " Indeed you come near me now, Hal; for we that take purses go by the moon and the seven stars and not by Phoebus, he, ' that wandering knight so fair.' " Here we have a sort of lyrical strain in Falstaff and then a tag of poetry which gives food for thought; but his next speech is unmistakable:

" Let us be Diana's foresters, gentlemen of the shade, minions of the moon; and let men say we be men of good government, being governed, as the sea is, by our noble and chaste mistress, the moon, under whose countenance we—steal."

This is Shakespeare speaking, and Shakespeare alone: the phrases sing to us in the unmistakable music of the master-poet, though the fall at the last to "—steal," seems to be an attempt to get into the character of Falstaff. It is, of course, difficult to make the first words of a person sharply characteristic; a writer is apt to work himself into a new character gradually; it is only the sensitive self-consciousness of our time that demands an absolute fidelity in characterization from the first word to the last. Yet this scene is so excellent and natural, that the uncertainty in the painting of Falstaff strikes me as peculiar. But this first speech is not the only speech of Falstaff in which Shakespeare

144

betrays himself; again and again we catch the very accent of the poet. It is not Falstaff but Shakespeare who says that "the poor abuses of the time want countenance"; and later in the play, when the character of Falstaff is fully developed, it is Shakespeare, the thinker, who calls Falstaff's ragged regiment "the cankers of a calm world and a long peace." In just the same way Hamlet speaks of the expedition of Fortinbras:

"This is the imposthume of much wealth and peace,
    That inward breaks."

But though the belief that Shakespeare sometimes falls out of the character and slips phrases of his own into Falstaff's mouth is well-founded, it should nevertheless be put aside as a heresy, for the true faith is that the white-bearded old footpad who cheered on his fellow-ruffians with:

"Strike. . . . Bacon-fed knaves! they hate us youth: down with them! fleece them!"

and again:

"On, bacons, on! What, ye knaves! young men must live!"

is the most splendid piece of humorous portraiture in the world's fiction.

Who but Falstaff would have found his self-justification in his youth?—*splendide mendax!* and yet the excuse is as true to his sack-heated blood when he uses it on Gadshill as it was true also to fact when he first used it forty years before. And who but Falstaff would have had the words of repentance always on his lips and never in his heart? I

ascribe these illuminating flashes to Falstaff, and
not to Shakespeare, for no imagination in the world
has yet accomplished such a miracle; as a miracle
of representment Falstaff is astonishing enough, as
a miracle of creation he is simply unthinkable. I
would almost as soon believe that Falstaff made
Shakespeare as that Shakespeare made Falstaff
without a living model. All hail to thee, inimitable,
incomparable Jack! Never before or since has poet
been blessed with such a teacher, as rich and laugh-
terful, as mendacious and corrupting as life itself.

I must not be taken to mean that the living
original of Falstaff was as richly humorous, as in-
exhaustibly diverting as the dramatic counterfeit
who is now a citizen and chief personage in that
world of literature which outlasts all the fleeting
shows of the so-called real world. It seems to me
to be possible for a good reader to notice, not only
Shakespeare's lapses and faults in the drawing of
this character, but also to make a very fair guess
at his heightening touches, and so arrive at last at
the humorous old lewdster who furnished the living
model for the inimitable portrait. The first scene
in which Falstaff appears talking with Prince Henry
will supply examples to illustrate my meaning.
Falstaff's very first speech after he asks Hal the
time of day gives us the key; he ends it with:

"And I pr'ythee, sweet wag, when thou art king,—
as, God save thy grace—majesty, I should say, for
grace thou wilt have none,——"

Here he is interrupted and breaks off, but a minute
or two later he come back again to his argument,
and curiously enough uses exactly the same words:

"But, I pr'ythee, sweet wag, shall there be gallows

146

standing in England when thou art king? and resolution thus fobbed as it is with the rusty curb of old father Antick, the law? "

Now, this question and the hope it expresses that justice would be put to shame in England on Prince Henry's accession to the throne is taken from a speech of the Prince in the old play, " The Famous Victories of Henry the Fifth." Shakespeare would have done better to leave it out, for Falstaff has far too good brains to imagine that all thieves could ever have his licence and far too much conceit ever to desire so unholy a consummation. And Shakespeare must have felt that the borrowed words were too shallow-common, for he immediately falls back on his own brains for the next phrase and gives us of his hoarded best. The second part of the question, " resolution thus fobbed," and so forth, is only another statement of the famous couplet in " Richard III." :

> " Conscience is but a word that cowards use,
> Devised at first to keep the strong in awe."

These faults show that Shakespeare is at first unsure of his personage; he fumbles a little; yet the vivacity, the roaring life, is certainly a quality of the original Falstaff, for it attends him as constantly as his shadow; the pun, too, is his, and the phrase " sweet wag " is probably taken from his mouth, for he repeats it again, " sweet wag," and again " mad wag." The shamelessness, too, and the lechery are marks of him, and the love of witty word-warfare, and, above all, the pretended repentance :

" O, thou hast damnable iteration, and art, indeed, able to corrupt a saint. Thou hast done much harm

147

upon me, Hal,—God forgive thee for it. Before I knew
thee, Hal, I knew nothing; and now am I, if a man
should speak truly, little better than one of the wicked.
I must give over this life, and I will give it over; by the
Lord, an I do not, I am a villain; I'll be damned for
never a king's son in Christendom."

In this first scene between Falstaff and Prince
Henry, Shakespeare is feeling his way, so to speak,
blindfold to Falstaff, with gropings of memory and
dashes of poetry that lead him past the mark. In
this first scene, as we noticed, he puts fine lyric
phrases in Falstaff's mouth; but he never repeats the
experiment; Falstaff and high poetry are antipodes
—all of which merely proves that at first Shakespeare had not got into the skin of his personage.
But the real Falstaff had probably tags of verse
in memory and lilts of song, for Shakespeare repeats this trait. Here we reach the test: Whenever
a feature is accentuated by repetition, we may guess
that it belongs to the living model. There was assuredly a strong dash of Puritanism in the real
Falstaff, for when Shakespeare comes to render this,
he multiplies the brush-strokes with perfect confidence; Falstaff is perpetually repenting.

After the first scene Shakespeare seems to have
made up his mind to keep closely to his model and
only to permit himself heightening touches.

In order to come closer to the original, I will now
take another passage later in the play, when Shakespeare is drawing Falstaff with a sure hand:

" *Fal.* A plague of all cowards, I say, and a vengeance too! marry and amen!—Give me a cup of sack,
boy.—Ere I lead this life long, I'll sew netherstocks,
and mend them, and foot them, too. A plague of all
cowards!—give me a cup of sack, roge.—Is there no
virtue extant?   [*Drinks.*] "

Falstaff

Here is surely the true Falstaff; he will not lead this life long; this is the soul of him; but the exquisite heightening phrase, " Is there no virtue extant? " is pure Shakespeare, Shakespeare generalizing as we saw him generalizing in just the same way in the scene where Cade is talked of in the Second Part of " King Henry VI." The form too is Shakespeare's. Who does not remember the magic line in " The Two Noble Kinsmen "?

"She is all the beauty extant."

And the next speech of Falstaff is just as illuminating:

" *Fal.* You rogue, here's lime in this sack, too; there is nothing but roguery to be found in villainous man: yet a coward is worse than a cup of sack with lime in it —a villainous coward.—Go thy ways, old Jack; die when thou wilt, if manhood, good manhood, be not forgot upon the face of the earth, then am I a shotten herring. There live not three good men unhanged in England, and one of them is fat and grows old: God help the while! A bad world I say——"

At the beginning the concrete fact, then generalization, and then merely a repetition of the traits marked in the first scene, with the addition of bragging. Evidently Shakespeare has the model in memory as he writes. I say " evidently," for Falstaff is the only character in Shakespeare that repeats the same words with damnable iteration, and in whom the same traits are shown again and again and again. When Shakespeare is painting himself in Richard II. he depicts irresolution again and again as he depicts it also in Hamlet; but neither Hamlet nor Richard repeats the same words, nor is

149

any trait in either of them accentuated so grossly as are the principal traits of Falstaff's character. The features in Falstaff which are so harped upon, are to me the features of the original model. Shakespeare did not know Falstaff quite as well as he knew himself; so he has to confine himself to certain qualities which he had observed, and stick, besides, to certain tags of speech, which were probably favourites with the living man.

In another important particular, too, Falstaff is unlike any other comic character in Shakespeare: he tells the truth about himself in a magical way. The passage I allude to is the first speech made by Falstaff in the Second Part of " Henry IV."; it shows us Shakespeare getting into the character again—after a certain lapse of time:

" *Fal*. Men of all sorts take a pride to gird at me; the brain of this foolish-compounded clay, man, is not able to invent anything that tends to laughter, more than I invent or is invented on me: I am not only witty in myself, but the cause that wit is in other men——"

Just as in the first act Shakespeare introducing Falstaff makes him talk poetically, so here there is a certain exaltation and lyrical swing which betrays the poet-creator. " Foolish-compounded," too, shows Shakespeare's hand, but the boast, I feel sure, was a boast often made by the original, and thus brings Shakespeare into intimate union with the character; for after this introduction Falstaff goes on to talk pure Falstaff, unmixed with any slightest dash of poetry.

Who was the original of Falstaff? Is a guess possible? It seems to me it must have been some lover of poetry—perhaps Chettle, the Chettle who years before had published Greene's attack upon

Shakespeare and who afterwards made amends for
it. In Dekker's tract, "A Knight's Conjuring,"
Chettle figures among the poets in Elysium: "In
comes Chettle sweating and blowing by reason of
his fatness; to welcome whom, because hee was of
olde acquaintance, all rose up, and fell presentlie on
their knees, to drinck a health to all the louers of
Hellicon." Here we have a fat man greeted with
laughter and mock reverence by the poets—just such
a model as Shakespeare needed, but the guess is
mere conjecture: we don't know enough about
Chettle to be at all sure. Yet Chettle was by way
of being a poet, and Falstaff uses tags of verse—still,
as I say, it is all pure guesswork. The only reason
I put his name forward is that some have talked of
Ben Jonson as Falstaff's original merely because he
was fat. I cannot believe that gentle Shakespeare
would ever have treated Jonson with such contempt;
but Chettle seems to have been a butt by nature.

That Falstaff was taken from one model is to me
certain. Shakespeare very seldom tells us what his
characters look like; whenever he gives us a photograph, so to speak, of a person, it is always taken
from life and extraordinarily significant. We have
several portraits of Falstaff: the Prince gives a picture of the "old fat man, . . ." that trunk of
humours ". . . that old white-bearded Satan "; the
Chief Justice gives us another of his "moist eye,
white beard, increasing belly and double chin."
Falstaff himself has another: "a goodly portly
man, i' faith and a corpulent; of a cheerful look, a
pleasing eye, and a most noble carriage." Such
physical portraiture alone would convince me that
there was a living model for Falstaff. But there
are more obvious arguments: the other humorous
characters of Shakespeare are infinitely inferior to

Falstaff, and the best of them are merely sides of Falstaff or poor reflections of him. Autolycus and Parolles have many of his traits, but they are not old, and taken together, they are only a faint *replica* of the immortal footpad.

Listening with my heart in my ears, I catch a living voice, a round, fat voice with tags of " pr'ythee," " wag," and " marry," and behind the inimitable dramatic counterfeit I see a big man with a white head and round belly who loved wine and women and jovial nights, a Triton among the minnows of boon companions, whose shameless effrontery was backed by cunning, whose wit though common was abundant and effective through long practice—a sort of licensed tavern-king, whose mere entrance into a room set the table in a roar. Shakespeare was attracted by the many-sided racy ruffian, delighted perhaps most by his easy mastery of life and men; he studied him with infinite zest, absorbed him wholly, and afterwards reproduced him with such richness of sympathy, such magic of enlarging invention that he has become, so to speak, the symbol of laughter throughout the world, for men of all races the true Comic Muse.

In any case I may be allowed one last argument. The Falstaff of " The Merry Wives of Windsor " is not the Falstaff of the two parts of " King Henry IV."; it is but a shadow of the great knight that we see, an echo of him that we hear in the later comedy. Falstaff would never have written the same letter to Mrs. Ford and Mrs. Page; there was too much fancy in him, too much fertility, too much delight in his own mind- and word-wealth ever to show himself so painfully stinted and barren. Nor is it credible that Falstaff would ever have fallen three times running into the same trap; Falstaff made traps; he did not fall into them. We know, too, that Falstaff would not fight " longer than he saw reason "; his instinct of self-preservation was largely developed; but he could face a sword; he drew on Pistol and chased him from the room; he was not such a pitiful coward as to take Ford's cudgelling. Finally, the Falstaff whom we all know could never have been befooled by the Welshman and his child-fairies. And this objection Shakespeare himself felt, for he meets it by making Falstaff explain how near he came to discovering the fraud, and how wit is made " a Jack-a-Lent when 'tis upon ill employment." But the fact that some explanation is necessary is an admission of the fault. Falstaff must indeed have laid his brains in the sun before he could have been taken in by foppery so gross and palpable. This is not the same man who at once recognized the Prince and Poins through their disguise as drawers. Yet there are moments when the Falstaff of " The Merry Wives " resumes his old nature. For example, when he is accused by Pistol of sharing in the proceeds of the theft, he answers with all the old shameless wit:

" Reason, you rogue, reason; think'st thou I'll endanger my soul gratis? "

and, again, when he has been cozened and beaten, he speaks almost in the old way:

" I never prospered since I forswore myself at primero. Well, if my wind were but long enough to say my prayers, I would repent."

But on the whole the Falstaff of " The Merry Wives " is but a poor thin shadow of the Falstaff of the two parts of " Henry IV."

Had " The Merry Wives " been produced under ordinary conditions, one would have had to rack one's brains to account for its feebleness. Not only is the genial Lord of Humour degraded in it into a buffoon, but the amusement of it is chiefly in situation; it is almost as much a farce as a comedy. For these and other reasons I believe in the truth of the tradition that Elizabeth was so pleased with the character of Falstaff that she ordered Shakespeare to write another play showing the fat knight in love, and that in obedience to this command Shakespeare wrote " The Merry Wives " in a fortnight. For what does a dramatist do when he is in a hurry to strike while the iron is hot and catch a Queen's fancy before it changes? Naturally he goes to his memory for his characters, to that vivid memory of youth which makes up by precision of portraiture for what it lacks in depth of comprehension. And this is the distinguishing characteristic of " The Merry Wives," particularly in the beginning. Even without " the dozen white luces " in his coat, one would swear that this Justice Shallow, with his pompous pride of birth and his stilted stupidity, is a portrait from life, some Sir Thomas Lucy or other, and Justice Shallow is not so deeply etched in as his cousin, Master Slender—" a little wee face, with a little yellow beard,—a cane-coloured beard." Such physical portraiture, as I have said, is very rare and very significant in Shakespeare. This photograph is slightly malevolent, too, as of one whose malice is protected by a Queen's commission. Those who do not believe tradition when thus circumstantially supported would not believe though one rose from the dead to witness to them. " The Merry Wives " is worthful to me as the only piece of Shakespeare's journalism that we possess; here

we find him doing task-work, and doing it at utmost
speed. Those who wish to measure the difference
between the conscious, deliberate work of the artist
and the hurried slap-dash performance of the jour-
nalist, have only to compare the Falstaff of " The
Merry Wives " with the Falstaff of the two parts of
" Henry IV." But if we take it for granted that
" The Merry Wives " was done in haste and to
order, can any inference be fairly drawn from the
feebleness of Falstaff and the unreality of his love-
making? I think so; it seems to me that, if Falstaff
had been a creation, Shakespeare must have reproduced him more effectively. His love-making in the
second part of " Henry IV." is real enough. But
just because Falstaff was taken from life, and
studied from the outside, Shakespeare having
painted him once could not paint him again, he
had exhausted his model and could only echo him.

The heart of the matter is that, whereas Shakespeare's men of action, when he is not helped by
history or tradition, are thinly conceived and poorly
painted, his comic characters—Falstaff, Sir Toby
Belch, and Dogberry; Maria, Dame Quickly, and
the Nurse, creatures of observation though they be,
are only inferior as works of art to the portraits of
himself which he has given us in Romeo, Hamlet,
Macbeth, Orsino, and Posthumus. It is his humour
which makes Shakespeare the greatest of dramatists,
the most complete of men.

BOOK II

CHAPTER I

SHAKESPEARE'S EARLY ATTEMPTS TO PORTRAY
HIMSELF AND HIS WIFE:

BIRON, ADRIANA, VALENTINE

IN the preceding chapters I have considered those
impersonations of Shakespeare which revealed
most distinctly the salient features of his character.
I now regard this part of my work as finished: the
outlines at least of his nature are established beyond dispute, and I may therefore be permitted to
return upon my steps, and beginning with the earliest
works pass in review most of the other personages
who discover him, however feebly or profoundly.
Hitherto I have rather challenged contradiction than
tried to conciliate or persuade; it was necessary to
convince the reader that Shakespeare was indeed
Hamlet-Orsino, plus an exquisite sense of humour;
and as the proofs of this were almost inexhaustible,
and as the stability of the whole structure depended
on the firmness of the foundations, I was more than
willing to call forth opposition in order once for all
to strangle doubt. But now that I have to put in
the finer traits of the portrait I have to hope for the
goodwill at least of my readers. Even then my task
is not easy. The subtler traits of a man's character
often elude accurate description, to say nothing of
exact proof; the differences in tone between a dramatist's own experiences of life and his observation of
the experiences of others are often so slight as to be
all but unnoticeable. In the case of some peculiarities I have only a mere suggestion to go upon, in

159

that of others a bare surmise, a hint so fleeting that it may well seem to the judicious as if the meshes of language were too coarse to catch such evanescent indication.

Fortunately in this work I am not called on to limit myself to that which can be proved beyond question, or to the ordinary man. I think my reader will allow me, or indeed expect me, now to throw off constraint and finish my picture as I please.

In this second book then I shall try to correct Shakespeare's portraits of himself by bringing out his concealed faults and vices—the shortcomings one's vanity slurs over and omits. Above all I shall try to notice anything that throws light upon his life, for I have to tell here the story of his passion and his soul's wreck. At the crisis of his life he revealed himself almost without affectation; in agony men forget to pose. And this more intimate understanding of the man will enable us to reconstruct, partially at least, the happenings of his life, and so trace not only his development, but the incidents of his life's journey from his school days in 1575 till he crept home to Stratford to die nearly forty years later.

The chief academic critics, such as Professor Dowden and Dr. Brandes, take pains to inform us that Biron in "Love's Labour's Lost" is nothing but an impersonation of Shakespeare. This would show much insight on the part of the Professors were it not that Coleridge as usual has been before them, and that Coleridge's statement is to be preferred to theirs. Coleridge was careful to say that the whole play revealed many of Shakespeare's characteristic features, and he added finely, " as in a portrait taken of him in his boyhood." This is far truer than Dowden's more precise statement that

" Berowne is the exponent of Shakespeare's own thought." For though, of course, Biron is especially the mouthpiece of the poet, yet Shakespeare reveals himself in the first speech of the King as clearly as he does in any speech of Biron:

"Let Fame, that all hunt after in their lives,
Live registered upon our brazen tombs,
And then grace us in the disgrace of death;
When, spite of cormorant devouring Time,
The endeavour of this present breath may buy
That honour which shall 'bate his scythe's keen edge,
And make us heirs of all eternity."

The King's criticism, too, of Armado in the first scene is more finely characteristic of Shakespeare than Biron's criticism of Boyet in the last act. In this, his first drama, Shakespeare can hardly sketch a sympathetic character without putting something of himself into it.

I regard " Love's Labour's Lost " as Shakespeare's earliest comedy, not only because the greater part of it is in rhymed verse, but also because he was unable in it to individualize his serious personages at all; the comic characters, on the other hand, are already carefully observed and distinctly differenced. Biron himself is scarcely more than a charming sketch: he is almost as interested in language as in love, and he plays with words till they revenge themselves by obscuring his wit; he is filled with the high spirits of youth; in fact, he shows us the form and pressure of the Renaissance as clearly as the features of Shakespeare. It is, however Biron-Shakespeare, who understands that the real world is built on broader natural foundations than the King's womanless Academe, and therefore predicts the failure of the ascetic experiment. Another

trait in Biron that brings us close to Shakespeare
is his contempt for book-learning:

> "Small have continual plodders ever won
> Save bare authority from others' books.
>
> .   .   .   .   .
>
> To much to know is to know nought but fame;
> And every godfather can give a name."

Again and again he returns to the charge:

> "To study now it is too late,
> Climb o'er the house to unlock the little gate."

The summing up is triumphant:

> "So, study evermore is overshot."

In fine, Biron ridicules study at such length and
with such earnestness and pointed phrase that it
is manifest the discussion was intensely interesting
to Shakespeare himself.   But we should have expected Shakespeare's *alter ego* to be arguing on the
other side; for again and again we have had to notice that Shakespeare was a confirmed lover of books;
he was always using bookish metaphors, and Hamlet
was a student by nature.   This attitude on the part
of Biron, then, calls for explanation, and it seems
to me that the only possible explanation is to be
found in Shakespeare's own experience.   Those who
know England as she was in the days of Elizabeth,
or as she is to-day, will hardly need to be told that
when Shakespeare first came to London he was regarded as an unlettered provincial ("with little
Latin and less Greek"), and had to bear the mocks
and flouts of his beschooled fellows, who esteemed
learning and gentility above genius.   In his very

first independent play he answered the scorners with scorn. But this disdain of study was not Shakespeare's real feeling; and his natural loyalty to the deeper truth forced him to make Biron contradict and excuse his own argument in a way which seems to me altogether charming; but is certainly undramatic:

"—Though I have for barbarism spoke more
Than for that angel knowledge you can say."

Undramatic the declaration is because it is at war with the length and earnestness with which Biron has maintained his contempt for learning; but here undoubtedly we find the true Shakespeare who as a youth speaks of " that angel, knowledge," just as in " Cymbeline " twenty years later he calls reverence, " that angel of the world."

When we come to his " Life " we shall see that Shakespeare, who was thrown into the scrimmage of existence as a youth, and had to win his own way in the world, had, naturally enough, a much higher opinion of books and book-learning than Goethe, who was bred a student and knew life only as an amateur:

" Einen Blick in's Buch hinein und zwei in's Leben
Das muss die rechte Form dem Geiste geben."

Shakespeare would undoubtedly have given " two glances " to books and one to life, had he been free to choose; but perhaps after all Goethe was right in warning us that life is more valuable to the artist than any transcript of it.

To return to our theme; Biron is not among Shakespeare's successful portraits of himself. As might be expected in a first essay, the drawing is

now over-minute, now too loose. When Biron talks
of study, he reveals, as we have seen, personal feelings that are merely transient; on the other hand,
when he talks about Boyet he talks merely to hear
" the music of his own vain tongue." He is, however, always nimble-witted and impulsive; "quick
Biron " as the Princess calls him, a gentleman of
charming manners, of incomparable fluent, graceful,
and witty speech, which qualities afterwards came
to blossom in Mercutio and Gratiano. The faults
in portraiture are manifestly due to inexperience:
Shakespeare was still too youthful-timid to paint
his chief features boldly, and it is left for Rosaline
to picture Biron for us as Shakespeare doubtless
desired to appear:

> " A merrier man,
> Within the limits of becoming mirth,
> I never spent an hour's talk withal.
> His eye begets occasion for his wit;
> For every object that the one doth catch,
> The other turns to a mirth-moving jest,
> Which his fair tongue, conceit's expositor,
> Delivers in such apt and gracious words
> That agèd ears play truant at his tales,
> And younger hearings are quite ravishèd,
> So sweet and voluble is his discourse."

Every touch of this self-painted portrait deserves to
be studied: it is the first photograph of our poet
which we possess—a photograph, too, taken in early
manhood. Shakespeare's wit we knew, his mirth
too, and that his conversation was voluble and sweet
enough to ravish youthful ears and enthrall the
aged we might have guessed from Jonson's report.
But it is delightful to hear of his mirth-moving
words and to know that he regarded himself as the
best talker in the world. But just as the play at the

end turns from love-making and gay courtesies to thoughts of death and " world-without-end " pledges, so Biron's merriment is only the effervescence of youth, and love brings out in him Shakespeare's characteristic melancholy:

" By heaven, I do love, and it hath taught me to rhyme, and to be melancholy."

Again and again, as in his apology to Rosaline, and his appeal at the end of the play to " honest plain words," he shows a deep underlying seriousness. The soul of quick, talkative, mirthful Biron is that he loves beauty whether of women or of words, and though he condemns " taffeta phrases," he shows his liking for the " silken terms precise " in the very form of his condemnation.

Of course all careful readers know that the greater seriousness of the last two acts of " Love's Labour's Lost," and the frequent use of blank verse instead of rhymed verse in them, are due to the fact that Shakespeare revised the play in 1597, some eight or nine years probably after he had first written it. Every one must have noticed the repetitions in Biron's long speech at the end of the fourth act, which show the original garment and the later, finer embroidery. As I shall have to return to this revision for other reasons, it will be enough here to remark that it is especially the speeches of Biron which Shakespeare improved in the second handling.

Dr. Brandes, or rather Coleridge, tells us that in Biron and his Rosaline we have the first hesitating sketch of the masterly Benedick and Beatrice of " Much Ado about Nothing "; but in this I think Coleridge goes too far. Unformed as Biron is, he is Shakespeare in early youth, whereas in Benedick the likeness is not by any means so clear. In fact, Benedick is merely an admirable stage silhouette and needs to be filled out with an actor's personality. Beatrice, on the other hand, is a woman of a very distinct type, whereas Rosaline needs pages of explanation, which Coleridge never dreamed of. A certain similarity rather of situation than of character seems to have misled Coleridge in this instance. Boyet jests with Maria and Rosaline just as Biron does, and just as Benedick jests with Beatrice: all these scenes simply show how intensely young Shakespeare enjoyed a combat of wits, spiced with the suggestiveness that nearly always shows itself when the combatants are of different sexes.

It is almost certain that " Love's Labour's Lost " was wholly conceived and constructed as well as written by Shakespeare; no play or story has yet been found which might, in this case, have served him as a model. For the first and probably the last time he seems to have taken the entire drama from his imagination, and the result from a playwright's point of view is unfortunate; " Love's Labour's Lost " is his slightest and feeblest play. It is scarcely ever seen on the stage—is, indeed, practically unactable. This fact goes to confirm the view already put forth more than once in these pages, that Shakespeare was not a good playwright and took little or no interest in the external incidents of his dramas. The plot and action of the story, so carefully worked out by the ordinary playwright and so highly esteemed by critics and spectators, he always borrows, as if he had recognized the weakness of this first attempt, and when he sets himself to construct a play, it has no action, no plot—is, indeed, merely a succession of fantastic occurrences that give occasion for light love-making and bril-

liant talk. Even in regard to the grouping of characters the construction of his early plays is puerile,
mechanical; in " Love's Labour's Lost " the King
with his three courtiers is set against the Princess
and her three ladies; in " The Two Gentlemen of
Verona " there is the faithful Valentine opposed to
the inconstant Proteus, and each of them has a comic
servant; and when later his plays from this point
of view were not manufactured but grew, and thus
assumed the beautiful irregular symmetry of life,
the incidents were still neglected. Neither the poet
nor the philosopher in Shakespeare felt much of the
child's interest in the story; he chose his tales for
the sake of the characters and the poetry, and
whether they were effective stage-tales or not
troubled him but little. There is hardly more plot
or action in " Lear " than in " Love's Labour's
Lost."

It is probable that " The Comedy of Errors "
followed hard on the heels of " Love's Labour's
Lost." It practically belongs to the same period:
it has fewer lines of prose in it than " Love's
Labour's Lost "; but, on the other hand, the in-
trigue-spinning is clever, and the whole play shows
a riper knowledge of theatrical conditions. Perhaps because the intrigue is more interesting, the
character-drawing is even feebler than that of the
earlier comedy: indeed, so far as the men go there is
hardly anything worth calling character-drawing at
all. Shakespeare speaks through this or that mask
as occasion tempts him: and if the women are
sharply, crudely differentiated, it is because Shakespeare, as I shall show later, has sketched his wife
for us in Adriana, and his view of her character is
decided enough if not over kind. Still, any and
every peculiarity of character deserves notice, for in

these earliest works Shakespeare is compelled to use his personal experience, to tell us of his own life and his own feelings, not having any wider knowledge to draw upon. Every word, therefore, in these first comedies, is important to those who would learn the story of his youth and fathom the idiosyncrasies of his being. When Ægeon, in the opening scenes, tells the Duke about the shipwreck in which he is separated from his wife and child, he declares that he himself " would gladly have embraced immediate death." No reason is given for this extraordinary contempt of living. It was the " incessant weepings " of his wife, the " piteous plainings of the pretty babes," that forced him, he says, to exert himself. But wives don't weep incessantly in danger, nor are the " piteous plainings of the pretty babes " a feature of shipwreck; I find here a little picture of Shakespeare's early married life in Stratford— a snapshot of memory. Ægeon concludes his account by saying that his life was prolonged in order

" To tell sad stories of my own mishaps "

—which reminds one of similar words used later by Richard II. This personal, melancholy note is here forced and false, for Ægeon surely lives in hope of finding his wife and child and not in order to tell of his misfortunes. Ægeon is evidently a breath of Shakespeare himself, and not more than a breath, because he only appears again when the play is practically finished. Deep-brooding melancholy was the customary habit of Shakespeare even in youth.

Just as in " Love's Labour's Lost " we find Shakespeare speaking first through the King and then more fully through the hero, Biron, so here he first speaks through Ægeon and then at greater length

through the protagonist Antipholus of Syracuse.
Antipholus is introduced to us as new come to
Ephesus, and Shakespeare is evidently thinking of
his own first day in London when he puts in his
mouth these words:

> " Within this hour it will be dinner-time:
> Till that, I'll view the manners of the town,
> Peruse the traders, gaze upon the buildings,
> And then return and sleep within mine inn;
> For with long travel I am stiff and weary."

Though " stiff and weary " he is too eager-young
to rest; he will see everything—even " peruse the
traders "—how the bookish metaphor always comes
to Shakespeare's lips!—before he will eat or sleep.
The utterly needless last line, with its emphatic description—" stiff and weary "—corroborates my
belief that Shakespeare in this passage is telling us
what he himself felt and did on his first arrival in
London. In the second scene of the third act Antipholus sends his servant to the port:

> " I will not harbour in this town to-night
> If any bark put forth."

From the fact that Shakespeare represented Antipholus to himself as wishing to leave Ephesus by
sea, it is probable that he pictured him coming to
Ephesus in a ship. But when Shakespeare begins
to tell us what he did on reaching London he recalls his own desires and then his own feelings; he
was " stiff and weary " on that first day because he
rode, or more probably walked, into London; one
does not become " stiff and weary " on board ship.
This is another snapshot at that early life of Shakespeare, and his arrival in London, which one would

not willingly miss. And surely it is the country-bred lad from Stratford, who, fearing all manner of town-tricks, speaks in this way:

> "They say this town is full of cozenage;
> As, nimble jugglers that deceive the eye,
> Dark-working sorcerers that change the mind,
> Soul-killing witches that deform the body,
> Disguised cheaters, prating mountebanks,
> And many such-like liberties of sin:
>
> I greatly fear my money is not safe."

This Antipholus is most ingenuous-talkative; without being questioned he tells about his servant:

> "A trusty villain, sir; that very oft,
> When I am dull with care and melancholy,
> Lightens my humour with his merry jests."

And as if this did not mark his peculiar thoughtful temperament sufficiently, he tells the merchant:

> "I will go lose myself,
> And wander up and down to view the city."

And when the merchant leaves him, commending him to his own content, he talks to himself in this strain:

> "He that commends me to mine own content,
> Commends me to the thing I cannot get,
>
> So I, to find a mother and a brother,
> In quest of them, unhappy, lose myself."

A most curious way, it must be confessed, to seek for any one; but perfectly natural to the refined, melancholy, meditative, book-loving temperament which was already Shakespeare's. In this " un-

happy " and " mother " I think I hear an echo of
Shakespeare's sorrow at parting from his own
mother.

This Antipholus, although very free and open,
has a reserve of dignity, as we see in the second
scene of the second act, when he talks with his
servant, who, as he thinks, has played with him:

> " Because that I familiarly sometimes
> Do use you for my fool, and chat with you,
> Your sauciness will jest upon my love,
> And make a common of my serious hours.
> When the sun shines let foolish gnats make sport,
> But creep in crannies when he hides his beams."

The self-esteem seems a little exaggerated here; but,
after all, it is only natural; the whole scene is taken
from Shakespeare's experience: the man who will
chat familiarly with his servant, and jest with him
as well, must expect to have to pull him up at times
rather sharply. Antipholus proceeds to play with
his servant in a fencing match of wit—a practice
Shakespeare seems to have delighted in. But it is
when Antipholus falls in love with Luciana that he
shows us Shakespeare at his most natural as a lover.
Luciana has just taken him to task for not loving
her sister Adriana, who, she thinks, is his wife.
Antipholus answers her thus:

> " Sweet mistress,—what your name is else, I know not,
> Nor by what wonder you do hit of mine,—
> Less in your knowledge and your face you show not,
> Than our earth's wonder; more than earth divine,
> Teach me, dear creature, how to think and speak;
> Lay open to my earthy-gross conceit,
> Smother'd in errors, feeble, shallow, weak,
> The folded meaning of your words' deceit. . . ."

He declares, in fact, that he loves her and not her sister:

" Sing, siren, for thyself and I will dote:
  Spread o'er the silver waves thy golden hairs,
  And as a bed I'll take them and there lie;

  .   .   .   .   .

  It is thyself, mine own self's better part,
  Mine eye's clear eye, my dear heart's dearer heart."

And as if this were not enough he goes on:

" My food, my fortune, and my sweet hope's aim,
  My sole earth's heaven, and my heaven's claim."

The word-conceits were a fashion of the time; but in spite of the verbal affectation, the courting shows the cunning of experience, and has, besides, a sort of echo of sincere feeling. How Shakespeare delights in making love! It reminds one of the first flutings of a thrush in early spring; over and over again he tries the notes with delighted iteration till he becomes a master of his music and charms the copses to silence with his song: and so Shakespeare sings of love again and again till at length we get the liquid notes of passion and the trills of joy all perfected in " Romeo and Juliet "; but the voice is the voice we heard before in " Venus and Adonis " and " The Comedy of Errors."

Antipholus' other appearances are not important. He merely fills his part till in the last scene he assures Luciana that he will make good his earlier protestations of love; but so far as he has any character at all, or distinctive individuality, he is young Shakespeare himself and his experiences are Shakespeare's.

Now a word or two about Adriana. Shakespeare

makes her a jealous, nagging, violent scold, who will have her husband arrested for debt, though she will give money to free him. But the comedy of the play would be better brought out if Adriana were pictured as loving and constant, inflicting her inconvenient affection upon the false husband as upon the true. Why did Shakespeare want to paint this unpleasant bitter-tongued wife?

When Adriana appears in the first scene of the second act she is at once sketched in her impatience and jealousy. She wants to know why her husband should have more liberty than she has, and declares that none but asses will be bridled so. Then she will strike her servant. In the first five minutes of this act she is sketched to the life, and Shakespeare does nothing afterwards but repeat and deepen the same strokes: it seems as if he knew nothing about her or would depict nothing of her except her jealousy and nagging, her impatience and violence. We have had occasion to notice more than once that when Shakespeare repeats touches in this way, he is drawing from life, from memory, and not from imagination. Moreover, in this case, he shows us at once that he is telling of his wife, because she defends herself against the accusation of age, which no one brings against her, though every one knows that Shakespeare's wife was eight years older than himself.

> " His company must do his minions grace,
> Whilst I at home starve for a merry look.
> Hath homely age the alluring beauty took
> From my poor cheek? then he hath wasted it . . .
>   . . . My decayed fair
> A sunny look of his would soon repair:
> But, poor unruly deer, he breaks the pale,
> And feeds from home; poor I am but his stale."

The appeal is pathetic; but Luciana will not see it. She cries:

> " Self-harming jealousy! fie, beat it hence! "

In the second scene of this second act Adriana goes on nagging in almost the same way.

In the second scene of the third act there is a phrase from the hero, Antipholus of Syracuse, about Adriana which I find significant:

> " She that doth call me husband, even my soul
> Doth for a wife abhor! "

There is no reason in the comedy for such strong words. Most men would be amused or pleased by a woman who makes up to them as Adriana makes up to Antipholus. I hear Shakespeare in this uncalled-for, over-emphatic " even my soul doth for a wife abhor."

In the fifth act Adriana is brought before the Abbess, and is proved to be a jealous scold. Shakespeare will not be satisfied till some impartial great person of Adriana's own sex has condemned her. Adriana admits that she has scolded her husband in public and in private, too; the Abbess replies:

> "And thereof came it that the man was mad."

And she adds:

> " The venom clamours of a jealous woman
> Poisons more deadly than a mad dog's tooth."

Again, a needlessly emphatic condemnation. But Adriana will not accept the reproof: she will have her husband at all costs. The whole scene discovers personal feeling. Adriana is the portrait that Shakespeare wished to give us of his wife.

The learned commentators have seemingly conspired to say as little about " The Two Gentlemen of Verona " as possible. No one of them identifies the protagonist, Valentine, with Shakespeare, though all of them identified Biron with Shakespeare, and yet Valentine, as we shall see, is a far better portrait of the master than Biron. This untimely blindness of the critics is, evidently, due to the fact that Coleridge has hardly mentioned " The Two Gentlemen of Verona," and they have consequently been unable to parrot his opinions.

" The Two Gentlemen of Verona " is manifestly a later work than " Love's Labour's Lost "; there is more blank verse and less rhyme in it, and a considerable improvement in character-drawing. Julia, for example, is individualized and lives for us in her affection and jealousy; her talks with her maid Lucetta are taken from life; they are indeed the first sketch of the delightful talks between Portia and Nerissa, and mark an immense advance upon the wordy *badinage* of the Princess and her ladies in " Love's Labour's Lost," where there was no attempt at differentiation of character. It seems indubitable to me that " The Two Gentlemen of Verona " is also later than " The Comedy of Errors," and just as far beyond doubt that it is earlier than " A Midsummer Night's Dream," in spite of Dr. Furnival's " Trial Table."

The first three comedies, " Love's Labour's Lost," " The Comedy of Errors," and " The Two Gentlemen of Verona," are all noteworthy for the light they throw on Shakespeare's early life.

In " The Two Gentlemen of Verona " Shakespeare makes similar youthful mistakes in portraiture to those we noticed in " Love's Labour's Lost "; mistakes which show that he is thinking of himself and his own circumstances. At the beginning of the play the only difference between Proteus and Valentine is that one is in love, and the other, heart-free, is leaving home to go to Milan. In this first scene Shakespeare speaks frankly through both Proteus and Valentine, just as he spoke through both the King and Biron in the first scene of " Love's Labour's Lost," and through both Ægeon and Antipholus of Syracuse in " The Comedy of Errors." But whilst the circumstances in the earliest comedy are imaginary and fantastic, the circumstances in " The Two Gentlemen of Verona " are manifestly, I think, taken from the poet's own experience. In the dialogue between Valentine and Proteus I hear Shakespeare persuading himself that he should leave Stratford. Some readers may regard this assumption as far-fetched, but it will appear the more plausible, I think, the more the dialogue is studied. Valentine begins the argument:

" Home-keeping youth have ever homely wits,"—

he will " see the wonders of the world abroad " rather than live " dully sluggardiz'd at home," wearing out " youth with shapeless idleness." But all these reasons are at once superfluous and peculiar. The audience needs no persuasion to believe that a young man is eager to travel and go to Court. Shakespeare's quick mounting spirit is in the lines, and the needlessness of the argument shows that we have here a personal confession. Valentine, then, mocks at love, because it was love that held Shakespeare so long in Stratford, and when Proteus defends it, he replies:

Biron, Adriana, Valentine

> " Even so by Love the young and tender wit
> Is turned to folly; blasting in the bud,
> Losing his verdure even in the prime,
> And all the fair effects of future hopes."

Here is Shakespeare's confession that his marriage had been a failure, not only because of his wife's mad jealousy and violent temper, which we have been forced to realize in " The Comedy of Errors," but also because love and its home-keeping ways threatened to dull and imprison the eager artist spirit. In the last charming line I find not only the music of Shakespeare's voice, but also one of the reasons—perhaps, indeed, the chief because the highest reason—which drew him from Stratford to London. And what the " future hope " was, he told us in the very first line of " Love's Labour's Lost." The King begins the play with:

> " Let Fame, that all hunt after in their lives."

Now all men don't hunt after fame; it was Shakespeare who felt that Fame pieced out Life's span and made us " heirs of all eternity "; it was young Shakespeare who desired fame so passionately that he believed all other men must share his immortal longing, the desire in him being a forecast of capacity, as, indeed, it usually is. If any one is inclined to think that I am here abusing conjecture let him remember that Proteus, too, tells us that Valentine is hunting after honour.

When Proteus defends love we hear Shakespeare just as clearly as when Valentine inveighs against it:

> " Yet writers say, as in the sweetest bud
> The eating canker dwells, so eating love
> Inhabits in the finest wits of all."

177

Shakespeare could not be disloyal to that passion of desire in him which he instinctively felt was, in some way or other, the necessary complement of his splendid intelligence. We must take the summing-up of Proteus when Valentine leaves him as the other half of Shakespeare's personal confession:

> " He after honour hunts, I after love:
> He leaves his friends to dignify them more;
> I leave myself, my friends, and all for love.
> Thou, Julia, thou hast metamorphosed me,—
> Made me neglect my studies, lose my time,
> War with good counsel, set the world at naught;
> Made wit with musing weak, heart sick with thought."

Young Shakespeare hunted as much after love as after honour, and these verses show that he has fully understood what a drag on him his foolish marriage has been. That all this is true to Shakespeare appears from the fact that it is false to the character of Proteus. Proteus is supposed to talk like this in the first blush of passion, before he has won Julia, before he even knows that she loves him. Is that natural? Or is it not rather Shakespeare's confession of what two wasted years of married life in Stratford had done for him? It was ambition—desire of fame and new love—that drove the tired and discontented Shakespeare from Anne Hathaway's arms to London.

When his father tells Proteus he must to Court on the morrow, instead of showing indignation or obstinate resolve to outwit tyranny, he generalizes in Shakespeare's way, exactly as Romeo and Orsino generalize in poetic numbers:

> " O, how this spring of love resembleth
> The uncertain glory of an April day."

Biron, Adriana, Valentine

Another reason for believing that this play deals
with Shakespeare's own experiences is to be found
in the curious change that takes place in Valentine.
In the first act Valentine disdains love: he prefers
to travel and win honour; but as soon as he reaches
Milan and sees Silvia, he falls even more desperately in love than Proteus.   What was the object,
then, in making him talk so earnestly against love
in the first act? It may be argued that Shakespeare
intended merely to contrast the two characters in the
first act; but he contrasts them in the first act on
this matter of love, only in the second act to annul
the distinction himself created.   Moreover, and this
is decisive, Valentine rails against love in the first
act as one who has experienced love's utmost rage:

> " To be
> In love: when scorn is bought with groans; coy looks,
> With heart-sore sighs; one fading moment's mirth,
> With twenty watchful, weary, tedious nights."

The man who speaks like this is not the man who
despises love and prefers honour, but one who has
already given himself to passion with an absolute
abandonment.   Such inconsistencies and flaws in
workmanship are in themselves trivial, but, from my
point of view, significant; for whenever Shakespeare
slips in drawing character, in nine cases out of ten
he slips through dragging in his own personality
or his personal experience, and not through carelessness, much less incompetence; his mistakes, therefore,
nearly always throw light on his nature or on his
life's story. From the beginning, too, Valentine,
like Shakespeare, is a born lover.

As soon, moreover, as he has gone to the capital
and fallen in love he becomes Shakespeare's avowed
favourite.   He finds Silvia's glove and cries:

"Sweet ornament that decks a thing divine—"

the exclamation reminding us of how Romeo talks
of Juliet's glove. Like other men, Shakespeare
learned life gradually, and in youth poverty of experience compels him to repeat his effects.

Again, when Valentine praises his friend Proteus
to the Duke, we find a characteristic touch of Shakespeare. Valentine says:

> "His years but young; but his experience old;
> His head unmellowed; but his judgement ripe."

In " The Merchant of Venice " Bellario, the learned
doctor of Padua, praises Portia in similar terms:

> " I never knew so young a body with so old a head."

But it is when Valentine confesses his love that
Shakespeare speaks through him most clearly:

> " Ay, Proteus, but that life is altered now,
> I have done penance for contemning love;
>
> .   .   .   .   .
>
> For in revenge of my contempt of love
> Love hath chased sleep from my enthrallèd eyes
> And made them watchers of my own heart's sorrow.
> O gentle Proteus, Love's a mighty lord,"—

and so on.

Every word in this confession is characteristic of
the poet and especially the fact that his insomnia is
due to love. Valentine then gives himself to passionate praise of Silvia, and ends with the " She is
alone " that recalls " She is all the beauty extant "
of " The Two Noble Kinsmen." Valentine the lover
reminds us of Romeo as the sketch resembles the
finished picture; when banished, he cries:

Biron, Adriana, Valentine

"And why not death, rather than living torment?
To die is to be banished from myself;
And Silvia is myself: banished from her,
Is self from self; a deadly banishment.
What light is light, if Silvia be not seen?
What joy is joy, if Silvia be not by?
Unless it be to think that she is by
And feed upon the shadow of perfection.
Except I be by Silvia in the night
There is no music in the nightingale,"

and so forth. I might compare this with what Romeo
says of his banishment, and perhaps infer from this
two-fold treatment of the theme that Shakespeare
left behind in Stratford some dark beauty who may
have given Anne Hathaway good cause for jealous
rage. It must not be forgotten here that Dryasdust
tells us he was betrothed to another girl when Anne
Hathaway's relations forced him to marry their
kinswoman.

A moment later and this lover Valentine uses the
very words that we found so characteristic in the
mouth of the lover Orsino in "Twelfth Night":

"O I have fed upon this woe already,
And now excess of it will make me surfeit."

Valentine, indeed, shows us traits of nearly all
Shakespeare's later lovers, and this seems to me interesting, because of course all the qualities were
in the youth, which were later differenced into various characters. His advice to the Duke, who pretends to be in love, is far too ripe, too contemptu-
ous-true, to suit the character of such a votary of
fond desire as Valentine was; it is mellow with experience and man-of-the-world wisdom, and the last
couplet of it distinctly foreshadows Benedick:

181

"Flatter and praise, commend, extol their graces;
Though ne'er so black, say they have angels' faces.
That man that hath a tongue, I say, is no man
If with his tongue he cannot win a woman."

But this is only an involuntary *aperçu* of Valentine,
as indeed Benedick is only an intellectual mood of
Shakespeare. And here Valentine is contrasted with
Proteus, who gives somewhat different advice to
Thurio, and yet advice which is still more characteristic of Shakespeare than Valentine-Benedick's
counsel. Proteus says:

"You must lay lime to tangle her desires
By wailful sonnets, whose composéd rhymes
Should be full fraught with serviceable vows."

In this way the young poet sought to give expression to different views of life, and so realize the
complexity of his own nature.

The other traits of Valentine's character that do
not necessarily belong to him as a lover are all characteristic traits of Shakespeare. When he is playing
the banished robber-chief far from his love, this is
how Valentine consoles himself:

"This shadowy desert, unfrequented woods,
I better brook than flourishing peopled towns:
Here can I sit alone unseen of any,
And to the nightingale's complaining notes
Tune my distresses and record my woes."

This idyllic love of nature, this marked preference
for the country over the city, however peculiar in a
highway robber, are characteristics of Shakespeare
from youth to age. Not only do his comedies lead
us continually from the haunts of men to the forest

and stream, but also his tragedies. He turns to
nature, indeed, in all times of stress and trouble for
its healing unconsciousness, its gentle changes that
can be foreseen and reckoned upon, and that yet
bring fresh interests and charming surprises; and
in times of health and happiness he pictures the
pleasant earth and its diviner beauties with a passionate intensity. Again and again we shall have
to notice his poet's love for " unfrequented woods,"
his thinker's longing for " the life removed."

At the end of the drama Valentine displays the
gentle forgivingness of disposition which we have
already had reason to regard as one of Shakespeare's most marked characteristics. As soon as
" false, fleeting Proteus " confesses his sin Valentine
pardons him with words that echo and re-echo
through Shakespeare's later dramas:

> " Then I am paid,
> And once again I do receive thee honest.
> Who by repentance is not satisfied
> Is nor of heaven nor earth; for these are pleased;
> By patience the Eternal's wrath's appeased."

He even goes further than this, and confounds our
knowledge of human nature by adding:

> " And that my love may appear plain and free
> All that was mine in Silvia I give thee."

And that the meaning may be made more distinct
than words can make it, he causes Julia to faint on
hearing the proposal. One cannot help recalling
the passage in " The Merchant of Venice " when
Bassanio and Gratiano both declare they would
sacrifice their wives to free Antonio, and a well-
known sonnet which seems to prove that Shakespeare

183

thought more of a man's friendship for a man than of a man's love for a woman. But as I shall have to discuss this point at length when I handle the Sonnets, I have, perhaps, said enough for the moment. Nor need I consider the fact here that the whole of this last scene of the last act was manifestly revised or rewritten by Shakespeare *circa* 1598—years after the rest of the play.

I think every one will admit now that Shakespeare revealed himself in " The Two Gentlemen of Verona," and especially in Valentine, much more fully than in Biron and in " Love's Labour's Lost." The three earliest comedies prove that from the very beginning of his career Shakespeare's chief aim was to reveal and realize himself.

CHAPTER II

NO one, so far as I know, has yet tried to identify Antonio, the Merchant of Venice, with Shakespeare, and yet Antonio is Shakespeare himself, and Shakespeare in what to us, children of an industrial civilization, is the most interesting attitude possible. Here in Antonio for the first time we discover Shakespeare in direct relations with real life, as real life is understood in the twentieth century. From Antonio we shall learn what Shakespeare thought of business men and business methods—of our modern way of living. Of course we must be on our guard against drawing general conclusions from this solitary example, unless we find from other plays that Antonio's attitude towards practical affairs was indeed Shakespeare's. But if this is the case, if Shakespeare has depicted himself characteristically in Antonio, how interesting it will be to hear his opinion of our money-making civilization. It will be as if he rose from the dead to tell us what he thinks of our doings. He has been represented by this critic and by that as a master of affairs, a prudent thrifty soul; now we shall see if this monstrous hybrid of tradesman-poet ever had any foundation in fact.

The first point to be settled is: Did Shakespeare reveal himself very ingenuously and completely in Antonio, or was the "royal merchant" a mere pose of his, a mood or a convention? Let us take

185

Antonio's first words, the words, too, which begin the play:

> " In sooth, I know not why I am so sad:
> It wearies me; you say it wearies you;
> But how I caught it, found it, or came by it,
> What stuff 'tis made of, whereof it is born,
> I am to learn;
> And such a want-wit sadness makes of me,
> That I have much ado to know myself."

It is this very sadness that makes it easy for us to know Shakespeare, even when he disguises himself as a Venetian merchant. A little later and Jaques will describe and define the disease as " humorous melancholy "; but here it is already a settled habit of mind.

Antonio then explains that his sadness has no cause, and incidentally attributes his wealth to fortune and not to his own brains or endeavour. The modern idea of the Captain of Industry who enriches others as well as himself, had evidently never entered into Shakespeare's head. Salarino says Antonio is " sad to think upon his merchandise "; but Antonio answers:

> " Believe me, no: I thank my fortune for it.
> My ventures are not in one bottom trusted,
> Nor to one place: nor is my whole estate
> Upon the fortune of this present year:
> Therefore my merchandise makes me not sad."

This tone of modest gentle sincerity is Shakespeare's habitual tone from about his thirtieth year to the end of his life: it has the accent of unaffected nature. In bidding farewell to Salarino Antonio shows us the exquisite courtesy which Shakespeare

186

used in life.   Salarino, seeing Bassanio approaching, says:

> " I would have stayed till I had made you merry,
>   If worthier friends had not prevented me."

Antonio answers:

> " Your worth is very dear in my regard.
>   I take it, your own business calls on you,
>   And you embrace the occasion to depart."

More characteristic still is the dialogue between Gratiano and Antonio in the same scene.   Gratiano, the twin-brother surely of Mercutio, tells Antonio that he thinks too much of the things of this world, and warns him:

> " They lose it that do buy it with much care."

Antonio replies:

> " I hold the world but as the world, Gratiano;
>   A stage, where every man must play a part,
>   And mine a sad one."

Every one who has followed me so far will admit that this is Shakespeare's most usual and most ingenuous attitude towards life; " I do not esteem worldly possessions," he says; " life itself is too transient, too unreal to be dearly held."   Gratiano's reflection, too, is Shakespeare's, and puts the truth in a nutshell:

> " They lose it that do buy it with much care."

We now come to the most salient peculiarity in

this play. When Bassanio, his debtor, asks him for more money, Antonio answers:

"My purse, my person, my extremest means,
Lie all unlocked to your occasions."

And, though Bassanio tells him his money is to be risked on a romantic and wild adventure, Antonio declares that Bassanio's doubt does him more wrong than if his friend had already wasted all he has, and the act closes by Antonio pressing Bassanio to use his credit " to the uttermost." Now, this contempt of money was, no doubt, a pose, if not a habit of the aristocratic society of the time, and Shakespeare may have been aping the tone of his betters in putting to show a most lavish generosity. But even if his social superiors encouraged him in a wasteful extravagance, it must be admitted that Shakespeare betters their teaching. The lord was riotously lavish, no doubt, because he had money, or could get it without much trouble; but, put in Antonio's position, he would not press his last penny on his friend, much less strain his credit " to the uttermost " for him as Antonio does for Bassanio. Here we have the personal note of Shakespeare: " Your affection," says the elder man to the younger, " is all to me, and money's less than nothing in the balance. Don't let us waste a word on it; a doubt of me were an injury!" But men will do that for affection which they would never do in cool blood, and therefore one cannot help asking whether Shakespeare really felt and practised this extreme contempt of wealth? For the moment, if we leave his actions out of the account, there can be, I think, no doubt about his feelings. His dislike of money makes him disfigure reality. No merchant, it may fairly be said, either of the sixteenth century or the twentieth, ever amassed or kept a fortune with Antonio's principles. In our day of world-wide speculation and immense wealth it is just possible for a man to be a millionaire and generous; but in the sixteenth century, when wealth was made by penurious saving, by slow daily adding of coin to coin, merchants like this Antonio were unheard of, impossible.

Moreover all the amiable characters in this play regard money with unaffected disdain; Portia no sooner hears of Shylock's suit than she cries:

> "Pay him six thousand, and deface the bond;
> Double six thousand, and then treble that,
> Before a friend of this description
> Shall lose a hair through Bassanio's fault."

And if we attribute this outburst to her love we must not forget that, when it comes to the test in court, and she holds the Jew in her hand and might save her gold, she again reminds him:

> "Shylock, there's thrice thy money offered thee."

A boundless generosity is the characteristic of Portia, and Bassanio, the penniless fortune-hunter, is just as extravagant; he will pay the Jew's bond twice over, and,

> "If that will not suffice,
> I will be bound to pay it ten times o'er,
> On forfeit of my hands, my head, my heart."

It may, of course, be urged that these Christians are all prodigal in order to throw Shylock's avarice and meanness into higher light; but that this disdain of money is not assumed for the sake of any artistic effect will appear from other plays. At

the risk of being accused of super-subtlety, I must
confess that I find in Shylock himself traces of
Shakespeare's contempt of money; Jessica says of
him:

> " I have heard him swear
> To Tubal and to Chus, his countrymen,
> That he would rather have Antonio's flesh
> Than twenty times the value of the sum
> That he did owe him."

Even Shylock, it appears, hated Antonio more than
he valued money, and this hatred, though it may
have its root in love of money, half redeems him in
our eyes. Shakespeare could not imagine a man who
loved money more than anything else; his hated and
hateful usurer is more a man of passion than a Jew.

The same prodigality and contempt of money are
to be found in nearly all Shakespeare's plays, and,
curiously enough, the persons to show this disdain
most strongly are usually the masks of Shakespeare
himself. A philosophic soliloquy is hardly more
characteristic of Shakespeare than a sneer at money.
It should be noted, too, that this peculiarity is not
a trait of his youth chiefly, as it is with most men
who are free-handed. It rather seems, as in the
case of Antonio, to be a reasoned attitude towards
life, and it undoubtedly becomes more and more
marked as Shakespeare grows older. Contempt of
wealth is stronger in Brutus than in Antonio;
stronger in Lear than in Brutus, and stronger in
Timon than in Lear.

But can we be at all certain that Antonio's view
of life in this respect was Shakespeare's? It may
be that Shakespeare pretended to this generosity
in order to loosen the purse-strings of his lordly
patrons. Even if his motive for writing in this strain

were a worthy motive, who is to assure us that he practised the generosity he preached? When I come to his life I think I shall be able to prove that Shakespeare was excessively careless of money; extravagant, indeed, and generous to a fault. Shakespeare did not win to eminence as a dramatist without exciting the envy and jealousy of many of his colleagues and contemporaries, and if these sharp-eyed critics had found him in drama after drama advocating lavish free-handedness while showing meanness or even ordinary prudence in his own expenditure, we should probably have heard of it as we heard from Greene how he took plays from other playwrights. But the silence of his contemporaries goes to confirm the positive testimony of Ben Jonson, that he was of " an open and free nature,"—openhanded always, and liberal, we may be sure, to a fault. In any case, the burden of proof lies with those who wish us to believe that Shakespeare was " a careful and prudent man of business," for in a dozen plays the personages who are his heroes and incarnations pour contempt on those who would lock " rascal counters " from their friends, and, in default of proof to the contrary, we are compelled to assume that he practised the generosity which he so earnestly and sedulously praised. At least it will be advisable for the moment to assume that he pictured himself as generous Antonio, without difficulty or conscious self-deception.

But this Antonio has not only the melancholy, courtesy and boundless generosity of Shakespeare; he has other qualities of the master which need to be thrown into relief.

First of all, Antonio has that submission to misfortune, that resignation in face of defeat and suffering which we have already seen as characteristics

191

of Richard II. The resignation might almost be called saintly, were it not that it seems to spring rather from the natural melancholy and sadness of Shakespeare's disposition; "the world is a hard, all-hating world," he seems to say, "and misery is the natural lot of man; defeat comes to all; why should I hope for any better fortune?" At the very beginning of the trial he recognizes that he is certain to lose; Bassanio and Gratiano appeal to the Duke for him; but he never speaks in his own defence; he says of his opponent at the outset:

> " I do oppose
> My patience to his fury, and am arm'd
> To suffer, with a quietness of spirit,
> The very tyranny and rage of his."

and again he will not contend, but begs the Court,

> " . . . . with all brief and plain conveniency
> Let me have judgement and the Jew his will."

Even when Bassanio tries to cheer him,

> "What, man, courage yet!
> The Jew shall have my flesh, blood, bones and all,
> Ere thou shalt lose for me one drop of blood."

Antonio answers:

> " I am a tainted wether of the flock,
> Meetest for death: the weakest kind of fruit
> Drops earliest to the ground: and so let me:
> You cannot better be employed, Bassanio,
> Than to live still and write mine epitaph."

He will not be saved; he gives himself at once to that " sweet way of despair " which we have found to be the second Richard's way and Shakespeare's way.

Just as we noticed, when speaking of Posthumus in " Cymbeline," that Shakespeare's hero and *alter ego* is always praised by the other personages of the drama, so this Antonio is praised preposterously by the chief personages of the play, and in the terms of praise we may see how Shakespeare, even in early manhood, liked to be considered. He had no ambition to be counted stalwart, or bold, or resolute like most young males of his race, much less " a good hater," as Dr. Johnson confessed himself; he wanted his gentle qualities recognized, and his intellectual gifts; Hamlet wished to be thought a courtier, scholar, gentleman; and here Salarino says of Antonio:

" A kinder gentleman treads not the earth,"

and he goes on to tell how Antonio, when parting from Bassanio, had " eyes big with tears ":

> " Turning his face, he put his hand behind him,
> And with affection wondrous sensible
> He wrung Bassanio's hand; and so they parted."

This Antonio is as tender-hearted and loving as young Arthur. And Lorenzo speaks of Antonio to Portia just as Salarino spoke of him:

> " *Lor.* But if you knew to whom you show this honour,
> How true a gentleman you send relief,
> How dear a lover of my lord your husband,
> I know you would be prouder of the work
> Than customary bounty can enforce you."

And finally Bassanio sums Antonio up in enthusiastic superlatives:

193

The Man Shakespeare

" The dearest friend to me, the kindest man,
The best-condition'd and unwearied spirit
In doing courtesies, and one in whom
The ancient Roman honour more appears
Than any that draws breath in Italy."

It is as a prince of friends and most courteous gentleman that Antonio acts his part from the beginning to the end of the play with one notable exception to which I shall return in a moment. It is astonishing to find this sadness, this courtesy, this lavish generosity and contempt of money, this love of love and friendship and affection in any man in early manhood; but these qualities were Shakespeare's from youth to old age.

I say that Antonio was most courteous to all with one notable exception, and that exception was Shylock.

It has become the custom on the English stage for the actor to try to turn Shylock into a hero; but that was assuredly not Shakespeare's intention. True, he makes Shylock appeal to the common humanity of both Jew and Christian.

" I am a Jew. Hath not a Jew eyes? hath not a Jew hands, organs, dimensions, senses, affections, passions? fed with the same food, hurt with the same weapons, subject to the same diseases, healed by the same means, warmed and cooled by the same winter and summer, as a Christian is? If you prick us, do we not bleed? if you tickle us, do we not laugh? if you poison us, do we not die? and if you wrong us, shall we not revenge? "

But if Shakespeare was far in advance of his age in this intellectual appreciation of the brotherhood of man; yet as an artist and thinker and poet he is particularly contemptuous of the usurer and

194

trader in other men's necessities, and therefore, when
Antonio meets Shylock, though he wants a favour
from him, he cannot be even decently polite to him.
He begins by saying in the third scene of the first
act:

> " Although I neither lend nor borrow
> By taking nor by giving of excess,
> Yet to supply the ripe wants of my friend,
> I'll break a custom."

The first phrase here reminds me of Polonius:
" neither a borrower nor a lender be." When Shylock attempts to defend himself by citing the way
Jacob cheated Laban, Antonio answers contemptuously " The devil can cite Scripture for his purpose." Shylock then goes on:

> " Signor Antonio, many a time and oft,
> In the Rialto you have rated me
> About my moneys and my usances:
> Still, I have borne it with a patient shrug,
> For sufferance is the badge of all our tribe.
> You call me mis-believer, cut-throat dog,
> And spit upon my Jewish gaberdine,
> And all for use of that which is mine own.
> Well then, it now appears you need my help:
> Go to, then; you come to me, and you say,
> ' Shylock, we would have moneys: ' you say so;
> You that did void your rheum upon my beard
> And foot me as you spurn a stranger cur
> Over your threshold: moneys is your suit.
> What should I say to you? Should I not say,
> ' Hath a dog money? is it possible
> A cur can lend three thousand ducats?' " . . .

Antonio answers this in words which it would be
almost impossible to take for Shakespeare's because
of their brutal rudeness, were it not, as we shall see

later, that Shakespeare loathed the Jew usurer more than any character in all his plays. Here are the words:

> " *Ant.* I am as like to call thee so again,
> To spit on thee again, to spurn thee too.
> If thou wilt lend this money, lend it not
> As to thy friends; for when did friendship take
> A breed for barren metal of his friend?
> But lend it rather to thine enemy
> Who, if he break, thou mayst with better face
> Exact the penalty."

Then Shylock makes peace, and proposes his modest penalty. Bassanio says:

> " You shall not seal to such a bond for me:
> I'll rather dwell in my necessity."

Antonio is perfectly careless and content: he says:

> " Content, i' faith: I'll seal to such a bond,
> And say there is much kindness in the Jew."

Antonio's heedless trust of other men and impatience are qualities most foreign to the merchant; but are shown again and again by Shakespeare's impersonations.

Perhaps it will be well here to prove once for all that Shakespeare did really hate the Jew. In the first place he excites our sympathy again and again for him on the broad grounds of common humanity; but the moment it comes to a particular occasion he represents him as hateful, even where a little thought would have taught him that the Jew must be at his best. It is a peculiarity of humanity which Shakespeare should not have overlooked, that all pariahs and outcasts display intense family affection; those whom the world scouts and hates are generally at their noblest in their own homes. The pressure from the outside, Herbert Spencer would say, tends to bring about cohesion among the members of the despised caste. The family affection of the Jew, his kindness to his kindred, have become proverbial. But Shakespeare admits no such kindness in Shylock: when his daughter leaves Shylock one would think that Shakespeare would picture the father's desolation and misery, his sorrow at losing his only child; but here there is no touch of sympathy in gentle Shakespeare:

" . . . . I would my daughter were dead at my foot, and the jewels in her ear! would she were hearsed at my foot, and the ducats in her coffin! "

But there is even better proof than this: when Shylock is defeated in his case and leaves the Court penniless and broken, Shakespeare allows him to be insulted by a gentleman. Shylock becomes pathetic in his defeat, for Shakespeare always sympathized with failure, even before he came to grief himself:

" *Shy.* Nay, take my life and all; pardon not that:
  You take my house when you do take the prop
  That doth sustain my house; you take my life
  When you do take the means whereby I live."

" *Por.* What mercy can you render him, Antonio?
" *Gra.* A halter gratis; nothing else for God's sake."

And then Antonio offers to " quit the fine for one-half his goods." Utterly broken now, Shylock says:

" I pray you, give me leave to go from hence;
  I am not well: send the deed after me,
  And I will sign it.

197

> *Duke.* Get thee gone, but do it.
> *Gra.* In christening shalt thou have two god-
>   fathers:
> Had I been judge, thou should'st have had ten
>   more,
> To bring thee to the gallows, not the font."

A brutal insult from a gallant gentleman to the broken Jew: it is the only time in all Shakespeare when a beaten and ruined man is so insulted.

Antonio, it must be confessed, is a very charming sketch of Shakespeare when he was about thirty years of age, and it is amusing to reflect that it is just the rich merchant with all his wealth at hazard whom he picks out to embody his utter contempt of riches. The "royal merchant," as he calls him, trained from youth to barter, is the very last man in the world to back such a venture as Bassanio's—much less would such a man treat money with disdain. But Shakespeare from the beginning of the play put himself quite naïvely in Antonio's place, and so the astounding antinomy came to expression.

CHAPTER III

THE SONNETS: PART I

EVER since Wordsworth wrote that the sonnets were the key to Shakespeare's heart, it has been taken for granted (save by those who regard even the sonnets as mere poetical exercises) that Shakespeare's real nature is discovered in the sonnets more easily and more surely than in the plays. Those readers who have followed me so far in examining his plays will hardly need to be told that I do not agree with this assumption. The author whose personality is rich and complex enough to create and vitalize a dozen characters, reveals himself more fully in his creations than he can in his proper person. It was natural enough that Wordsworth, a great lyric poet, should catch Shakespeare's accent better in his sonnets than in his dramas; but that is owing to Wordsworth's limitations. And if the majority of later English critics have agreed with Wordsworth, it only shows that Englishmen in general are better judges of lyric than of dramatic work. We have the greatest lyrics in the world; but our dramas, with the exception of Shakespeare's, are not remarkable. And in that modern extension of the drama, the novel, we are distinctly inferior to the French and Russians. This inferiority must be ascribed to the new-fangled prudery of language and thought which emasculates all our later fiction; but as that prudery is not found in our lyric verse it is evident that here alone the inspiration is full and rich enough to overflow the limits of epicene convention.

Whether the reader agrees with me or not on this point, it may be accepted that Shakespeare revealed himself far more completely in his plays than as a lyric poet. Just as he chose his dramatic subjects with some felicity to reveal his many-sided nature, so he used the sonnets with equal artistry to discover that part of himself which could hardly be rendered objectively. Whatever is masculine in a man can be depicted superbly on the stage, but his feminine qualities—passionate self-abandonment, facile for-givingness, self-pity—do not show well in the dra-matic struggle. What sort of a drama would that be in which the hero would have to confess that when in the vale of years he had fallen desperately in love with a girl, and that he had been foolish enough to send a friend, a young noble, to plead his cause, with the result that the girl won the friend and gave her-self to him? The protagonist would earn mocking laughter and not sympathy, and this Shakespeare no doubt foresaw. Besides, to Shakespeare, this story, which is in brief the story of the sonnets, was terribly real and intimate, and he felt instinctively that he could not treat it objectively; it was too near him, too exquisitely painful for that.

At some time or other life overpowers the strongest of us, and that defeat we all treat lyrically; when the deepest depth in us is stirred we cannot feign, or depict ourselves from the outside dispassionately; we can only cry our passion, our pain and our despair; this once we use no art, simple truth is all we seek to reach. The crisis of Shakespeare's life, the hour of agony and bloody sweat when his weak-ness **found** him out and life's handicap proved **too** heavy even for his strength—that is the subject of the sonnets.

Now what was Shakespeare's weakness? his besetting temptation? " Love is my sin," he says; " Love of love and her soft hours " was his weakness: passion the snare that meshed his soul. No wonder Antony cries:

> " Whither hast thou led me, Egypt? "

for his gipsy led Shakespeare from shame to shame, to the verge of madness. The sonnets give us the story, the whole terrible, sinful, magical story of Shakespeare's passion.

As might have been expected, Englishmen like Wordsworth, with an intense appreciation of lyric poetry, have done good work in criticism of the sonnets, and one Englishman has read them with extraordinary understanding. Mr. Tyler's work on the sonnets ranks higher than that of Coleridge on the plays. I do not mean to say that it is on the same intellectual level with the work of Coleridge, though it shows wide reading, astonishing acuteness, and much skill in the marshalling of argument. But Mr. Tyler had the good fortune to be the first to give to the personages of the sonnets a local habitation and a name, and that unique achievement puts him in a place by himself far above the mass of commentators. Before his book appeared in 1890 the sonnets lay in the dim light of guess-work. It is true that Hallam had adopted the hypothesis of Boaden and Bright, and had identified William Herbert, Earl of Pembroke, with the high-born, handsome youth for whom Shakespeare, in the sonnets, expressed such passionate affection; but still, there were people who thought that the Earl of Southampton filled the requirements even better than William

Herbert, and as I say, the whole subject lay in the twilight of surmise and supposition.

Mr. Tyler, working on a hint of the Rev. W. A. Harrison, identified Shakespeare's high-born mistress, the " dark lady " of the sonnets, with Mistress Mary Fitton, a maid of honour to Queen Elizabeth.

These, then, are the personages of the drama, and the story is very simple: Shakespeare loved Mistress Fitton and sent his friend, the young Lord Herbert, to her on some pretext, but with the design that he should commend Shakespeare to the lady. Mistress Fitton fell in love with William Herbert, wooed and won him, and Shakespeare had to mourn the loss of both friend and mistress.

It would be natural to speak of this identification of Mr. Tyler's as the best working hypothesis yet put forward; but it would be unfair to him; it is more than this. Till his book appeared, even the date of the sonnets was not fixed; many critics regarded them as an early work, as early, indeed, as 1591 or 1592; he was the first person to prove that the time they cover extends roughly from 1598 to 1601. Mr. Tyler then has not only given us the names of the actors, but he has put the tragedy in its proper place in Shakespeare's life, and he deserves all thanks for his illuminating work.

I bring to this theory fresh corroboration from the plays. Strange to say, Mr. Tyler has hardly used the plays, yet, as regards the story told in the sonnets, the proof that it is a real and not an imaginary story can be drawn from the plays. I may have to point out, incidentally, what I regard as mistakes and oversights in Mr. Tyler's work; but in the main it stands four-square, imposing itself on the reason and satisfying at the same time instinct and sympathy.

Shakespeare's Love-Story

Let us first see how far the story told in the sonnets is borne out by the plays. For a great many critics, even to-day, reject the story altogether, and believe that the sonnets were nothing but poetic exercises.

The sonnets fall naturally into two parts: from 1 to 126 they tell how Shakespeare loved a youth of high rank and great personal beauty; sonnet 127 is an *envoi*; from 128 to 152 they tell of Shakespeare's love for a " dark lady." What binds the two series together is the story told in both, or at least told in one and corroborated in the other, that Shakespeare first sent his friend to the lady, most probably to plead his cause, and that she wooed his friend and gave herself to him. Now this is not a common or easily invented story. No one would guess that Shakespeare could be so foolish as to send his friend to plead his love for him. That's a mistake that no man who knows women would be likely to make; but the unlikelihood of the story is part of the evidence of its truth—*credo quia incredibile* has an element of persuasion in it.

No one has yet noticed that the story of the sonnets is treated three times in Shakespeare's plays. The first time the story appears it is handled so lightly that it looks to me as if he had not then lived through the incidents which he narrates. In the " Two Gentlemen of Verona " Proteus is asked by the Duke to plead Thurio's cause with Silvia, and he promises to do so; but instead, presses his own suit and is rejected. The incident is handled so carelessly (Proteus not being Thurio's friend) that it seems to me to have no importance save as a mere coincidence. When the scene between Proteus and Silvia was written Shakespeare had not yet been deceived by his friend. Still in " The Two Gentlemen of Verona " there is one speech which certainly betrays personal passion. It is in the last scene of the fifth act, when Valentine surprises Proteus offering violence to Silvia.

> " *Val.* (*coming forward*) Ruffian, let go that rude
>   uncivil touch,—
> Thou friend of an ill fashion!
>   *Pro.*   Valentine!
>   *Val. Thou common friend, that's without faith or*
>   *love,—*
> *For such is a friend now;*—treacherous man!
> Thou hast beguiled my hopes: nought but mine eye
> Could have persuaded me.   Now I dare not say
> I have one friend alive: thou would'st disprove me.
> Who should be trusted when one's own right hand
> Is perjured to the bosom?   Proteus,
> I am sorry I must never trust thee more,
> But count the world a stranger for thy sake.
> *The private wound is deepest: time most accurst*
> *'Mongst all foes that a friend should be the worst!* "

The first lines which I have italicised are too plain to be misread; when they were written Shakespeare had just been cheated by his friend; they are his passionate comment on the occurrence—" For such is a friend now "—can hardly be otherwise explained. The last couplet, too, which I have also put in italics, is manifestly a reflection on his betrayal: it is a twin rendering of the feeling expressed in sonnet 40:

> " And yet love knows it is a greater grief
>   To bear love's wrong than hate's known injury."

It contrasts " foe and friend," just as the sonnet contrasts " love and hate."

Mr. Israel Gollancz declares that " several critics

are inclined to attribute this final scene to another hand," and to his mind " it bears evident signs of hasty composition." No guess could be wider from the truth. The scene is most manifestly pure Shakespeare—I take the soliloquy of Valentine, with which the scene opens, as among Shakespeare's most characteristic utterances—but the whole scene is certainly later than the rest of the play. The truth probably is that after his friend had deceived him, " The Two Gentleman of Verona " was played again, and that Shakespeare rewrote this last scene under the influence of personal feeling. The 170 lines of it are full of phrases which might be taken direct from the sonnets. Here's such a couplet:

> " O, 'tis the curse in love, and still approved,
> When women cannot love where they're beloved."

The whole scene tells the story a little more frankly than we find it in the sonnets, as might be expected, seeing that Shakespeare's rival was a great noble and not to be criticised freely. This fact explains to me Valentine's unmotived renunciation of Silvia; explains, too, why he is reconciled to his friend with such unseemly haste. Valentine's last words in the scene are illuminating:

> " 'Twere pity two such friends should be long foes."

The way this scene in " The Two Gentlemen of Verona " is told throws more light on Shakespeare's feelings at the moment of his betrayal than the sonnets themselves. Under the cover of fictitious names Shakespeare ventured to show the disgust and contempt he felt for Lord Herbert's betrayal more plainly than he cared, or perhaps dared, to do when speaking in his own person.

There is another play where the same incident
is handled in such fashion as to put the truth of
the sonnet-story beyond all doubt.

In " Much Ado about Nothing " the incident is
dragged in by the ears, and the whole treatment is
most remarkable. Every one will remember how
Claudio tells the Prince that he loves Hero, and asks
his friend's assistance: " your highness now may do
me good." There's no reason for Claudio's shyness:
no reason why he should call upon the Prince for
help in a case where most men prefer to use their
own tongues; but Claudio is young, and so we glide
over the inherent improbability of the incident. The
Prince at once promises to plead for Claudio with
Hero and with her father:

> " And thou shalt have her. Was't not to this end
>   That thou began'st to twist so fine a story? "

Now comes the peculiar handling of the incident.
Claudio knows the Prince is wooing Hero for him,
therefore when Don John tells him that the Prince
" is enamoured on Hero," he should at once infer
that Don John is mistaken through ignorance of this
fact; but instead of that he falls suspicious, and
questions:

> " How know you he loves her?
>   *D. John.* I heard him swear his affection.
>   *Bor.* So did I too, and he swore he would marry her
>   to-night."

There is absolutely nothing even in this corroboration by Borachio to shake Claudio's trust in the
Prince: neither Don John nor Borachio knows what
he knows, that the Prince is wooing for him
(Claudio) and at his request. He should therefore

smile at the futile attempt to excite his jealousy.
But at once he is persuaded of the worst, as a man
would be who had already experienced such dis-
loyalty: he cries:

" 'Tis certain so; the prince woos for himself."

And then we should expect to hear him curse the
prince as a traitorous friend, and dwell on his own
loyal service by way of contrast, and so keep turn-
ing the dagger in the wound with the thought that
no one but himself was ever so repaid for such
honesty of love. But, no! Claudio has no bitterness
in him, no reproachings; he speaks of the whole
matter as if it had happened months and months
before, as indeed it had; for " Much Ado about
Nothing" was written about 1599. Reflection had
already shown Shakespeare the unreason of revolt,
and he puts his own thought in the mouth of
Claudio:

" 'Tis certain so; the prince woos for himself.
Friendship is constant in all other things
Save in the office and affairs of love:
Therefore all hearts in love use their own tongues;
Let every eye negotiate for itself,
And trust no agent; for beauty is a witch,
Against whose charms faith melteth into blood.
This is an accident of hourly proof,
Which I mistrusted not. Farewell, therefore, Hero."

The Claudio who spoke like this in the first madness of love lost and friendship cheated would be a
monster. Here we have Shakespeare speaking in
all calmness of something that happened to himself a considerable time before. The lines I have
put in italics admit no other interpretation: they
show Shakespeare's philosophic acceptance of things

as they are; what has happened to him is not to be assumed as singular but is the common lot of man— " an accident of hourly proof "—which he blames himself for not foreseeing. In fact, Claudio's temper here is as detached and impartial as Benedick's. Benedick declares that Claudio should be whipped:

> " *D. Pedro.* To be whipped! What's his fault?
> *Benedick.* The flat transgression of a schoolboy, who being overjoyed with finding a bird's nest, shows it his companion and he steals it."

That is the view of the realist who knows life and men, and plays the game according to the rules accepted. Shakespeare understood this side of life as well as most men. But Don Pedro is a prince —a Shakespearean prince at that—full of all loyalties and ideal sentiments; he answers Benedick from Shakespeare's own heart:

> " Wilt thou make a trust a transgression?
> The transgression is in the stealer."

It is curious that Shakespeare doesn't see that Claudio must feel this truth a thousand times more keenly than the Prince. As I have said, Claudio's calm acceptance of the fact is a revelation of Shakespeare's own attitude, an attitude just modified by the moral reprobation put in the mouth of the Prince. The recital itself shows that the incident was a personal experience of Shakespeare, and as one might expect in this case it does not accelerate but retard the action of the drama; it is, indeed, altogether foreign to the drama, an excrescence upon it and not an improvement but a blemish. Moreover, the reflective, disillusioned, slightly pessimistic tone of the narrative is alien and strange to the optimistic temper of the play; finally, this garb of patient sadness does not suit Claudio, who should be all love and eagerness, and diminishes instead of increasing our sympathy with his later actions. Whoever considers these facts will admit that we have here Shakespeare telling us what happened to himself, and what he really thought of his friend's betrayal.

"The transgression is in the stealer."

That is Shakespeare's mature judgement of Lord Herbert's betrayal.

The third mention of this sonnet-story in a play is later still: it is in "Twelfth Night." The Duke, as we have seen, is an incarnation of Shakespeare himself, and, indeed, the finest incarnation we have of his temperament. In the fourth scene of the first act he sends Viola to plead his cause for him with Olivia, much in the same way, no doubt, as Shakespeare sent Pembroke to Miss Fitton. The whole scene deserves careful reading.

"Cesario,
Thou know'st no less but all; I have unclasp'd
To thee the book even of my secret soul:
Therefore, good youth, address thy gait unto her;
Be not denied access, stand at her doors,
And tell them, there thy fixed foot shall grow
Till thou have audience.
    Vio.   Sure, my noble lord,
If she be so abandon'd to her sorrow
As it is spoke, she never will admit me.
    Duke. Be clamorous and leap all civil bounds
Rather than make unprofited return.
    Vio. Say I do speak with her, my lord, what then?
    Duke. O, then unfold the passion of my love,
Surprise her with discourse of my dear faith:
It shall become thee well to act my woes;

She will attend it better in thy youth
Than in a nuncio's of more grave aspect.
    Vio. I think not so, my lord.
    Duke.   Dear lad, believe it;
For they shall yet belie thy happy years,
That say thou art a man: Diana's lip
Is not more smooth and rubious; thy small pipe
Is as the maiden's organ, shrill and sound;
And all is semblative a woman's part.
I know thy constellation is right apt
For this affair. Some four or five attend him;
All if you will; for I myself am best
When least in company."

I do not want to find more here than is in the
text: the passage simply shows that this idea of
sending some one to plead his love was constantly
in Shakespeare's mind in these years. The curious
part of the matter is that he should pick a youth
as ambassador, and a youth who is merely his page.
He can discover no reason for choosing such a boy
as Viola, and so simply asserts that youth will be
better attended to, which is certainly not the fact.
Lord Herbert's youth was in his mind: but he
could not put the truth in the play that when he
chose his ambassador he chose him for his high
position and personal beauty and charm, and not
because of his youth. The whole incident is treated
lightly as something of small import; the bitterness
in " Much Ado " has died out: " Twelfth Night "
was written about 1601, a year or so later than
" Much Ado."

I do not want to labour the conclusion I have
reached; but it must be admitted that I have found
in the plays, and especially in " The Two Gentlemen of Verona " and " Much Ado," the same story
which is told in the sonnets; a story lugged into the

plays, where, indeed, its introduction is a grave fault in art and its treatment too peculiar to be anything but personal. Here in the plays we have, so to speak, three views of the sonnet-story; the first in " The Two Gentlemen of Verona," when the betrayal is fresh in Shakespeare's memory and his words are embittered with angry feeling:

" Thou common friend that's without faith or love."

The second view is taken in " Much Ado About Nothing " when the pain of the betrayal has been a little salved by time. Shakespeare now moralizes the occurrence. He shows us how it would be looked upon by a philosopher (for that is what the lover, Claudio, is in regard. to his betrayal) and by a soldier and man of the world, Benedick, and by a Prince. Shakespeare selects the prince to give effect to the view that the fault is in the transgressor and not in the man who trusts. The many-sided treatment of the story shows all the stages through which Shakespeare's mind moved, and the result is to me a more complete confession than is to be found in the sonnets. Finally the story is touched upon in " Twelfth Night," when the betrayal had faded into oblivion, but the poet lets out the fact that his ambassador was a youth, and the reason he gives for this is plainly insufficient. If after these three recitals any one can still believe that the sonnet-story is imaginary, he is beyond persuasion by argument.

CHAPTER IV

NOW that we have found the story of the sonnets repeated three times in the plays, it may be worth our while to see if we can discover in the plays anything that throws light upon the circumstances or personages of this curious triangular drama. At the outset, I must admit that save in these three plays I can find no mention whatever of Shakespeare's betrayer, Lord Herbert. He was " a false friend," the plays tell us, a " common friend without faith or love," " a friend of an ill fashion "; young, too, yet trusted; but beyond this summary superficial characterization there is silence. *Me judice* Lord Herbert made no deep or peculiar impression on Shakespeare; an opinion calculated to give pause to the scandal-mongers. For there can be no doubt whatever that Shakespeare's love, Mistress Fitton, the " dark lady " of the sonnet-series from 128 to 152, is to be found again and again in play after play, profoundly modifying the poet's outlook upon life and art. Before I take in hand this identification of Miss Fitton and her influence upon Shakespeare, let me beg the reader to bear in mind the fact that Shakespeare was a sensualist by nature, a lover, which is as rare a thing as consummate genius. The story of his idolatrous passion for Mary Fitton is the story of his life. This is what the commentators and critics hitherto have failed to appreciate. Let us now get at the facts and see what light the dramas throw upon the chief personage of the story, Mistress Fitton. The study will probably teach us that Shakespeare was the most impassioned lover and love-poet in all literature.

History tells us that Mary Fitton became a maid of honour to Queen Elizabeth in 1595 at the age of seventeen. From a letter addressed by her father to Sir Robert Cecil on January 29th, 1599, it is fairly certain that she had already been married at the age of sixteen; the union was probably not entirely valid, but the mere fact suggests a certain reckless-ness of character, or overpowering sensuality, or both, and shows that even as a girl Mistress Fitton was no shrinking, timid, modest maiden. Wrapped in a horseman's cloak she used to leave the Palace at night to meet her lover, Lord William Herbert. Though twice married, she had an illegitimate child by Herbert, and two later by Sir Richard Leveson.

This extraordinary woman is undoubtedly the sort of woman Shakespeare depicted as the " dark lady " of the sonnets. Nearly every sonnet of the twenty-six devoted to his mistress contains some accusation against her; and all these charges are manifestly directed against one and the same woman. First of all she is described in sonnet 131 as " tyrannous "; then in sonnet 133 as " faithless "; in sonnet 137 as " the bay where all men ride . . . the wide world's commonplace "; in sonnet 138 as " false "; in 139, she is " coquettish "; 140, " proud "; 142, " false to the bonds of love "; 147, " black as hell . . . dark as night "—in both looks and char-acter; 148, " full of foul faults "; 149, " cruel "; 150, " unworthy," but of " powerful" personality; 152, " unkind—inconstant . . . unfaithful . . . forsworn."

Now, the first question is: Can we find this " dark lady " of the sonnets in the plays? The sonnets tell us she was of pale complexion with black eyes and hair; do the plays bear out this description? And if they do bear it out do they throw any new light upon Miss Fitton's character? Did Miss Fitton seem proud and inconstant, tyrannous and wanton, to Shakespeare when he first met her, and before she knew Lord Herbert?

The earliest mention of the poet's mistress in the plays is to be found, I think, in " Romeo and Juliet." " Romeo and Juliet " is dated by Mr. Furnival 1591-1593; it was first mentioned in 1595 by Meres; first published in 1597. I think in its present form it must be taken to date from 1597. Romeo, who, as we have already seen, is an incarnation of Shakespeare, is presented to us in the very first scene as in love with one Rosaline. This in itself tells me nothing; but the proof that Shakespeare stands in intimate relation to the girl called Rosaline comes later, and so the first introductory words have a certain significance for me. Romeo himself tells us that " she hath Dian's wit," one of Shakespeare's favourite comparisons for his love, and speaks of her chastity, or rather of her unapproachableness; he goes on:

" O she is rich in beauty, only poor
That, when she dies, with beauty dies her store."

which reminds us curiously of the first sonnets.

In the second scene Benvolio invites Romeo to the feast of Capulet, where his love, " the fair Rosaline," is supping, and adds:

" Compare her face with some that I shall shew,
And I will make thee think thy swan a crow."

Romeo replies that there is none fairer than his love, and Benvolio retorts:

"Tut! You saw her fair, none else being by."

This bantering is most pointed if we assume that Rosaline was dark rather than fair.

In the second act Mercutio comes upon the scene, and, mocking Romeo's melancholy and passion, cries:

> "I conjure thee, by Rosaline's bright eyes,
> By her high forehead and her scarlet lip. . . ."

This description surprises me. Shakespeare rarely uses such physical portraiture of his personages, and Mercutio is a side of Shakespeare himself; a character all compact of wit and talkativeness, a character wholly invented by the poet.

A little later my suspicion is confirmed. In the fourth scene of the second act Mercutio talks to Benvolio about Romeo; they both wonder where he is, and Mercutio says:

> "Ah, that same pale-hearted wench, that Rosaline,
> Torments him so that he will sure run mad."

And again, a moment later, Mercutio laughs at Romeo as already dead, "stabbed with a white wench's black eye." Now, here is confirmation of my suspicion. It is most unusual for Shakespeare to give the physical peculiarities of any of his characters; no one knows how Romeo looked, or Juliet or even Hamlet or Ophelia; and here he repeats the description.

The only other examples we have as yet found in Shakespeare of such physical portraiture is the sketching of Falstaff in "Henry IV." and the snapshot of Master Slender in "The Merry Wives of Windsor," as a "little wee face, with a little yellow beard,—a cane-coloured beard." Both these photo-

graphs, as we noticed at the time, were very significant, and Slender's extraordinarily significant by
reason of its striking and peculiar realism.   Though
an insignificant character, Slender is photographed
for us by Shakespeare's contempt and hatred, just as
this Rosaline is photographed by his passionate love,
photographed again and again.

Shakespeare's usual way of describing the physical
appearance of a man or woman, when he allowed
himself to do it at all, which was seldom, was what
one might call the ideal or conventional way.   A
good example is to be found in Hamlet's description
of his father; he is speaking to his mother:

> "Hyperion's curls, the front of Jove himself,
>   An eye like Mars, to threaten and command,
> A station like the herald Mercury
>   New-lighted on a heaven-kissing hill."

In the special case I am considering Rosaline is
less even than a secondary character; she is not a
personage in the play at all.   She is merely mentioned casually by Benvolio and then by Mercutio,
and even Mercutio is not the protagonist; yet his
mention of her is strikingly detailed, astonishingly
realistic, in spite of its off-hand brevity.   We have
a photographic snapshot, so to speak, of this girl:
she " torments " Romeo; she is " hard-hearted "; a
" white wench " with " black eyes "; twice in four
lines she is called now " pale," now " white "—
plainly her complexion had no red in it, and was
in startling contrast to her black eyes and hair.
Manifestly this picture is taken from life, and it is
just as manifestly the portrait of the " dark lady "
of the sonnets.

As if to make assurance doubly sure, there is an-

other description of this same Rosaline in another
play, so detailed and striking, composed as it is of
contrasting and startling peculiarities that I can
only wonder that its full significance has not been
appreciated ages ago. To have missed its meaning
only proves that men do not read Shakespeare with
love's fine wit.

The repetition of the portrait is fortunate for
another reason: it tells us when the love story took
place. The allusion to the " dark lady " in " Romeo
and Juliet " is difficult to date exactly; the next
mention of her in a play can be fixed in time with
some precision. " Love's Labour's Lost " was revised by Shakespeare for production at Court during
the Christmas festivities of 1597. When the quarto
was published in 1598 it bore on its title-page the
words, " A pleasant conceited comedy called ' Love's
Labour's Lost.' As it was presented before Her
Highnes this last Christmas. Newly corrected and
augmented By W. Shakespeare." It is in the revised part that we find Shakespeare introducing his
dark love again, and this time, too, curiously enough,
under the name of Rosaline. Evidently he enjoyed
the mere music of the word. Biron is an incarnation
of Shakespeare himself, as we have already seen,
and the meeting of Biron and his love, Rosaline, in
the play is extremely interesting for us as Shakespeare in this revised production, one would think,
would wish to ingratiate himself with his love, more
especially as she would probably be present when the
play was produced. Rosaline is made to praise Biron,
before he appears, as a merry man and a most excellent talker; but when they meet they simply indulge in a tourney of wit, in which Rosaline more
than holds her own, showing indeed astounding self-
assurance, spiced with a little contempt of Biron;

" hard-hearted " Mercutio called it. Every word deserves to be weighed:

" *Biron.* Did not I dance with you in Brabant once?
Ros. Did not I dance with you in Brabant once?
Biron. I know you did.
Ros. How needless was it, then, to ask the question?
Biron. You must not be so quick.
Ros. 'Tis long of you that spur me with such questions.
Biron. Your wit's too hot, it speeds too fast, 'twill tire.
Ros. Not till it leave the rider in the mire.
Biron. What time o' day?
Ros. The hour that fools should ask.
Biron. Now fair befall your mask!
Ros. Fair fall the face it covers!
Biron. And send you many lovers!
Ros. Amen, so you be none.
Biron. Nay, then will I be gone."

Clearly this Rosaline, too, has Dian's wit and is not in love with Biron, any more than the Rosaline of " Romeo and Juliet " was in love with Romeo.

The next allusion is even more characteristic. Biron and Longaville and Boyet are talking; Longaville shows his admiration for one of the Princess's women, " the one in the white" he declares, " is a most sweet lady. . . ."

" *Biron.* What is her name in the cap?
Boyet. Rosaline, by good hap.
Biron. Is she wedded or no?
Boyet. To her will, sir, or so.
Biron. You are welcome, sir: adieu."

This, " To her will, sir, or so," is exactly in the spirit of the sonnets: every one will remember the first two lines of sonnet 135:

" Whoever hath her wish, thou hast thy *Will*,
And *Will* to boot, and *Will* in overplus;"

That, " To her will, sir, or so," I find astonishingly
significant, for not only has it nothing to do with the
play and is therefore unexpected, but the character-
drawing is unexpected, too; maids are not usually
wedded to their will in a double sense, and no other
of these maids of honour is described at all.

A little later Biron speaks again of Rosaline in
a way which shocks expectation. First of all, he
rages at himself for being in love at all. " And I,
forsooth in love! I, that have been love's whip!"
Here I pause again, it seems to me that Shakespeare
is making confession to us, just as when he admitted
without reason that Jaques was lewd. Be that as it
may, he certainly goes on in words which are astounding, so utterly unforeseen are they, and therefore the more characteristic:

" Nay, to be perjured, which is worst of all;
And, among three, to love the worst of all;"

The first line of this couplet, that he is perjured in
loving Rosaline may be taken as applying to the
circumstances of the play; but Shakespeare also
talks of himself in sonnet 152 as " perjured," for
he only swears in order to misuse his love, or with
a side glance at the fact that he is married and
therefore perjured when he swears love to one not
his wife. It is well to keep this " perjured " in
memory.

But it is the second line which is the more astonishing; there Biron tells us that among the three
of the Princess's women he loves " the worst of
all." Up to this moment we have only been told
kindly things of Rosaline and the other ladies; we

had no idea that any one of them was bad, much less that Rosaline was " the worst of all." The suspicion grows upon us, a suspicion which is confirmed immediately afterwards, that Shakespeare is speaking of himself and of a particular woman; else we should have to admit that his portraiture of Rosaline's character was artistically bad, and bad without excuse, for why should he lavish all this wealth of unpleasant detail on a mere subsidiary character? He goes on, however, to make the fault worse; he next speaks of his love Rosaline as—

> " A whitely wanton with a velvet brow,
> With two pitch-balls stuck in her face for eyes;
>   Ay, and by heaven, one that will do the deed;
> Though Argus were her eunuch and her guard:
>   And I to sigh for her! to watch for her!
> To pray for her! Go to! it is a plague."

It is, of course, a blot upon the play for Biron to declare that his love is a wanton of the worst. It is not merely unexpected and uncalled-for; it diminishes our sympathy with Biron and his love, and also with the play. But we have already found the rule trustworthy that whenever Shakespeare makes a mistake in art it is because of some strong personal feeling and not for want of wit, and this rule evidently holds good here. Shakespeare-Biron is picturing the woman he himself loves; for not only does he describe her as a wanton to the detriment of the play; but he pictures her precisely, and this Rosaline is the only person in the play of whom we have any physical description at all. Moreover, he has given such precise and repeated photographs of no other character in any of his plays:

> " A whitely wanton with a velvet brow,
> With two pitch-balls stuck in her face for eyes."

Shakespeare's Love-Story

This is certainly the same Rosaline we found depicted in "Romeo and Juliet"; but the portraiture here, both physical and moral, is more detailed and peculiar than it was in the earlier play. Shakespeare now knows his Rosaline intimately. The mere facts that here again her physical appearance is set forth with such particularity, and that the "hard-heartedness" which Mercutio noted in her has now become "wantonness" is all-important, especially when we remember that Miss Fitton was probably listening to the play. Even at Christmas, 1597, Shakespeare's passion has reached the height of a sex-duel. Miss Fitton has tortured him so that he delights in calling her names to her face in public when the play would have led one to expect ingratiating or complimentary courtesies. It does not weaken this argument to admit that the general audience would not perhaps have understood the allusions.

It is an almost incredible fact that not a single one of his hundreds of commentators has even noticed any peculiarity in this physical portraiture of Rosaline; Shakespeare uses this realism so rarely one would have thought that every critic would have been astounded by it; but no, they all pass over it without a word, Coleridge, Mr. Tyler, all of them.

The fourth act of "Love's Labour's Lost" begins with a most characteristic soliloquy of Biron:

"*Biron.* The king he is hunting the deer; I am coursing myself: they have pitched a toil; I am toiling in a pitch—pitch that defiles: defile! a foul word."

Here Biron is manifestly playing on the "pitch-balls" his love has for eyes, and also on the "foul faults" Shakespeare speaks of in the sonnets and in Othello. Biron goes on:

The Man Shakespeare

" O, but her eye—by this light, but for her eye, I
would not love her; yes, for her two eyes. Well, I do
nothing in the world but lie, and lie in my throat. By
heaven, I do love: and it hath taught me to rhyme, and
to be melancholy; and here is part of my rhyme, and
here my melancholy. Well, she hath one o' my sonnets
already: the clown bore it, the fool sent it, and the lady
hath it: sweet clown, sweeter fool, sweetest lady!"

This proves to me that some of Shakespeare's
sonnets were written in 1597. True, Mr. Tyler
would try to bind all the sonnets within the three
years from 1598 to 1601, the three years which
Shakespeare speaks about in sonnet 104:

> " Three winters cold
> Have from the forests shook three summers' pride,
> Three beauteous springs to yellow autumn turn'd
> In process of the seasons have I seen.
> Three April perfumes in three hot Junes burn'd,
> Since first I saw you fresh, which yet are green."

Lord Herbert first came to Court in the spring
of 1598, and so sonnet 104 may have represented
the fact precisely so far as Herbert was concerned;
but I am not minded to take the poet so literally.
Instead of beginning in the spring of 1598, some
of the sonnets to the lady were probably written in
the autumn of 1597, or even earlier, and yet Shakespeare would be quite justified in talking of three
years, if the period ended in 1601. A poet is not
to be bound to an almanack's exactitude.

In the fourth act of " Love's Labour's Lost," when
Biron confesses his love for " the heavenly Rosaline,"
the King banters him in the spirit of the time:

> " *King.* By heaven, thy love is black as ebony.
> *Biron.* Is ebony like her? O wood divine!

A wife of such wood were felicity.
O, who can give an oath? Where is a book?
That I may swear beauty doth beauty lack,
If that she learn not of her eye to look:
No face is fair that is not full so black."

Here we have Shakespeare again describing his
mistress for us, though he has done it better earlier
in the play; he harps upon her dark beauty here
to praise it, just as he praised it in Sonnet 127; it
is passion's trick to sound the extremes of blame and
praise alternately.

In the time of Elizabeth it was customary for
poets and courtiers to praise red hair and a fair
complexion as "beauty's ensign," and so compli-
ment the Queen. The flunkeyism, which is a characteristic of all the Germanic races, was peculiarly
marked in England from the earliest times, and induced men, even in those "spacious days," not only
to overpraise fair hair, but to run down dark hair
and eyes as ugly. The King replies:

"O paradox! Black is the badge of hell,
    The hue of dungeons and the school of night;
And beauty's crest becomes the heavens well."

Biron answers:

" Devils soonest tempt, resembling spirits of light.
    O, if in black my lady's brow be deck'd
It mourns that painting and usurping hair
    Should ravish doters with a false aspect;
And therefore is she born to make black fair.
    Her favour turns the fashion of the days,
For native blood is counted painting now;
    And therefore red that would avoid dispraise,
Paints itself black, to imitate her brow."

Our timid poet is bold enough, when cloaked under a stage-name, to uphold the colour of his love's hair against the Queen's; the mere fact speaks volumes to those who know their Shakespeare.

Sonnet 127 runs in almost the same words; though now the poet speaking in his own person is less bold:

" In the old age black was not counted fair,
    Or, if it were, it bore not beauty's name;
But now is black beauty's successive heir,
    And beauty slandered with a bastard shame:
For since each hand hath put on nature's power,
    Fairing the soul with art's false borrow'd face,
Sweet beauty hath no name, no holy bower,
    But is profaned, if not lives in disgrace.
Therefore my mistress' eyes are raven black,
    Her eyes so suited, and they mourners seem
At such who, not born fair, no beauty lack,
    Slandering creation with a false esteem:
Yet so they mourn, becoming of their woe
    That every tongue says beauty should look so."

There can be no doubt that in this Rosaline of " Romeo and Juliet " and of " Love's Labour's Lost," Shakespeare is describing the " dark lady " of the second sonnet-series, and describing her, against his custom in play-writing, even more exactly than he described her in the lyrics.

There is a line at the end of this act which is very characteristic when considered with what has gone before; it is clearly a confession of Shakespeare himself, and a perfect example of what one might call the conscience that pervades all his mature work:

" Light wenches may prove plagues to men forsworn."

We were right, it seems, in putting some stress on that " perjured " when we first met it.

In the second scene of the fifth act, which opens with a talk between the Princess and her ladies, our view of Rosaline is confirmed. Katherine calls Rosaline light, and jests upon this in lewd fashion; declares, too, that she is " a merry, nimble, stirring spirit," in fact, tells her that she is

> " A light condition in a beauty dark."

All these needless repetitions prove to me that Shakespeare is describing his mistress as she lived and moved. Those who disagree with me should give another instance in which he has used or abused the same precise portraiture. But there is more in this light badinage of the girls than a description of Rosaline. When Rosaline says that she will torture Biron before she goes, and turn him into her vassal, the Princess adds,

> " None are so surely caught when they are catch'd
> As wit turned fool."

Rosaline replies,

> " The blood of youth burns not with such excess
> As gravity's revolt to wantonness."

This remark has no pertinence or meaning in Rosaline's mouth. Biron is supposed to be young in the play, and he has never been distinguished for his gravity, but for his wit and humour: the Princess calls him " quick Biron." The two lines are clearly Shakespeare's criticism of himself. When he wrote the sonnets he thought himself old, and certainly his years (thirty-four) contrasted badly with those of Mary Fitton who was at this time not more than nineteen.

Late in 1597 then, before William Herbert came upon the scene at all, Shakespeare knew that his mistress was a wanton:

> " Ay, and by heaven, one that will do the deed;
> Though Argus were her eunuch and her guard."

Shakespeare has painted his love for us in these plays as a most extraordinary woman: in person she is tall, with pallid complexion and black eyes and black brows, " a gipsy," he calls her; in nature imperious, lawless, witty, passionate—a " wanton "; moreover, a person of birth and position. That a girl of the time has been discovered who united all these qualities in herself would bring conviction to almost any mind; but belief passes into certitude when we reflect that this portrait of his mistress is given with greatest particularity in the plays, where in fact it is out of place and a fault in art. When studying the later plays we shall find this gipsy wanton again and again; she made the deepest impression on Shakespeare; was, indeed, the one love of his life. It was her falseness that brought him to self-knowledge and knowledge of life, and turned him from a light-hearted writer of comedies and histories into the author of the greatest tragedies that have ever been conceived. Shakespeare owes the greater part of his renown to Mary Fitton.

CHAPTER V

THE most interesting question in the sonnets, the question the vital importance of which dwarfs all others, has never yet been fairly tackled and decided. As soon as English critics noticed, a hundred years or so ago, that the sonnets fell into two series, and that the first, and longer, series was addressed to a young man, they cried, " shocking! shocking! " and registered judgement with smug haste on evidence that would not hang a cat. Hallam, " the judicious," held that " it would have been better for Shakespeare's reputation if the sonnets had never been written," and even Heine, led away by the consensus of opinion, accepted the condemnation, and regretted " the miserable degradation of humanity " to be found in the sonnets. But before giving ourselves to the novel enjoyment of moral superiority over Shakespeare, it may be worth while to ask, is the fact proved? is his guilt established?

No one, I think, who has followed me so far will need to be told that I take no interest in white-washing Shakespeare: I am intent on painting him as he lived and loved, and if I found him as vicious as Villon, or as cruel as a stoat, I would set it all down as faithfully as I would give proof of his generosity or his gentleness.

Before the reader can fairly judge of Shakespeare's innocence or guilt, he must hold in mind two salient peculiarities of the man which I have

already noted; but which must now be relieved out
into due prominence so that one will make instinctive
allowance for them at every moment, his sensuality
and his snobbishness.

His sensuality is the quality, as we have seen,
which unites the creatures of his temperament with
those of his intellect, his poets with his thinkers,
and proves that Romeo and Jaques, the Duke of
" Twelfth Night " and Hamlet, are one and the same
person. If the matter is fairly considered it will be
found that this all-pervading sensuality is the
source, or at least a natural accompaniment of his
gentle kindness and his unrivalled sympathy.

Shakespeare painted no portrait of the hero or
of the adventurer; found no new word for the virile
virtues or virile vices, but he gave immortal expression to desire and its offspring, to love, jealousy,
and despair, to every form of pathos, pleading and
pity, to all the gentler and more feminine qualities.
Desire in especial has inspired him with phrases
more magically expressive even than those gasped
out by panting Sappho when lust had made her body
a lyre of deathless music. Her lyric to the belovèd
is not so intense as Othello's:

> " O, thou weed
> Who art so lovely fair and smell'st so sweet
> That the sense aches at thee ";

or as Cleopatra's astonishing:

> " There is gold, and here
> My bluest veins to kiss ";

—the revelation of a lifetime devoted to vanity and
sensuality, sensuality pampered as a god and adored
with an Eastern devotion.

Shakespeare's Love-Story

I do not think I need labour this point further; as I have already noticed, Orsino, the Duke of "Twelfth Night," sums up Shakespeare's philosophy of love in the words:

> "Give me excess of it, that, surfeiting,
> The appetite may sicken, and so die."—

Shakespeare told us the truth about himself when he wrote in sonnet 142, "Love is my sin." We can expect from him new words or a new method in the painting of passionate desire.

The second peculiarity of Shakespeare which we must establish firmly in our minds before we attempt to construe the sonnets is his extraordinary snobbishness.

English snobbishness is like a London fog, intenser than can be found in any other country; it is so extravagant, indeed, that it seems different in kind. One instance of this: when Mr. Gladstone was being examined once in a case, he was asked by counsel, Was he a friend of a certain lord? Instead of answering simply that he was, he replied that he did not think it right to say he was a friend of so great a noble: "he had the honour of his acquaintance." Only in England would the man who could make noblemen at will be found bowing before them with this humility of soul.

In Shakespeare's time English snobbishness was stronger than it is to-day; it was then supported by law and enforced by penalties. To speak of a lord without his title was regarded as defamation, and was punished as such more than once by the Star Chamber. Shakespeare's position, too, explains how this native snobbishness in him was heightened to flunkeyism. He was an aristocrat born, as we have seen, and felt in himself a kinship for the courtesies, chivalries, and generosities of aristocratic life. This tendency was accentuated by his calling. The middle class, already steeped in Puritanism, looked upon the theatre as scarcely better than the brothel, and showed their contempt for the players in a thousand ways. The groundlings and common people, with their " greasy caps " and " stinking breath " were as loathsome to Shakespeare as the crop-headed, gain-loving citizens who condemned him and his like pitilessly. He was thrown back, therefore, upon the young noblemen who had read the classics and loved the arts. His works show how he admires them. He could paint you Bassanio or Benedick or Mercutio to the life. Everybody has noticed the predilection with which he lends such characters his own poetic spirit and charm. His lower orders are all food for comedy or farce: he will not treat them seriously.

His snobbishness carries him to astounding lengths. One instance: every capable critic has been astonished by the extraordinary fidelity to fact he shows in his historical plays; he often takes whole pages of an earlier play or of Plutarch, and merely varying the language uses them in his drama. He is punctiliously careful to set down the fact, whatever it may be, and explain it, even when it troubles the flow of his story; but as soon as the fact comes into conflict with his respect for dignitaries, he loses his nice conscience. He tells us of Agincourt without ever mentioning the fact that the English bowmen won the battle; he had the truth before him; the chronicler from whom he took the story vouched for the fact; but Shakespeare preferred to ascribe the victory to Henry and his lords. Shakespeare loved a lord with a passionate admiration, and when he paints himself it is usually as a duke or prince.

Shakespeare's Love-Story

Holding these truths in our mind, Shakespeare's intense sensitiveness and sensuality, and his almost inconceivable snobbishness, we may now take up the sonnets.

The first thing that strikes one in the sonnets is the fact that, though a hundred and twenty-five of them are devoted to a young man, and Shakespeare's affection for him, and only twenty-six to the woman, every one of those to the woman is characterized by a terrible veracity of passion, whereas those addressed to the youth are rather conventional than convincing. He pictures the woman to the life; strong, proud, with dark eyes and hair, pale complexion—a wanton with the rare power of carrying off even a wanton's shame. He finds a method new to literature to describe her. He will have no poetic exaggeration; snow is whiter than her breasts; violets sweeter than her breath:

> "And yet, by heaven, I think my love as rare
> As any she belied with false compare."

His passion is so intense that he has no desire to paint her seduction as greater than it was. She has got into his blood, so to speak, and each drop of it under the microscope would show her image. Take any sonnet at haphazard, and you will hear the rage of his desire.

But what is the youth like?—" the master-mistress " of his passion, to give him the title which seems to have convinced the witless of Shakespeare's guilt. Not one word of description is to be found anywhere; no painting epithet—nothing. Where is the cry of this terrible, shameless, outrageous passion that mastered Shakespeare's conscience and enslaved his will? Hardly a phrase that goes beyond

affection—such affection as Shakespeare at thirty-
four might well feel for a gifted, handsome aristocrat like Lord Herbert, who had youth, beauty,
wealth, wit to recommend him. Herbert was a poet,
too: a patron unparagoned! "If Southampton
gave me a thousand pounds," Shakespeare may well
have argued, "perhaps Lord Herbert will get me
made Master of the Revels, or even give me a higher
place." An aristocratic society tends to make para-
sites even of the strong, as Dr. Johnson's famous
letter to Lord Chesterfield proves.

But let us leave supposition and come to the
sonnets themselves, which are addressed to the youth.
The first sonnet begins:

> " From fairest creatures we desire increase,
>   That thereby beauty's rose might never die."

This is a very good argument indeed when addressed to a woman; but when addressed to a man
by a man it rings strained and false. Yet it is the
theme of the first seventeen sonnets. It is precisely
the same argument which Shakespeare set forth in
" Venus and Adonis " again and again:

> " Seeds spring from seeds and beauty breedeth beauty;
>   Thou wast begot; to get it is thy duty."
>   (167-8.)
> " And so, in spite of death, thou dost survive,
>   In that thy likeness still is left alive . . ."
>   (173-4.)
> " Foul cankering rust the hidden treasure frets,
>   But gold that's put to use more gold begets."
>   (767-8.)

At the end of the third sonnet we find the same
argument:

" But if thou live, remember'd not to be,
Die single, and thine image dies with thee."

Again, in the fourth, sixth, and seventh sonnets the same plea is urged. In the tenth sonnet the poet cries:

" Make thee another self, for love of me,
That beauty still may live in thine or thee."

And again at the end of the thirteenth sonnet:

" You had a father; let your son say so."

Every one of these sonnets contains simply the argument which is set forth with equal force and far superior pertinence in " Venus and Adonis."

That is, Shakespeare makes use of the passion he has felt for a woman to give reality to the expression of his affection for the youth. No better proof could be imagined of the fact that he never loved the youth with passion.

In sonnet 18 Shakespeare begins to alter his note. He then tells the youth that he will achieve immortality, not through his children, but through Shakespeare's verses. Sonnet 19 is rounded with the same thought:

" Yet do thy worst, old Time: despite thy wrong,
My love shall in my verse ever live young."

Sonnet 20 is often referred to as suggesting intimacy:

" A woman's face with Nature's own hand painted,
Hast thou, the master-mistress of my passion;
A woman's gentle heart, but not acquainted
With shifting change, as is false woman's fashion;

An eye more bright than theirs, less false in rolling
Gilding the object whereupon it gazeth;
A man in hue, all ' hues ' in his controlling,
Which steals men's eyes and women's souls amazeth.
And for a woman wert thou first created;
Till Nature, as she wrought thee, fell a-doting,
And by addition me of thee defeated,
By adding one thing to my purpose nothing.
  But since she prick'd thee out for women's pleasure
  Mine be thy love, and thy love's use their treasure."

The sextet of this sonnet absolutely disproves guilty intimacy, and is, I believe, intended to disprove it; Shakespeare had already fathomed the scandal-loving minds of his friends and wanted to set forth the noble disinterestedness of his affection.

Sonnet 22 is more sincere, though not so passionate; it neither strengthens nor rebuts the argument. Sonnet 23 is the sonnet upon which all those chiefly rely who wish to condemn Shakespeare. Here it is:

" As an unperfect actor on the stage,
Who with his fear is put beside his part,
Or some fierce thing replete with too much rage,
Whose strength's abundance weakens his own heart;
So I, for fear of trust, forget to say
The perfect ceremony of love's rite,
And in mine own love's strength seem to decay,
O'ercharged with burthen of mine own love's might
O, let my looks be then the eloquence
And dumb presages of my speaking breast;
Who plead for love, and look for recompense,
More than that tongue that more hath more express'd.
  O, learn to read what silent love hath writ:
  To hear with eyes belongs to love's fine wit."

We can interpret the phrases, " the perfect ceremony of love's rite " and " look for recompense " as we will; but it must be admitted that even when used to the uttermost they form an astonishingly small base on which to raise so huge and hideous a superstructure.

But we shall be told that the condemnation of Shakespeare is based, not upon any sonnet or any line; but upon the way Shakespeare speaks as soon as he discovers that his mistress has betrayed him in favour of his friend. One is inclined to expect that he will throw the blame on the friend, and, after casting him off, seek to win again the affections of his mistress. Nine men out of ten would act in this way. But the sonnets tell us with iteration and most peculiar emphasis that Shakespeare does not condemn the friend. As soon as he hears of the traitorism he cries (sonnet 33):

" Full many a glorious morning have I seen
   Flatter the mountain-tops with sovereign eye,
   Kissing with golden face the meadows green,
   Gilding pale streams with heavenly alchemy;
   Anon permit the basest clouds to ride
   With ugly rack on his celestial face,
   And from the forlorn world his visage hide,
   Stealing unseen to west with this disgrace:
   Even so my sun one early morn did shine
   With all triumphant splendour on my brow;
   But out! alack! he was but one hour mine,
   The region cloud hath mask'd him from me now.
    Yet him for this my love no whit disdaineth;
    Suns of the world may stain, when heaven's sun
     staineth."

It is the loss of his friend he regrets, rather than the loss of his mistress; she is not mentioned save by comparison with " base clouds." Yet even when read by Gradgrind and his compeers the thirteenth line of this sonnet is utterly inconsistent with passion.

In the next sonnet the friend repents, and weeps the " strong offence," and Shakespeare accepts the sorrow as salve that " heals the wound "; his friend's tears are pearls that " ransom all ill deeds." The next sonnet begins with the line:

" No more be griev'd at that which thou hast done ";

Shakespeare will be an " accessory " to his friend's " theft," though he admits that the robbery is still sour. Then come four sonnets in which he is content to forget all about the wrong he has suffered, and simply exhausts himself in praise of his friend. Sonnet 40 begins:

" Take all my loves, my love, yea, take them all;
What hast thou then more than thou hadst before?
No love, my love, that thou may'st true love call;
All mine was thine, before thou hadst this more."

This is surely the very soul of tender affection; but it is significant that even here the word " true " is emphasized and not " love "; he goes on:

" I do forgive thy robbery, gentle thief,
Although thou steal thee all my poverty;
And yet love knows it is a greater grief
To bear love's wrong, than hate's known injury."

Never before was a man so gentle-kind; we might be listening to the lament of a broken-hearted woman who smiles through her tears to reassure her lover; yet there is no attempt to disguise the fact that Herbert has done " wrong." The next sonnet puts the poet's feeling as strongly as possible.

"Those pretty wrongs that liberty commits,
When I am sometime absent from thy heart,
Thy beauty and thy years full well befits,
For still temptation follows where thou art.
Gentle thou art, and therefore to be won,
Beauteous thou art, therefore to be assail'd;
And when a woman woos, what woman's son
Will sourly leave her till she have prevail'd?
Ay me! but yet thou might'st my seat forbear,
And chide thy beauty and thy straying youth,
Who lead thee in their riot even there
Where thou art forced to break a twofold truth;
    Hers, by thy beauty tempting her to thee,
    Thine by thy beauty being false to me."

The first lines show that Shakespeare is pretending; he attempts not only to minimize the offence, but to find it charming. A mother who caught her young son kissing a girl would reproach him in this fashion; to her his faults would be the " pretty wrongs that liberty commits." But this is not the way passion speaks, and here again the sextet condemns Herbert in the plainest terms. At length we have the summing-up:

"That thou hast her, it is not all my grief,
And yet it may be said I lov'd her dearly;
That she hath thee, is of my wailing chief,
A loss in love that touches me more nearly.
Loving offenders, thus I will excuse ye:
Thou dost love her, because thou know'st I love her;
And for my sake even so doth she abuse me,
Suffering my friend for my sake to approve her.
If I lose thee, my loss is my love's gain,
And losing her, my friend hath found that loss;
Both find each other, and I lose both twain,
And both for my sake lay on me this cross:
    But here's the joy; my friend and I are one;
    Sweet flattery! then she loves but me alone."

This sonnet, with its affected word-play and wire-drawn consolation, leaves one gaping: Shakespeare's verbal affectations had got into his very blood. To my mind the whole sonnet is too extravagant to be sincere; it is only to be explained by the fact that Shakespeare's liking for Herbert was heightened by snobbishness and by the hope of patronage. None of it rings true except the first couplet. Yet the argument of it is repeated, strange to say, and emphasized in the sonnets addressed to the " dark lady " whom Shakespeare loved. Sonnet 144 is clear enough:

> " Two loves I have of comfort and despair,
>   Which like two spirits do suggest me still:
>   The better angel is a man, right fair,
>   The worser spirit a woman, colour'd ill.
>   To win me soon to hell, my female evil
>   Tempteth my better angel from my side,
>   And would corrupt my saint to be a devil,
>   Wooing his purity with her foul pride.
>   And whether that my angel be turn'd fiend
>   Suspect I may, yet, not directly tell;
>   But being both from me, both to each friend,
>   I guess one angel in another's hell:
>   Yet this shall I ne'er know, but live in doubt,
>   Till my bad angel fire my good one out."

As soon as his mistress comes on the scene Shakespeare's passionate sincerity cannot be questioned. The truth is the intensity of his passion leads him to condemn and spite the woman, while the absence of passion allows him to pretend affection for the friend. Sonnet 133, written to the woman, is decisive:

> " Beshrew that heart that makes my heart to groan
>   For that deep wound it gives my friend and me!

Is't not enough to torture me alone,
But slave to slavery my sweet'st friend must be?
Me from myself thy cruel eye hath taken,
And my next self thou harder hast engross'd:
Of him, myself, and thee, I am forsaken;
A torment thrice threefold thus to be cross'd.
Prison my heart in thy steel bosom's ward,
But then my friend's heart let my poor heart bail;
Whoe'er keeps me, let my heart be his guard;
Thou canst not then use rigour in my gaol:
  And yet thou wilt; for I, being pent in thee,
  Perforce am thine, and all that is in me."

The last couplet is to me " perforce " conclusive.

But let us take it that these sonnets prove the contention of the cry of critics that Shakespeare preferred friendship to love, and held his friend dearer than his mistress, and let us see if the plays corroborate the sonnets on this point. We may possibly find that the plays only strengthen the doubt which the sonnets implant in us.

" The Merchant of Venice " has always seemed to me important as helping to fix the date of the sonnets. Antonio, as I have shown, is an impersonation of Shakespeare himself. It seems to me Shakespeare would have found it impossible to write of Antonio's self-sacrificing love for Bassanio after he himself had been cheated by his friend. This play then must have been written shortly before his betrayal, and should give us Shakespeare's ordinary attitude. Many expressions in the play remind us of the sonnets, and one in especial of sonnet 41. In the sixth scene of the second act, Jessica, when escaping from her father's house, uses Shakespeare's voice to say:

" But love is blind and lovers cannot see
The pretty follies that themselves commit."

Here we have " the pretty follies " which is used again as " pretty wrongs " in sonnet 41. Immediately afterwards Lorenzo, another mask of Shakespeare, praises Jessica as " wise, fair, and true," just as in sonnet 105 Shakespeare praises his friend as " kind, fair, and true," using again words which his passion for a woman has taught him.

The fourth act sets forth the same argument we find in the sonnets. When it looks as if Antonio would have to give his life as forfeit to the Jew, Bassanio exclaims:

> " Antonio, I am married to a wife
> Which is as dear to me as life itself;
> But life itself, my wife and all the world
> Are not with me esteem'd above thy life.
> I would lose all, ay, sacrifice them all
> Here to this devil to deliver you."

This is the language of passionate exaggeration, one might say. Antonio is suffering in Bassanio's place, paying the penalty, so to speak, for Bassanio's happiness. No wonder Bassanio exaggerates his grief and the sacrifice he would be prepared to make. But Gratiano has no such excuse for extravagant speech, and yet Gratiano follows in the self-same vein:

> " I have a wife whom, I protest, I love:
> I would she were in heaven, so she could
> Entreat some power to change this currish Jew."

The peculiarity of this attitude is heightened by the fact that the two wives, Portia and Nerissa, both take the ordinary view. Portia says:

> " Your wife would give you little thanks for that
> If she were by to hear you make the offer."

240

And Nerissa goes a little further:

> " 'Tis well you offer it behind her back,
> The wish would make else an unquiet house."

The blunder is monstrous; not only is the friend prepared to sacrifice all he possesses, including his wife, to save his benefactor, but the friend's friend is content to sacrifice his wife too for the same object. Shakespeare then in early manhood was accustomed to put friendship before love; we must find some explanation of what seems to us so unnatural an attitude.

In the last scene of " The Two Gentlemen of Verona," which is due to a later revision, the sonnet-case is emphasized. And at this time Shakespeare has suffered Herbert's betrayal. As soon as the false friend Proteus says he is sorry and asks forgiveness, Valentine, another impersonation of Shakespeare, replies:

> "Then I am paid;
> And once again I do receive thee honest:
> Who by repentance is not satisfied,
> Is nor of heaven nor earth, for these are pleas'd;
> By penitence the Eternal's wrath's appeased;
> And that my love may appear plain and free,
> All that was mine in Silvia I give thee."

This incarnation of Shakespeare speaks of repentance in Shakespeare's most characteristic fashion, and then coolly surrenders the woman he loves to his friend without a moment's hesitation, and without even considering whether the woman would be satisfied with the transfer. The words admit of no misconstruction; they stand four-square, not to be shaken by any ingenuity of reason, and Shakespeare supplies us with further corroboration of them.

" Coriolanus " was written fully ten years after " The Merchant of Venice," and long after the revision of " The Two Gentlemen of Verona." And yet Shakespeare's attitude at forty-three is, in regard to this matter, just what it was at thirty-three. When Aufidius finds Coriolanus in his house, and learns that he has been banished from Rome and is now prepared to turn his army against his countrymen, he welcomes him as " more a friend than e'er an enemy," and this is the way he takes to show his joy:

> " Know thou first,
> I loved the maid I married: never man
> Sigh'd truer breath; but that I see thee here,
> Thou noble thing! more dances my rapt heart
> Than when I first my wedded mistress saw
> Bestride my threshold."

Here's the same attitude; the same extravagance; the same insistence on the fact that the man loves the maid and yet has more delight in the friend. What does it mean? When we first find it in " The Merchant of Venice " it must give the reader pause; in " The Two Gentlemen of Verona " it surprises us; in the sonnets, accompanied as it is by every flattering expression of tender affection for the friend, it brings us to question; but its repetition in " Coriolanus " must assure us that it is a mere pose. Aufidius was not such a friend of Coriolanus that we can take his protestation seriously. The argument is evidently a stock argument to Shakespeare: a part of the ordinary furniture of his mind: it is like a fashionable dress of the period—the wearer does not notice its peculiarity.

The truth is, Shakespeare found in the literature of his time, and in the minds of his contemporaries,

242

a fantastically high appreciation of friendship, coupled with a corresponding disdain for love as we moderns understand it. In " Wit's Commonwealth," published in 1598, we find: " The love of men to women is a thing common and of course, but the friendship of man to man, infinite and immortal." Passionate devotion to friendship is a sort of mark of the Renaissance, and the words " love " and " lover " in Elizabethan English were commonly used for " friend " and " friendship." Moreover, one must not forget that Lyly, whose euphuistic speech affected Shakespeare for years, had handled this same incident in his " Campaspe," where Alexander gives up his love to his rival, Apelles. Shakespeare, not to be outdone in any loyalty, sets forth the same fantastical devotion in the sonnets and plays. He does this, partly because the spirit of the time infected him, partly out of sincere admiration for Herbert, but oftener, I imagine, out of self-interest. It is pose, flunkeyism and the hope of benefits to come and not passion that inspired the first series of sonnets.

Whoever reads the scene carefully in " Much Ado About Nothing," cannot avoid seeing that Shakespeare at his best not only does not minimize his friend's offence, but condemns it absolutely:

" The transgression is in the stealer."

And in the sonnets, too, in spite of himself, the same true feeling pierces through the snobbish and affected excuses.

" Ay me! but yet thou might'st my seat forbear,
And chide thy beauty and thy straying youth,
Who lead thee in their riot even there

243

> Where thou art forced to break a twofold truth,
> Hers, by thy beauty tempting her to thee,
> Thine, by thy beauty being false to me."

Shakespeare was a sycophant, a flunkey if you will, but nothing worse.

Further arguments suggest themselves. Shakespeare lived, as it were, in a glass house with a score of curious eyes watching everything he did and with as many ears pricked for every word he said; but this foul accusation was never even suggested by any of his rivals. In especial Ben Jonson was always girding at Shakespeare, now satirically, now good-humouredly. Is it not manifest that if any such sin had ever been attributed to him, Ben Jonson would have given the suspicion utterance? There is a passage in his " Bartholomew Fair " which I feel sure is meant as a skit upon the relations we find in the Sonnets. In Act V., scene iii., there is a puppet-show setting forth " the ancient modern history of Hero and Leander, otherwise called the Touchstone of true Love, with as true a trial of Friendship between Damon and Pythias, two faithful friends o' the Bankside." Hero is a " wench o' the Bankside," and Leander swims across the Thames to her. Damon and Pythias meet at her lodgings, and abuse each other violently, only to finish as perfect good friends.

" *Damon.* Whore-master in thy face;
Thou hast lain with her thyself, I'll prove it in this place.
    Leatherhead. They are whore-masters both, sir, that's
        a plain case.
    Pythias. Thou lie like a rogue.
    Leatherhead. Do I lie like a rogue?
    Pythias. A pimp and a scab.
    Leatherhead. A pimp and a scab!
I say, between you you have both but one drab.

Pythias and Damon. Come, now we'll go together to
breakfast to Hero.
Leatherhead. Thus, gentles, you perceive without
any denial
'Twixt Damon and Pythias here friendship's true trial."

Rare Ben Jonson would have been delighted to set
forth the viler charge if it had ever been whis-
pered.

Then again, it seems to me certain that if Shakespeare had been the sort of man his accusers say
he was, he would have betrayed himself in his plays.
Consider merely the fact that young boys then
played the girls' parts on the stage. Surely if
Shakespeare had had any leaning that way, we
should have found again and again ambiguous or
suggestive expressions given to some of these boys
when aping girls; but not one. The temptation
was there; the provocation was there, incessant and
prolonged for twenty-five years, and yet, to my
knowledge, Shakespeare has never used one word
that malice could misconstrue. Yet he loved suggestive and lewd speech.

Luckily, however, there is stronger proof of Shakespeare's innocence than even his condemnation of
his false friend, proof so strong, that if all the arguments for his guilt were tenfold stronger than they
are, this proof would outweigh them all and bring
them to nought. Nor should it be supposed, because
I have only mentioned the chief arguments for and
against, that I do not know all those that can be
urged on either side. I have confined myself to
the chief ones simply because by merely stating
them, their utter weakness must be admitted by
every one who can read Shakespeare, by every one
who understands his impulsive sensitiveness, and

the facility with which affectionate expressions came
to his lips. Moreover, it must not be forgotten that
while the sonnets were being written he was in
rivalry with Chapman for this very patron's favour,
and this rivalry alone would explain a good deal of
the fervour, or, should I say, the affected fervour
he put into the first series of sonnets; but now for
the decisive and convincing argument for Shakespeare's innocence.

Let us first ask ourselves how it is that real
passion betrays itself and proves its force. Surely
it is by its continuance; by its effect upon the
life later. I have assumed, or inferred, as my
readers may decide, that Shakespeare's liking for
Herbert was chiefly snobbish, and was deepened by
the selfish hope that he would find in him a patron
even more powerful and more liberally disposed
than Lord Southampton. He probably felt that
young Herbert owed him a great deal for his companionship and poetical advice; for Herbert was
by way of being a poet himself. If my view is correct, after Shakespeare lost Lord Herbert's affection, we should expect to hear him talking of man's
forgetfulness and ingratitude, and that is just what
Lord Herbert left in him, bitterness and contempt.
Never one word in all his works to show that the
loss of this youth's affection touched him more
nearly. As we have seen, he cannot keep the incident out of his plays. Again and again he drags
it in; but in none of these dramas is there any
lingering kindness towards the betrayer. And as
soon as the incident was past and done with, as
soon as the three or four years' companionship
with Lord Herbert was at an end, not one word
more do we catch expressive of affection. Again
and again Shakespeare rails at man's ingratitude,
but nothing more. Think of it. Pembroke, under

James, came to great power; was, indeed, made Lord Chamberlain, and set above all the players, so that he could have advanced Shakespeare as he pleased with a word: with a word could have made him Master of the Revels, or given him a higher post. He did not help him in any way. He gave books every Christmas to Ben Jonson, but we hear of no gift to Shakespeare, though evidently from the dedication to him of the first folio, he remained on terms of careless acquaintance with Shakespeare. Ingratitude is what Shakespeare found in Lord Pembroke; ingratitude is what he complains of in him.

What a different effect the loss of Mary Fitton had upon Shakespeare. Just consider what the plays teach us when the sonnet-story is finished. The youth vanishes; no reader can find a trace of him, or even an allusion to him. But the woman comes to be the centre, as we shall see, of tragedy after tragedy. She flames through Shakespeare's life, a fiery symbol, till at length she inspires perhaps his greatest drama, "Antony and Cleopatra," filling it with the disgrace of him who is "a strumpet's fool," the shame of him who has become "the bellows and the fan to cool a harlot's lust."

The passion for Mary Fitton was the passion of Shakespeare's whole life. The adoration of her, and the insane desire of her, can be seen in every plays he wrote from 1597 to 1608. After he lost her, he went back to her; but the wound of her frailty cankered and took on proud flesh in him, and tortured him to nervous breakdown and madness. When at length he won to peace, after ten years, it was the peace of exhaustion. His love for his "gipsy-wanton" burned him out, as one is burnt to ashes at the stake, and his passion only ended with his life.

There is no room for doubt in my mind, no faintest suspicion. Hallam and Heine, and all the cry of critics, are mistaken in this matter. Shakespeare admired Lord Herbert's youth and boldness and beauty, hoped great things from his favour and patronage; but after the betrayal, he judged him inexorably as a mean traitor, " a stealer" who had betrayed " a twofold trust "; and later, cursed him for his ingratitude, and went about with wild thoughts of bloody revenge, as we shall soon see in " Hamlet " and " Othello," and then dropped him into oblivion without a pang.

It is bad enough to show that Shakespeare, the sweetest spirit and finest mind in all literature, should have degraded himself to pretend such an affection for the profligate Herbert as has given occasion for misconstruction. It is bad enough, I say, to know that Shakespeare could play flunkey to this extent; but after all, that is the worst that can be urged against him, and it is so much better than men have been led to believe that there may be a certain relief in the knowledge.

CHAPTER VI

THE FIRST-FRUIT OF THE TREE OF KNOWLEDGE:
BRUTUS

THE play of " Julius Caesar " was written about
1600 or 1601. As " Twelfth Night " was the
last of the golden comedies, so " Julius Caesar " is
the first of the great tragedies, and bears melancholy witness to us that the poet's young-eyed
confidence in life and joy in living are dying, if
not dead. " Julius Caesar " is the first outcome of
disillusion. Before it was written Shakespeare had
been deceived by his mistress, betrayed by his
friend; his eyes had been opened to the fraud and
falsehood of life; but, like one who has just been
operated on for cataract, he still sees realities as
through a mist, dimly. He meets the shock of
traitorous betrayal as we should have expected
Valentine or Antonio or Orsino to meet it—with
pitying forgiveness. Suffering, instead of steeling
his heart and drying up his sympathies, as it does
with most men, softened him, induced him to give
himself wholly to that " angel, Pity." He will not
believe that his bitter experience is universal; in
spite of Herbert's betrayal, he still has the courage
to declare his belief in the existence of the ideal.
At the very last his defeated Brutus cries:

" My heart doth joy that yet in all my life
I found no man but he was true to me."

The pathos of this attempt still to believe in man

and man's truth is over the whole play. But the belief was fated to disappear. No man who lives in the world can boast of loyalty as Brutus did; even Jesus had a Judas among the Twelve. But when Shakespeare wrote " Julius Caesar " he still tried to believe, and this gives the play an important place in his life's story.

Before I begin to consider the character of Brutus I should like to draw attention to three passages which place Brutus between the melancholy Jaques of "As You Like It," whose melancholy is merely temperamental, and the almost despairing Hamlet. Jaques says:

"Invest me in my motley; give me leave
    To speak my mind, and I will through and through
    Cleanse the foul body of the infected world,
    If they will patiently receive my medicine."

This is the view of early manhood which does not doubt its power to cure all the evils which afflict mortality. Then comes the later, more hopeless view, to which Brutus gives expression:

" Till then, my noble friend, chew upon this;
    Brutus had rather be a villager
    Than to repute himself a son of Rome
    Under these hard conditions as this time
    Is like to lay upon us."

And later still, and still more bitter, Hamlet's:

" The time is out of joint; O cursed spite,
    That ever I was born to set it right! "

But Shakespeare is a meliorist even in Hamlet, and believes that the ailments of man can all be set right.

The likenesses between Brutus and Hamlet are so marked that even the commentators have noticed them. Professor Dowden exaggerates the similarities. "Both (dramas)," he writes, "are tragedies of thought rather than of passion; both present in their chief characters the spectacle of noble natures which fail through some weakness or deficiency rather than through crime; upon Brutus as upon Hamlet a burden is laid which he is not able to bear; neither Brutus nor Hamlet is fitted for action, yet both are called to act in dangerous and difficult affairs." Much of this is Professor Dowden's view and not Shakespeare's. When Shakespeare wrote "Julius Caesar" he had not reached that stage in self-understanding when he became conscious that he was a man of thought rather than of action, and that the two ideals tend to exclude each other. In the contest at Philippi Brutus and his wing win the day; it is the defeat of Cassius which brings about the ruin; Shakespeare evidently intended to depict Brutus as well "fitted for action."

Some critics find it disconcerting that Shakespeare identified himself with Brutus, who failed, rather than with Caesar, who succeeded. But even before he himself came to grief in his love and trust, Shakespeare had always treated the failures with peculiar sympathy. He preferred Arthur to the Bastard, and King Henry VI. to Richard III., and Richard II. to proud Bolingbroke. And after his agony of disillusion, all his heroes are failures for years and years: Brutus, Hamlet, Macbeth, Lear, Troilus, Antony, and Timon—all fail as he himself had failed.

There is some matter for surprise in the fact that Brutus is an ideal portrait of Shakespeare. Disillusion usually brings a certain bitter sincerity, a measure of realism, into artistic work; but its first effect on Shakespeare was to draw out all the kindliness in him; Brutus is Shakespeare at his sweetest and best. Yet the soul-suffering of the man has assuredly improved his art: Brutus is a better portrait of him than Biron, Valentine, Romeo, or Antonio, a more serious and bolder piece of self-revealing even than Orsino. Shakespeare is not afraid now to depict the deep underlying kindness of his nature, his essential goodness of heart. A little earlier, and occupied chiefly with his own complex growth, he could only paint sides of himself; a little later, and the personal interest absorbed all others, so that his dramas became lyrics of anguish and despair. Brutus belongs to the best time, artistically speaking, to the time when passion and pain had tried the character without benumbing the will or distracting the mind: it is a masterpiece of portraiture, and stands in even closer relation to Hamlet than Romeo stands to Orsino. As Shakespeare appears to us in Brutus at thirty-seven, so he was when they bore him to his grave at fifty-two—the heart does not alter greatly.

Let no one say or think that in all this I am drawing on my imagination; what I have said is justified by all that Brutus says and does from one end of the play to the other. According to his custom, Shakespeare has said it all of himself very plainly, and has put his confession into the mouth of Brutus on his very first appearance (Act i. sc. 2):

> " Cassius
> Be not deceived: if I have veiled my look
> I turn the trouble of my countenance
> Merely upon myself. Vexed I am
> Of late with passions of some difference,

Tree of Knowledge: Brutus

> Conceptions only proper to myself,
> Which gives some soil, perhaps, to my behaviours,
> But let not therefore my good friends be grieved,—
> Among which number, Cassius, be you one,—
> Nor construe any further in neglect,
> Than that poor Brutus, with himself at war,
> Forgets the shows of love to other men."

What were these "different passions," complex personal passions, too, which had vexed Brutus and changed his manners even to his friends? There is no hint of them in Plutarch, no word about them in the play. It was not "poor Brutus," but poor Shakespeare, racked by love and jealousy, tortured by betrayal, who was now "at war with himself."

I assume the identity of Brutus with Shakespeare before I have absolutely proved it because it furnishes the solution to the difficulties of the play. As usual, Coleridge has given proof of his insight by seeing and stating the chief difficulty, without, however, being able to explain it, and as usual, also, the later critics have followed him as far as they can, and in this case have elected to pass over the difficulty in silence. Coleridge quotes some of the words of Brutus when he first thinks of killing Caesar, and calls the passage a speech of Brutus, but it is in reality a soliloquy of Brutus, and must be considered in its entirety. Brutus says:

> "It must be by his death: and for my part,
> I know no personal cause to spurn at him
> But for the general. He would be crowned:—
> How that might change his nature, there's the
>   question?
> It is the bright day that brings forth the adder,
> And that craves wary walking. Crown him?—that;

And then, I grant, we put a sting in him
That at his will he may do danger with.
The abuse of greatness is, when it disjoins
Remorse from power: and to speak truth of Caesar,
I have known his affections swayed
More than his reason. But 'tis a common proof,
That lowliness is young ambition's ladder,
Whereto the climber-upwards turns his face;
But when he once attains the topmost round,
He then unto the ladder turns his back,
Looks in the clouds, scorning the base degrees
By which he did ascend. So Caesar may:
Then, lest he may, prevent. And since the quarrel
Will bear no colour for the thing he is,
Fashion it thus: that, what he is, augmented,
Would run to these and these extremities:
And therefore think him as a serpent's egg,
Which, hatched, would as his kind grow mischievous;
And kill him in the shell."

Coleridge's comment on this deserves notice.
He wrote: " This speech is singular; at least, I do
not at present see into Shakespeare's motive, his
rationale, or in what point of view he meant
Brutus' character to appear. For surely . . . nothing can seem more discordant with our historical
preconceptions of Brutus, or more lowering to the
intellect of the Stoico-Platonic tyrannicide, than
the tenets here attributed to him—to him, the stern
Roman republican; namely, that he would have no
objection to a king, or to Caesar, a monarch in
Rome, would Caesar but be as good a monarch as
he now seems disposed to be! How, too, could
Brutus say that he found no personal cause—none
in Caesar's past conduct as a man? Had he not
passed the Rubicon? Had he not entered Rome
as a conquerer? Had he not placed his Gauls in
the Senate? Shakespeare, it may be said, has not

brought these things forward. True;—and this is just the ground of my perplexity. What character did Shakespeare mean his Brutus to be? "

All this is sound criticism, and can only be answered by the truth that Shakespeare from the beginning of the play identified himself with Brutus, and paid but little attention to the historic Brutus whom he had met in Plutarch. Let us push criticism a little further, and we shall see that this is the only possible way to read the riddle. We all know why Plutarch's Brutus killed Caesar; but why does Shakespeare's Brutus kill the man he so esteems? Because Caesar may change his nature when king; because like the serpent's egg he may " grow mischievous "? But when he speaks " truth " of Caesar he has to admit Caesar's goodness. The " serpent's egg " reason then is inapplicable. Besides, when speaking of himself on the plains of Philippi, Shakespeare's Brutus explicitly contradicts this false reasoning:

> " I know not how
> But I do find it cowardly and vile,
> *For fear of what might fall,* so to prevent
> The term of life."

It would seem, therefore, that Brutus did not kill Caesar, as one crushes a serpent's egg, to prevent evil consequences. It is equally manifest that he did not do it for " the general," for if ever " the general " were shown to be despicable and worthless it is in this very play, where the citizens murder Cinna the poet because he has the same name as Cinna the conspirator, and the lower classes are despised as the " rabblement," " the common herd," with " chapped hands," " sweaty night-caps," and " stinking breath."

255

The Man Shakespeare

It is Dr. Brandes' idea and not Shakespeare's that Brutus is a "man of uncompromising character and principle." That is the Brutus of Plutarch, who finds in his stern republican love of the common good an ethical motive for killing the ambitious Caesar. But Shakespeare had no understanding of the republican ideal, and no sympathy with the public; accordingly, his Brutus has no adequate reason for contriving Caesar's death. Shakespeare followed Plutarch in freeing Brutus from the suspicion of personal or interested motive, but he didn't see that by doing this he made his Brutus a conspirator without a cause, a murderer without a motive. The truth is our gentle poet could never find a convincing ground for coldblooded murder. It will be remembered that Macbeth only murders, as the deer murders, out of fear, and the fact that his Brutus can find no justification of any sort for killing Caesar, confirms our view of Shakespeare's gentle kindness. The "uncompromising character and principle" of the severe republican we find in Plutarch, sit uneasily on Shakespeare's Brutus; it is apparent that the poet had no conception of what we call a fanatic. His difficulties arise from this limitation of insight. He begins to write the play by making Brutus an idealized po........ self; he, therefore, dwells on Brutus' perfect nobility, sincerity, and unselfishness, but does not realize that the more perfect he makes Brutus, the more clear and cogent Brutus' motive must be for undertaking Caesar's assassination.

In this confusion Shakespeare's usually fine instinct is at fault, and he blunders from mistake to mistake. His idealizing tendency makes him present Brutus as perfect, and at the same time he uses the historical incident of the anonymous letters, which goes to show Brutus as conceited and vain. If these letters influenced Brutus—and they must be taken to have done so, or else why were they introduced?—we have a noble and unselfish man murdering out of paltry vanity. In Plutarch, where Brutus is depicted as an austere republican, the incident of the letters only throws a natural shade of doubt on the rigid principles by which alone he is supposed to be guided. We all feel that rigid principles rest on pride, and may best be led astray through pride. But Shakespeare's Brutus is pure human sweetness, and the letters are worse than out of place when addressed to him. Shakespeare should never have used this incident; it is a blot on his conception.

All through the first acts of the play Brutus is incredible, for he is in an impossible position. Shakespeare simply could not find any valid reason why his *alter ego*, Brutus, should kill Caesar. But from the moment the murder is committed to the end of the play Brutus-Shakespeare is at peace with himself. And as soon as the dramatist lets himself go and paints Brutus with entire freedom and frankness, he rises to the height of tragic pathos, and we can all recognize the original of the portrait. At first Brutus is merely ideal; his perfect unsuspiciousness—he trusts even Antony; his transparent honesty—he will have no other oath among the conspirators

" Than honesty to honesty engaged ";

his hatred of bloodshed—he opposes Cassius, who proposes to murder Antony; all these noble qualities may be contrasted with the subtler short-comings

257

which make of Hamlet so vital a creation. Hamlet
is suspicious even of Ophelia; Hamlet is only " indifferent honest "; Hamlet makes his friends swear to
keep the ghost's appearance a profound secret;
Hamlet lives from the beginning, while Brutus at
first is a mere bundle of perfections individualized
only by that personal intimate confession which I
have already quoted, which, however, has nothing
to do with the play. But later in the drama Shakespeare begins to lend Brutus his own weaknesses,
and forthwith Brutus lives. His insomnia is pure
Shakespeare:

> " Since Cassius first did whet me against Caesar,
>   I have not slept."

The character of Brutus is superbly portrayed in
that wonderful scene with Cassius in the fourth act.
With all the superiority of conscious genius he
treats his confederate as a child or madman, much
as Hamlet treats Rosencrantz and Guildenstern:

> " Shall I be frighted when a madman stares? "

Cassius is mean, too, whereas Brutus is kindly and
generous to a degree:

> " For I can raise no money by vile means:
>   By heaven, I had rather coin my heart,
>   And drop my blood for drachmas, than to wring
>   From the hard hands of peasants their vile trash
>   By any indirection. . . .
>
>   .   .   .   .   .
>
>   When Marcus Brutus grows so covetous,
>   To lock such rascal counters from his friends,
>   Be ready, gods, with all your thunderbolts,
>   Dash him to pieces."

258

And, above all, as soon as Cassius appeals to his affection, Brutus is disarmed:

> "O Cassius, you are yoked with a lamb
> That carries anger, as the flint bears fire;
> Who, much enforced, shows a hasty spark,
> And straight is cold again."

This is the best expression of Shakespeare's temper; the "hasty spark" is Hamlet's temper, as we have seen, and Macbeth's, and Romeo's.

And now everything that Brutus does or says is Shakespeare's best. In a bowl of wine he buries "all unkindness." His affection for Cassius is not a virtue to one in especial. The scene in the fourth act, in which he begs the pardon of his boy Lucius, should be learned by heart by those who wish to understand our loving and lovable Shakespeare. This scene, be it remarked, is not in Plutarch, but is Shakespeare's own invention. His care for the lad's comfort, at a time when his own life is striking the supreme hour, is exquisitely pathetic. Then come his farewell to Cassius and his lament over Cassius' body; then the second fight and the nobly generous words that hold in them, as flowers their perfume, all Shakespeare's sweetness of nature:

> "My heart doth joy, that yet in all my life
> I found no man, but he was true to me."

And then night hangs upon the weary, sleepless eyes, and we are all ready to echo Antony's marvellous valediction:

> "This was the noblest Roman of them all;
>
> His life was gentle; and the elements
> So mixed in him, that Nature might stand up
> And say to all the world, 'This was a man!'"

But this Brutus was no murderer, no conspirator, no narrow republican fanatic, but simply gentle Shakespeare discovering to us his own sad heart and the sweetness which suffering had called forth in him.

CHAPTER VII

"A beautiful, pure and most moral nature, without the strength of nerve which makes the hero, sinks beneath a burden which it can neither bear nor throw off; every duty is holy to him,—this too hard. The impossible is required of him,—not the impossible in itself, but the impossible to him. How he winds, turns, agonizes, advances and recoils, ever reminded, ever reminding himself, and at last almost loses his purpose from his thoughts, without ever again recovering his peace of mind. . . ."—*"Hamlet" by Goethe.*

GOETHE'S criticism of "Hamlet" is so much finer than any English criticism that I am glad to quote it. It will serve, I think, as a standard to distinguish the best criticism of the past from what I shall set forth in the course of this analysis. In this chapter I shall try to show what new light our knowledge of Shakespeare throws on the play, and conversely what new light the play throws on its maker.

The first moment of disillusion brought out, as we have seen in Brutus, all the kindness in Shakespeare's nature. He will believe in men in spite of experience; but the idealistic pose could not be kept up; sooner or later Shakespeare had to face the fact that he had been befooled and scorned by friend and mistress—how did he meet it? "Hamlet" is the answer: Shakespeare went about nursing dreams of revenge and murder. Disillusion had

261

deeper consequences; forced to see other men as they were, he tried for a moment to see himself as he was. The outcome of that objective vision was Hamlet—a masterpiece of self-revealing.

Yet, when he wrote " Hamlet," nothing was clear to him; the significance of the catastrophe had only dawned upon him; he had no notion how complete his soul-shipwreck was, still less did he dream of painting himself realistically in all his obsequious flunkeyism and ungovernable sensuality. He saw himself less idealistically than heretofore, and, trying to look at himself fairly, honestly, he could not but accuse himself of irresolution at the very least; he had hung on with Herbert, as the sonnets tell us, hoping to build again the confidence which had been ruined by betrayal, hoping he knew not what of gain or place, to the injury of his own self-respect; while brooding all the time on quite impossible plans of revenge, impossible, for action had been " sicklied o'er with the pale cast of thought." Hamlet could not screw his courage to the sticking point, and so became a type for ever of the philosopher or man of letters who, by thinking, has lost the capacity for action.

Putting ourselves in Shakespeare's place for the moment we see at once why he selected this story for treatment at this time. He knew, none better, that no young aristocrat would have submitted patiently to the wrong he had suffered from Lord Herbert; he created Laertes to show how instant and determined such a man would be in taking murderous revenge; but he still felt that what others would regard as faults, his irresolution and shrinking from bloodshed were in themselves nobler, and so, whilst half excusing, half realizing himself, he brought forth a masterpiece. This brooding on revenge, which is the heart and explanation of his great play, shows us how little Shakespeare cared for Herbert, how completely he had condemned him. The soliloquy on this point in " Hamlet " is the most characteristic thing in the drama:

> " This is most brave,
> That I, the son of a dear father murder'd
> Prompted to my revenge by heaven and hell,
> Must, like a whore, unpack my heart with words,
> And fall a-cursing like a very drab."

Shakespeare is thinking of Herbert's betrayal: " here I am," he says, " prompted to revenge by reason and custom, yet instead of acting I fall a-cursing like a drab." But behind his irresolution is his hatred of bloodshed: he could whip out his sword and on a sudden kill Polonius, mistaking him for the king (Herbert), but he could not, in cold blood, make up his mind to kill and proceed to execution. Like his own Hubert, Shakespeare had to confess:

> " Within this bosom never enter'd yet
> The dreadful motion of a murderous thought."

He had none of the direct, passionate, con-scienceless resolution of Laertes. He whips him-self to anger against the king by thinking of Her-bert in the king's place; but lackey-like has to admit that mere regard for position and power gives him pause: Lord Herbert was too far above him:

> " There's such divinity doth hedge a king,
> That treason can but peep to what it would."

Shakespeare's personal feeling dominates and

inspires the whole play. One crucial instance will prove this. Why did Hamlet hate his mother's lechery? Most men would hardly have condemned it, certainly would not have suffered their thoughts to dwell on it beyond the moment; but to Hamlet his mother's faithlessness was horrible, shameful, degrading, simply because Hamlet-Shakespeare had identified her with Miss Fitton, and it was Miss Fitton's faithlessness, it was her deception he was condemning in the bitterest words he could find. He thus gets into a somewhat unreal tragedy, a passionate intensity which is otherwise wholly inexplicable. This is how he talks to his mother:

> " Have you eyes?
> Could you on this fair mountain leave to feed,
> And batten on this moor? Ha! have you eyes . . .
> . . . . What devil was't
> That thus cozen'd you at hoodman-blind?
> Eyes without feeling, feeling without sight,
> Ears without hands or eyes, smelling sans all,
> Or but a sickly part of one true sense
> Could not so mope.
> O, shame! where is thy blush?"

If anyone can imagine that this is the way a son thinks of a mother's slip he is past my persuading. In all this Shakespeare is thinking of himself in comparison with Herbert; and his advice to his mother is almost as self-revealing, showing, as it does, what he would wish to say to Miss Fitton:

> " Repent what's past; avoid what is to come;
> And do not spread the compost on the weeds
> To make them ranker. . . .
> Assume a virtue if you have it not. . . ."

In his description of the king and queen we get

Revenge and Jealousy: Hamlet

Shakespeare's view of Lord Herbert and Miss Fitton: the king (Herbert) is " mildew'd " and foul in comparison with his modest poet-rival—" A satyr to Hyperion."

Hamlet's view of his mother (Miss Fitton), though bitterer still, is yet the bitterness of disappointed love: he will have her repent, refrain from the adultery, and be pure and good again.   When the Queen asks:

> "What shall I do?"

Hamlet answers:

> " Not this, by no means, that I bid you do:
> Let the king tempt you again to bed;
> Pinch wanton on your cheek; call you his mouse;
> And let him, for a pair of reechy kisses,
> Or paddling in your neck with his damned fingers . . ."

Maddened with jealousy he sees the act, scourges himself with his own lewd imagining as Posthumus scourges himself.   No one ever felt this intensity of jealous rage about a mother or a sister.   The mere idea is absurd; it is one's own passion-torture that speaks in such words as I have here quoted.

Hamlet's treatment of Ophelia, too, and his advice to her are all the outcome of Shakespeare's own disappointment:

> " Get thee to a nunnery: why wouldst thou be a breeder of sinners?"

We all expect from Hamlet some outburst of divine tenderness to Ophelia; but the scenes with the pure and devoted girl whom he is supposed to love are not half realized, are nothing like so intense as the scenes with the guilty mother.   It is jealousy that is blazing in Shakespeare at this time, and not love; when Hamlet speaks to the Queen we hear Shakespeare speaking to his own faithless, guilty love. Besides, Ophelia is not even realized; she is submissive affection, an abstraction, and not a character. Shakespeare did not take interest enough in her to give her flesh and blood.

Shakespeare's jealousy and excessive sensuality come to full light in the scene between Hamlet and Ophelia, when they are about to witness the play before the king: he persists in talking smut to her, which she pretends not to understand. The lewdness, we all feel, is out of place in " Hamlet," horribly out of place when Hamlet is talking to Ophelia, but Shakespeare's sensuality has been stung to ecstasy by Miss Fitton's frailty, and he cannot but give it voice. As soon as Ophelia goes out of her mind she, too, becomes coarse—all of which is but a witness to Shakespeare's tortured animality. Yet Goethe can talk of Hamlet's " pure and most moral nature." A goat is hardly less pure, though Hamlet was moral enough in the high sense of the word.

There are one or two minor questions still to be considered, and the chief of these is how far, even in this moment of disillusion, did our Shakespeare see himself as he was? Hamlet says:

" I am very proud, revengeful, ambitious; with more offences at my beck than I have thoughts to put them in, imagination to give them shape, or time to act them in. What should such fellows as I do crawling between heaven and earth? We are arrant knaves, all; believe none of us."

All this is mere rhetoric, and full of clever self-excusing. Hamlet is not very revengeful or ambitious; he is weakly-irresolute, and excessively sensual, with all the faults that accompany these frailties. Even at this moment, when he must know that he is not very revengeful, that forgiveness were easier to him, Shakespeare will pose to himself, and call himself revengeful: he is such an idealist that he absolutely refuses to see himself as he is. In later dramas we shall find that he grows to deeper self-knowledge. Hamlet is but the half-way house to complete understanding.

Fortunately we have each of us an infallible touchstone by which we can judge of our love of truth. Any of us, man or woman, would rather be accused of a mental than a physical shortcoming. Do we see our bodily imperfections as they are? Can we describe ourselves pitilessly with snub nose, or coarse beak, bandy legs or thin shanks; gross paunch or sedgy beard? Shakespeare in Hamlet can hardly bear even to suggest his physical imperfections. Hamlet lets out inadvertently that he was fat, but he will not say so openly. His mother says to Hamlet:

"You are fat and scant of breath."

Many people, especially actors, have been so determined to see Hamlet as slight and student-like, that they have tried to criticize this phrase, and one of them, Mr. Beerbohm Tree, even in our day, went so far as to degrade the text to "faint and scant of breath." But the fatness is there, and comes to view again in another phrase of Hamlet:

"O, that this too, too solid flesh would melt,
Thaw, and resolve itself into a dew."

267

No thin man ever spoke of his flesh in that way.

Shakespeare was probably small, too. We know that he used to play Adam in " As You Like it," and in the play Orlando has to take Adam up and carry him off the stage, a thing no actor would attempt if the Adam had been a big man. Shakespeare was probably of middle height, or below it, and podgy. I always picture him to myself as very like Swinburne. Yet even in Hamlet he would make himself out to be a devil of a fellow: " valiant Hamlet," a swordsman of the finest, a superb duellist, who can touch Laertes again and again, though lacking practice. At the last push of fate Shakespeare will pose and deceive himself.

It is curiously characteristic of Shakespeare that when Hamlet broods on retaliation he does not brood like a brave man, who gloats on challenging his enemy to a fair fight, and killing him by sheer force or resolution; his passion, his revenge, is almost that of an Italian bravo. Not once does Hamlet think of forcing the king (Herbert) to a duel; he goes about with ideas of assassination, and not of combat.

" Now might I do it pat "

he cries as he sees the king praying; and he does not do it because he would thus send the king's soul to Heaven—shrill wordy intensity to excuse want of nerve. Whenever we get under the skin, it is Shakespeare's femininity which startles us.

One cannot leave this great picture of Hamlet-Shakespeare without noticing one curious fact, which throws a flood of light on the relations of literary art to life. Shakespeare, as we have seen, is boiling with jealous passion, brooding continually on murderous revenge, and so becomes conscious of his own irresolution. He dwells on this, and makes this irresolution the chief feature of Hamlet's character, and yet because he is writing about himself he manages to suggest so many other qualities, and such amiable and noble ones, that we are all in love with Hamlet, in spite of his irresolution, erotic mania and bloody thoughts.

In later dramas Shakespeare went on to deal with the deeper and more elemental things in his nature, with jealousy in " Othello," and passionate desire in " Antony and Cleopatra "; but he never, perhaps, did much better work than in this drama where he chooses to magnify a secondary and ancillary weakness into the chief defect of his whole being. The pathos of the drama is to be found in the fact that Shakespeare realizes he is unable to take personal vengeance on Herbert. " Hamlet " is a drama of pathetic weakness, strengthened by a drama of revenge and jealousy. In these last respects it is a preparatory study for " Othello."

In " Hamlet " Shakespeare let out some of the foul matter which Herbert's mean betrayal had bred in him. Even in " Hamlet," however, his passion for Mary Fitton, and his jealousy of her, constitute the real theme. We shall soon see how this passion coloured all the rest of his life and art, and at length brought about his ruin.

CHAPTER VIII

DRAMAS OF REVENGE AND JEALOUSY: PART II
" OTHELLO "

THERE is perhaps no single drama which throws such light on Shakespeare and his method of work as " Othello ": it is a long conflict between the artist in him and the man, and, in the struggle, both his artistic ideals and his passionate soul come to clearest view. From it we see that Shakespeare's nature gave itself gradually to jealousy and revenge. The fire of his passion burned more and more fiercely for years; was infinitely hotter in 1604, when " Othello " was written, than it had been when " Julius Caesar " was written in 1600. This proves to me that Shakespeare's connection with Mary Fitton did not come to an end when he first discovered her unfaithfulness. The intimacy continued for a dozen years. In sonnet 136 he prays her to allow him to be one of her lovers. That she was liberal enough to consent appears clearly from the growth of passion in his plays. It is certain, too, that she went on deceiving him with other lovers, or his jealousy would have waned away, ebbing with fulfilled desire. But his passion increases in intensity from 1597 to 1604, whipped no doubt to ecstasy by continual deception and wild jealousy. Both lust and jealousy swing to madness in " Othello." But Shakespeare was so great an artist that, when he took the story from Cinthio, he tried to realize it without bringing in his own personality: hence arises a conflict between his art and his passion.

At first sight " Othello " reminds one of a picture by Titian or Veronese; it is a romantic conception; the personages are all in gala dress; the struggle between Iago and the Moor is melodramatic; the whole picture aglow with a superb richness of colour. It is Shakespeare's finest play, his supreme achievement as a playwright. It is impossible to read " Othello " without admiring the art of it. The beginning is so easy: the introduction of the chief characters so measured and impressive that when the action really begins, it develops and increases in speed as by its own weight to the inevitable end; inevitable—for the end in this case is merely the resultant of the shock of these various personalities. But if the action itself is superbly ordered, the painting of character leaves much to be desired, as we shall see. There is one notable difference between " Othello " and those dramas, " Hamlet," " Macbeth," and " Cymbeline," wherein Shakespeare has depicted himself as the protagonist. In the self-revealing dramas not only does Shakespeare give his hero licence to talk, in and out of season, and thus hinder the development of the story, but he also allows him to occupy the whole stage without a competitor. The explanation is obvious enough. Dramatic art is to be congratulated on the fact that now and then Shakespeare left himself for a little out of the play, for then not only does the construction of the play improve but the play grows in interest through the encounter of evenly-matched antagonists. The first thing we notice in " Othello " is that Iago is at least·as important a character as the hero himself. " Hamlet," on the other hand, is almost a lyric; there is no counterpoise to the student-prince.

Now let us get to the play itself. Othello's first appearance in converse with Iago in the second scene of the first act does not seem to me to deserve the praise that has been lavished on it. Though Othello knows that " boasting is (not) an honour," he nevertheless boasts himself of royal blood. We have noticed already Shakespeare's love of good blood, and belief in its wondrous efficacy; it is one of his permanent and most characteristic traits. The passage about royal descent might be left out with advantage; if these three lines are omitted, Othello's pride in his own nature—his " parts and perfect soul "—is far more strongly felt. But such trivial flaws are forgotten when Brabantio enters and swords are drawn.

" Keep up your bright swords, for the dew will rust
        them."

is excellent in its contemptuous irony. A little later, however, Othello finds an expression which is intensely characteristic of a great man of action:

                    " Hold your hands,
Both you of my inclining, and the rest;
Were it my cue to fight, I should have known it
Without a prompter."

This last line and a half is addressed especially to Iago who is bent on provoking a fight, and is, I think, the best piece of character-painting in all " Othello "; the born general knows instinctively the moment to attack just as the trained boxer's hand strikes before he consciously sees the opening. When Othello speaks before the Duke, too, he

reveals himself with admirable clearness and truth
to nature. His pride is so deep-rooted, his self-
respect so great, that he respects all other dignitaries: the Senators are his "very noble and
approved good masters." Every word weighed and
effectual. Admirable, too, is the expression "round
unvarnished tale."

But pride and respect for others' greatness are
not qualities peculiar to the man of action; they
belong to all men of ability. As soon as Othello
begins to tell how he won Desdemona, he falls out
of his character. Feeling certain that he has placed
his hero before us in strong outlines, Shakespeare
lets himself go, and at once we catch him speaking
and not Othello. In "antres vast and deserts idle"
I hear the poet, and when the verse swings to—

"... men whose heads
Do grow beneath their shoulders,"

it is plain that Othello, the lord and lover of realities, has deserted the firm ground of fact. But
Shakespeare pulls himself in almost before he has
yielded to the charm of his own words, and again
Othello speaks:

"This to hear
Would Desdemona seriously incline,
But still the house-affairs would draw her thence,"

and so forth.

The temptation, however, was overpowering, and
again Shakespeare yields to it:

"And often did beguile her of her tears
When I did speak of some distressful stroke
That my youth suffered."

It is a characteristic of the man of action that he thinks lightly of reverses; he loves hard buffets as a swimmer high waves, and when he tells his life-story he does not talk of his " distress." This " distressful stroke that my youth suffered " is manifestly pure Shakespeare—tender-hearted Shakespeare, who pitied himself and the distressful strokes his youth suffered very profoundly. The characterization of Othello in the rest of this scene is anything but happy. He talks too much; I miss the short sharp words which would show the man used to command, and not only does he talk too much, but he talks in images like a poet, and exaggerates:

> " The tyrant Custom, most grave senators,
> Hath made the flinty and steel couch of war
> My thrice-driven bed of down."

Even the matter here is insincere; this is the poet's explanation of the Captain's preference for a hard bed and hard living: " he has been accustomed to it," says Shakespeare, not understanding that there are born hunter and soldier natures who absolutely prefer hardships to effeminate luxury. Othello's next speech is just as bad; he talks too much of things particular and private, and the farther he goes, the worse he gets, till we again hear the poet speaking, or rather mouthing:

> " No, when light-winged toys
> Of feathered Cupid seel with wanton dullness
> My speculative and officed instruments,
> That my disports corrupt and taint my business
> Let housewives make a skillet of my helm,
> And all indign and base adversities
> Make head against my estimation."

Again when he says—

> " Come, Desdemona: I have but an hour
> Of love, of worldly matters and direction
> To spend with thee; we must obey the time,"

I find no sharp impatience to get to work such as Hotspur felt, but a certain reluctance to leave his love—a natural touch which indicates that the poet was thinking of himself and not of his puppet.

The first scene of the second act shows us how Shakespeare, the dramatist, worked. Cassio is plainly Shakespeare the poet; any of his speeches taken at haphazard proves it. When he hears that Iago has arrived he breaks out:

> " He has had most favourable and happy speed;
> Tempests themselves, high seas, and howling winds,
> The guttered rocks and congregated sands—
> Traitors ensteeped to clog the guiltless keel—
> As having sense of beauty, do omit
> Their mortal natures, letting go safely by
> The divine Desdemona."

And when Desdemona lands, Cassio's first exclamation is sufficient to establish the fact that he is merely the poet's mask:

> " O, behold,
> The riches of the ship is come on shore! "

And just as clearly as Cassio is Shakespeare, the lyric poet, so is Iago, at first, the embodiment of Shakespeare's intelligence. Iago has been described as immoral; he does not seem to me to be immoral, but amoral, as the intellect always is. He says to the women:

" Come on, come on; you're pictures out of doors,
Bells in your parlours, wild cats in your kitchens,
Saints in your injuries, devils being offended,
Players in your housewifery, and housewives in
    your beds."

Iago sees things as they are, fairly and not
maliciously; he is " nothing if not critical," but
his criticism has a touch of Shakespeare's erotic
mania in it. Think of that " housewives in your
beds "! He will not deceive himself, however; in
spite of Cassio's admiration of Desdemona Iago does
not imagine that Cassio is in love with her; " well
kissed," he says, " an excellent courtesy," finding
at once the true explanation.[1]

But having taken up this intellectual attitude in
order to create Iago, Shakespeare tries next to make
his puppet concrete and individual by giving him
revenge for a soul, but in this he does not succeed,
for intellect is not maleficent. At moments Iago
lives for us; " drown cats and blind puppies . . .
put money in your purse "—his brains delight us;
but when he pursues Desdemona to her end, we
revolt; such malignity is inhuman. Shakespeare
was so little inclined to evil, knew so little of hate
and revenge that his villain is unreal in his cruelty.
Again and again the reader asks himself why Iago

[1] At the end of this scene Iago says:

" That Cassio loves her I do well believe it,"

but that is merely one of the many inconsistencies in Shakespeare's drawing of Iago. There are others; at one time he
talks of Cassio as a mere book soldier, at another equals him
with Caesar. Had Coleridge noted these contradictions he
would have declared them to be a higher perfection than logical
unity, and there is something to be said for the argument,
though in these instances I think the contradictions are due to
Shakespeare's carelessness rather than to his deeper insight.

is so venomous. He hates Othello because Othello
has passed him over and preferred Cassio; because
he thinks he has had reason to be jealous of Othello,
because—but everyone feels that these are reasons
supplied by Shakespeare to explain the inexplicable;
taken altogether they are inadequate, and we are
apt to throw them aside with Coleridge as the
" motive hunting of motiveless malignity." But
such a thing as " motiveless malignity " is not in
nature. Iago's villainy is too cruel, too steadfast to
be human; perfect pitiless malignity is as impossible
to man as perfect innate goodness.

Though Iago and Othello hold the stage for nine-
tenths of the play Shakespeare does not realize
them so completely as he realizes Cassio, an altogether subordinate character. The drinking episode
of Cassio was not found by Shakespeare in Cinthio,
and is, I think, clearly the confession of Shakespeare
himself, for though aptly invented to explain Cassio's dismissal, it is unduly prolonged, and thus com-
stitutes perhaps the most important fault in the
construction of the play. Consider, too, how the
moral is applied by Iago to England in especial,
with which country neither Iago nor the story has
anything whatever to do.

Othello's appearance stilling the riot, his words
to Iago and his dismissal of Cassio are alike honest
work. The subsequent talk between Cassio and
Iago about " reputation " is scarcely more than a
repetition of what Falstaff said of " honour."

Coleridge has made a great deal of the notion
that Othello was justified in describing himself as
" not easily jealous "; but poor Coleridge's perverse
ingenuity never led him further astray. The exact
contrary must, I think, be admitted; Othello was
surely very quick to suspect Desdemona; he

remembers Iago's first suspicious phrase, ponders it
and asks its meaning; he is as quick as Posthumus
was to believe the worst of Imogen, as quick as
Richard II. to suspect his friends Bagot and Green
of traitorism, and this proneness to suspicion is the
soul of jealousy.   And Othello is not only quick to
suspect but easy to convince—impulsive at once
and credulous.   His quick wits jump to the conclusion that Iago, " this honest creature! " doubtless

" Sees and knows more, much more, than he unfolds."

On hinted imputation he is already half persuaded,
and persuaded as only a sensualist would be that it
is lust which has led Desdemona astray:

> " O curse of marriage!
> That we can call these delicate creatures ours,
> And not their appetite."

He is, indeed, so disposed to catch the foul infection that Iago cries:

> " Trifles light as air
> Are to the jealous confirmations strong
> As proofs of holy writ."

And well he may, for before he uses the handkerchief or any evidence, on mere suspicion Othello
is already racked with doubt, distraught with
jealousy, maddened with passion; " his occupation's
gone "; he rages against Iago and demands proof.
Iago answers:
> " I do not like the office;
> But, sith I am entered in this cause so far
> .   .   .   .   .
> I will go on."

Revenge and Jealousy: Othello

This is the same paltry reason Richard III. and Macbeth adduced for adding to the number of their crimes, the truth being that Shakespeare could find no reason in his own nature for effective hatred.

Othello gives immediate credence to Iago's dream, thinks it "a shrewd doubt"; he is a "credulous fool," as Iago calls him, and it is only our sense of Iago's devilish cleverness that allows us to excuse Othello's folly. The strawberry-spotted handkerchief is not needed: the magic in its web is so strong that the mere mention of it blows his love away and condemns both Cassio and Desdemona to death. If this Othello is not easily jealous then no man is prone to doubt and quick to turn from love to loathing.

The truth of the matter is that in the beginning of the play Othello is a marionette fairly well shaped and exceedingly picturesque; but as soon as jealousy is touched upon, the mask is thrown aside; Othello, the self-contained captain, disappears, the poet takes his place and at once shows himself to be the aptest subject for the green fever. The emotions then put into Othello's mouth are intensely realized; his jealousy is indeed Shakespeare's own confession, and it would be impossible to find in all literature pages of more sincere and terrible self-revealing. Shakespeare is not more at home in showing us the passion of Romeo and Juliet or the irresolution of Richard II. or the scepticism of Hamlet than in depicting the growth and paroxysms of jealousy; his overpowering sensuality, the sensuality of Romeo and of Orsino, has sounded every note of love's mortal sickness:

"*Oth.* I had been happy if the general camp,
Pioneers and all, had tasted her sweet body,

So I had nothing known.

. . . . .

Damn her, lewd minx! O, damn her!"

We have here the proof that the jealousy of Othello was Shakespeare's jealousy; it is all compounded of sensuality. But, and this is the immediate point of my argument, the captain, Othello, is not presented to us as a sensualist to whom such a suspicion would be, of course, the nearest thought. On the contrary, Othello is depicted as sober [1] and solid, slow to anger, and master of himself and his desire; he expressly tells the lords of Venice that he does not wish Desdemona to accompany him:

> " To please the palate of my appetite
> Nor to comply with heat—the young affects,
> In me defunct—and proper satisfaction."

Shakespeare goes out of his way to put this unnecessary explanation in Othello's mouth; he will not have us think of him as passion's fool, but as passion's master; Othello is not to be even suspicious; he tells Iago:

> " 'Tis not to make me jealous
> To say—my wife is fair, feeds well, loves company,
> Is free of speech, sings, plays and dances well;
> Where virtue is, thesè are more virtuous:
> Nor from mine own weak merits will I draw
> The smallest fear or doubt of her revolt;
> For she had eyes and chose me."

[1] Shakespeare makes Lodovico speak of Othello's "solid virtue"—"the nature whom passion could not shake." Even Iago finds Othello's anger ominous because of its rarity:

> "There's matter in't, indeed, if he be angry."

Revenge and Jealousy: Othello

It was all this, no doubt, that misled Coleridge. He did not realize that this Othello suddenly changes his nature; the sober lord of himself becomes in an instant very quick to suspect, and being jealous, is nothing if not sensual; he can think of no reason for Desdemona's fall but her appetite; the imagination of the sensual act throws him into a fit; it is this picture which gives life to his hate. The conclusion is not to be avoided; as soon as Othello becomes jealous he is transformed by Shakespeare's own passion. For this is the way Shakespeare conceived jealousy and the only way. The jealousy of Leontes in "The Winter's Tale" is precisely the same; Hermione gives her hand to Polixenes, and at once Leontes suspects and hates, and his rage is all of "paddling palms [1] and pinching fingers." The jealousy of Posthumus, too, is of the same kind:

> "Never talk on't;
> She hath been colted by him."

It is the imagining of the sensual act that drives him to incoherence and the verge of madness, as it drove Othello. In all these characters Shakespeare is only recalling the stages of the passion that desolated his life.

The part that imagination usually plays in tormenting the jealous man with obscene pictures is now played by Iago; the first scene of the fourth act is this erotic self-torture put in Iago's mouth. As Othello's passion rises to madness, as the self-analysis becomes more and more intimate and per-

[1] Iago's expression, too; cf. "Othello," II. 1, and "Hamlet," III. 4.

sonal, we have Shakespeare's re-lived agony clothing itself in his favourite terms of expression:

> " O! it comes o'er my memory,
> As doth the raven o'er the infected house,
> Boding to all,—he had my handkerchief."

The interest swings still higher; the scene in which Iago uses Cassio's conceit and laughter to exasperate further the already mad Othello is one of the notable triumphs of dramatic art. But just as the quick growth of his jealousy, and its terrible sensuality, have shown us that Othello is not the self-contained master of his passions that he pretends to be and that Shakespeare wishes us to believe, so this scene, in which the listening Othello rages in savagery, reveals to us an intense femininity of nature. For generally the man concentrates his hatred upon the woman who deceives him, and is only disdainful of his rival, whereas the woman for various reasons gives herself to hatred of her rival, and feels only angry contempt for her lover's traitorism. But Othello—or shall we not say Shakespeare?—discovers in the sincerest ecstasy of this passion as much of the woman's nature as of the man's. After seeing his handkerchief in Bianca's hands he asks:

> " How shall I murder him, Iago? "

Manifestly, Shakespeare is thinking of Herbert and his base betrayal. Othello would have Cassio thrown to the dogs, would have him " nine years a-killing "; and though he adds that Desdemona shall " rot and perish and be damned to-night," immediately afterwards we see what an infinite affection for her underlies his anger:

282

"O, the world hath not a sweeter creature: she might lie by an emperor's side and command him tasks."

And then Shakespeare uses his brains objectively, so to speak, to excuse his persistent tenderness, and at once he reveals himself and proves to us that he is thinking of Mary Fitton, and not of poor Desdemona:

"Hang her! I do but say what she is.—So delicate with her needle!—An admirable musician! O, she will sing the savageness out of a bear.—Of so high and plenteous wit and invention."

Shakespeare himself speaks in this passage. For when has Desdemona shown high and plenteous wit or invention? She is hardly more than a symbol of constancy. It is Mary Fitton who has "wit and invention," and is "an admirable musician."

The feminine tenderness in Shakespeare comes to perfect expression in the next lines; no woman has a more enduring affection:

"*Iago.* She's the worse for all this.
Oth. O! a thousand, a thousand times. And, then of so gentle a condition!
Iago. Ay, too gentle.
Oth. Nay, that's certain:—but yet the pity of it, Iago!—O, Iago, the pity of it, Iago!"

The tenderness shrills to such exquisite poignancy that it becomes a universal cry, the soul's lament for traitorism: "The pity of it, Iago! O, Iago, the pity of it!" Othello's jealous passion is at its height in the scene with Desdemona when he gives his accusations precise words, and flings money to Emilia as the guilty confidante. And yet even here,

283

where he delights to soil his love, his tenderness
reaches its most passionate expression:

> "O thou weed,
> Who art so lovely fair, and smell'st so sweet,
> That the sense aches at thee—would thou hadst ne'er
> been born!"

As soon as jealousy reaches its end, and passes
into revenge, Shakespeare tries to get back into
Othello the captain again. Othello's first speech
in the bedchamber is clear enough in all conscience,
but it has been so mangled by unintelligent actors
such as Salvini that it cries for explanation. Every
one will remember how Salvini and others playing
this part stole into the room like murderers, and
then bellowed so that they would have waked the
dead. And when the foolish mummers were criticized
for thus misreading the character, they answered
boldly that Othello was a Moor, that his passion was
Southern, and I know not what besides. It is clear
that Shakespeare's Othello enters the room quietly
as a justice with a duty to perform: he keeps his
resolution to the sticking-point by thinking of the
offence; he says solemnly:

> "It is the cause, it is the cause, my soul——"

and, Englishman-like, finds a moral reason for his
intended action:

> "Yet she must die, else she'll betray more men."

But the reason fades and the resolution wavers
in the passion for her "body and beauty," and the
tenderness of the lover comes to hearing again:

Revenge and Jealousy: Othello

" [*Kissing her.*] O balmy breath,—that dost almost per-
suade
Justice to break her sword! one more, one more.—
Be thus when thou art dead, and I will kill thee,
And love thee after.—One more, and this the last.
So sweet was ne'er so fatal.   I must weep,
But they are cruel tears; this sorrow's heavenly;
It strikes where it doth love.—She wakes."

So gentle a murderer was never seen save Macbeth, and the " heavenly sorrow " that strikes where
it doth love is one of the best examples in literature
of the Englishman's capacity for hypocritical self-
deception.   The subsequent dialogue shows us in
Othello the short, plain phrases of immitigable resolution; in this scene Shakespeare comes nearer to
realizing strength than anywhere else in all his work.
But even here his nature shows itself; Othello has to
be misled by Desdemona's weeping, which he takes
to be sorrow for Cassio's death, before he can pass
to action, and as soon as the murder is accomplished, he regrets:

" O, insupportable!   O heavy hour! "

His frank avowal, however, is excellently characteristic of the soldier Othello:

" 'Twas I that killed her."

A moment later there is a perfect poetic expres-
sion of his love:
" Nay, had she been true
If Heaven would make me such another world
Of one entire and perfect chrysolite,
I'd not have sold her for it."

Then comes a revelation of sensuality and physical

fastidiousness so peculiar that by itself it proves much of what I have said of Shakespeare:

> " *Oth.* . . . Ay, 'twas he that told me first;
> An honest man he is, and hates the slime
> That sticks on filthy deeds."

For a breathing-space now before he is convinced of his fatal error, Othello speaks as the soldier, but in spite of the fact that he has fulfilled his revenge, and should be at his sincerest, we have no word of profound self-revealing. But as soon as he realizes his mistake, his regret becomes as passionate as a woman's and magical in expression:

> " Cold, cold, my girl!
> Even like thy chastity."

Another proof that Shakespeare discards the captain, Othello, in order to give utterance to his own jealousy and love, is to be found in the similarity between this speech of Othello and the corresponding speech of Posthumus in " Cymbeline." As soon as Posthumus is convinced of his mistake, he calls Iachimo " Italian fiend " and himself " most credulous fool," " egregious murderer," and so forth. He asks for " some upright justicer " to punish him as he deserves with " cord or knife or poison," nay, he will have " tortures ingenious." He then praises Imogen as " the temple of virtue," and again shouts curses at himself and finally calls upon his love:

> " O Imogen!
> My queen, my life, my wife! O Imogen,
> Imogen, Imogen! "

Othello behaves in precisely the same manner; he

calls Iago that " demi-devil," and himself " an honourable murderer "; and Iago calls him a " credulous fool." Othello, too, cries for punishment; instead of " tortures ingenious," he will have " devils "
to " whip " him, and " roast him in sulphur." He
praises Desdemona as chaste, " ill-starred wench,"
" my girl," and so forth; then curses himself lustily
and ends his lament with the words:

"O Desdemon! dead, Desdemon! dead! O!"

The same changes in mood, the same words even
—the likeness is so close that it can only be explained as I have explained it; from beginning to
end of " Cymbeline " Posthumus is Shakespeare, and
as soon as jealousy, pity, remorse, or any tender
emotion seizes Othello he becomes Shakespeare too,
and speaks with Shakespeare's voice.

From here on, it is all good work if not great
work to Othello's last speech, which merits particular consideration. He begins as the captain, but
soon passes into the poet; and then towards the end
talks again in quick measure as the man of action.
I quote the whole speech,[1] putting into italics the
phrases in which the poet betrays himself:

" *Oth.* Soft you; a word or two, before you go.
I have done the State some service, and they know it;
No more of that.—*I pray you in your letters,*
When you shall these unlucky deeds relate,
Speak of me as I am; nothing extenuate,
Nor set down aught in malice; then must you speak
Of one that loved not wisely, but too well;

1 This speech is curiously like the long speech of Richard II.
which I have already noticed; at the beginning Shakespeare
speaks as a king for a few lines, then naturally as a poet, and
at the end pulls himself up and tries to resume the character.

The Man Shakespeare

'Of one not easily jealous, but being wrought
Perplexed in the extreme; of one whose hand,
Like the base Indian, threw a pearl away
Richer than all his tribe; of one whose subdued eyes,
Albeit unusèd to the melting mood,
Drop tears as fast as the Arabian trees
Their medicinal gum. Set you down this;
And say, besides, that in Aleppo once,
When a malignant and a turban'd Turk
Beat a Venetian, and traduced the State,
I took by the throat the circumcized dog
And smote him—thus."

All the memorable words here are the words of the gentle poet revealing his own nature ingenuously. The relief given by tears is exquisitely expressed, but the relief itself is a feminine experience; men usually find that tears humiliate them, and take refuge from their scalding shame in anger. The deathless phrases of the poet's grief must be contrasted with the braggart mouthings of the captain at the end in order to realize how impossible it was for Shakespeare to depict a man of deeds.

In the first two acts Shakespeare has tried to present Othello with some sincerity and truth to the dramatic fiction. But as soon as jealousy touches Othello, he becomes the transparent vessel of Shakespeare's own emotion, and is filled with it as with his heart's blood. All the magical phrases in the play are phrases of jealousy, passion, and pity. The character of the captain in Othello is never deeply realized. It is a brave sketch, but, after all, only the merest sketch when compared with Hamlet or Macbeth. We know what they thought of life and death, and of all things in the world and over it; but what do we know of Othello's thoughts upon the deepest matters that concern man? Did he believe even in his stories to Desdemona?—in the men whose heads do grow beneath their shoulders? in his magic handkerchief? in what Iago calls his " fantastical lies "?   This, I submit, is another important indication that Shakespeare drew Othello, the captain, from the outside; the jealous, tender heart of him is Shakespeare's, but take that away and we scarcely know more of him than the colour of his skin.   What interests us in Othello is not his strength, but his weakness, Shakespeare's weakness—his passion and pity, his torture, rage, jealousy and remorse, the successive stages of his soul's Calvary!

CHAPTER IX

Troilus and Cressida

> " He probed from hell to hell
> Of human passions, but of love deflowered
> His wisdom was not. . . ."
> —*Meredith's Sonnet on Shakespeare.*

WITH " Hamlet " and his dreams of an impossible revenge Shakespeare got rid of some of the perilous stuff which his friend's traitorism had bred in him. In " Othello " he gave deathless expression to the madness of his jealous rage and so cleared his soul, to some extent, of that poisonous infection. But passion in Shakespeare survived hatred of the betrayer and jealousy of him; he had quickly finished with Herbert; but Mary Fitton lived still for him and tempted him perpetually—the lust of the flesh, the desire of the eye, insatiable, cruel as the grave. He will now portray his mistress for us dramatically—unveil her very soul, show the gipsy-wanton as she is. He who has always painted in high lights is now going to paint French fashion, in blackest shadows, for with the years his passion and his bitterness have grown in intensity. Mary Fitton is now " false Cressid." Pandarus says of her in the first scene of the first act:

" An her hair were not somewhat darker than Helen's —well, go to—there were no more comparison between the women."

Mary Fitton's hair, we know, was raven-black, but

the evidence connecting Shakespeare's mistress with "false Cressid" is stronger, as we shall see, than any particular line or expression.

"Troilus and Cressida" is a wretched, invertebrate play without even a main current of interest. Of course there are fine phrases in it, as in most of the productions of Shakespeare's maturity; but the characterization is worse than careless, and at first one wonders why Shakespeare wrote the tedious, foolish stuff except to get rid of his own bitterness in the railing of Thersites, and in the depicting of Cressida's shameless wantonness. It is impossible to doubt that "false Cressid" was meant for Mary Fitton. The moment she appears the play begins to live; personal bitterness turns her portrait into a caricature; every fault is exaggerated and lashed with rage; it is not so much a drama as a scene where Shakespeare insults his mistress.

Let us look at this phase of his passion in perspective. Almost as soon as he became acquainted with Miss Fitton, about Christmas 1597, Shakespeare wrote of her as a wanton; yet so long as she gave herself to him he appears to have been able to take refuge in his tenderness and endure her strayings. But passion in him grew with what it fed on, and after she faulted with Lord Herbert, we find him in a sonnet threatening her that his "pity-wanting pain" may induce him to write of her as she was. No doubt her pride and scornful strength revolted under this treatment and she drew away from him. Tortured by desire he would then praise her with some astonishing phrases; call her "the heart's blood of beauty, love's invisible soul," and after some hesitation she would yield again. No sooner was the "ruined love" rebuilt than she would offend again, and again he would curse and threaten, and so the wretched, half-miserable, half-ecstatic life of passion stormed along, one moment in Heaven, the next in Hell.

All the while Shakespeare was longing, or thought he was longing, for truth and constancy, and at length he gave form and name to his desire for winnowed purity of love and perfect constancy, and this consoling but impalpable ideal he called Ophelia, Desdemona, Cordelia. But again and again Miss Fitton reconquered him and at length his accumulated bitterness compelled him to depict his mistress realistically. Cressida is his first attempt, the first dramatic portrait of the mistress who got into Shakespeare's blood and infected the current of his being, and the portrait is spoiled by the poet's hatred and contempt just as the whole drama is spoiled by a passion of bitterness that is surely the sign of intense personal suffering. Cressida is depicted as a vile wanton, a drab by nature; but it is no part even of this conception to make her soulless and devilish. On the contrary, an artist of Shakespeare's imaginative sympathy loves to put in high relief the grain of good in things evil and the taint of evil in things good that give humanity its curious complexity. Shakespeare observed this rule of dramatic presentation more consistently than any of his predecessors or contemporaries—more consistently, more finely far than Homer or Sophocles, whose heroes had only such faults as their creators thought virtues; why then did he forget nature so far as to picture " false Cressida " without a redeeming quality? He first shows her coquetting with Troilus, and her coquetry even is unattractive, shallow, and obvious; then she gives herself to Troilus out of passionate desire; but Shakespeare omits to tell us why she takes up with Diomedes immediately afterwards. We are to understand merely that she is what Ulysses calls a " sluttish spoil of opportunity," and " daughter of the game." But as passionate desire is not of necessity faithless we are distressed and puzzled by her soulless wantonness. And when she goes on to present Diomedes with the scarf that Troilus gave her, we revolt; the woman is too full of blood to be so entirely heartless. Here is the scene embittered by the fact that Troilus witnesses Cressida's betrayal:

> " *Diomedes.* I had your heart before, this follows it.
> *Troilus.* [*Aside.*] I did swear patience.
> *Cressida.* You shall not have it, Diomed, faith you
> shall not;
> I'll give you something else.
> *Diomedes.* I will have this: whose was it?
> *Cressida.*   It is no matter.
> *Diomedes.* Come, tell me whose it was?
> *Cressida.* 'Twas one that loved me better than you
> will,
> But, now you have it, take it."

The scene is a splendid dramatic scene, a piece torn from life, so realistic that it convinces, and yet we revolt; we feel that we have not got to the heart of the mystery. There is so much evil in Cressida that we want to see the spark of goodness in her, however fleeting and ineffective the spark may be. But Shakespeare makes her attempt at justification a confession of absolute faithlessness:

> " Troilus, farewell! one eye yet looks on thee
> But with my heart the other eye doth see.
> Ah! poor our sex! This fault in us I find,
> The error of our eye directs our mind."

This is plainly Shakespeare's reflection and not

Cressida's apology, and if we contrast this speech with the dialogue given above, it becomes plain, I think, that the terrible scene with Diomedes is taken from life, or is at least Shakespeare's vision of the way Mary Fitton behaved. There's a magic in those devilish words of Cressida that outdoes imagination:

> " 'Twas one that loved me better than you will,
>   But, now you have it, take it."

And then:

> " Sweet, honey Greek, tempt me no more to folly: "

The very power of the characterization makes the traitress hateful. If Mary Fitton ever gave any gift of Shakespeare to Lord Herbert, the dramatist should have known that she no longer loved him, had in reality already forgotten him in her new passion; but to paint a woman as remembering a lover, indeed as still loving him, and yet as giving his gift to another, is an offence in art though it may be true to nature. It is a fault in art because it is impossible to motive it in a few lines. The fact of the gift is bad enough; without explanation it is horrible. For this and other reasons I infer that Shakespeare took the fact from his own experience: he had suffered, it seems to me, from some such traitorism on the part of his mistress, or he ascribed to Mary Fitton some traitorism of his own.

In sonnet 122 he finds weighty excuse for having given away the table-book which his friend had given to him. His own confessed shortcoming might have taught him to exercise more lenient judgement towards his frail love.

But when Shakespeare wrote " Troilus and Cres-

sida " a passion of bitterness possessed him; he not
only vilified Cressida but all the world, Agamemnon,
Nestor, Achilles, Ajax; he seems indeed to have
taken more pleasure in the railing of Thersites than
in any other part of the work except the scourging
of Cressida. He shocks us by the picture of Achilles
and his myrmidons murdering Hector when they
come upon him unarmed.

One or two incidental difficulties must be settled
before we pass to a greater play.

" Troilus and Cressida " has always been regarded
as a sort of enigma. Professor Dowden asks: " With
what intention and in what spirit did Shakespeare
write this strange comedy? All the Greek heroes
who fought against Troy are pitilessly exposed to
ridicule." And from this fact and the bitterness
of " Timon " some German critics have drawn the
inference that Shakespeare was incapable of comprehending Greek life, and that indeed he only
realized his Romans so perfectly because the Roman
was very like the Briton in his mastery of practical
affairs, of the details of administration and of government. This is an excellent instance of German
prejudice. No one could have been better fitted
than Shakespeare to understand Greek civilization
and Greek art with its supreme love of plastic
beauty, but his master Plutarch gave him far better
pictures of Roman life than of Greek life, partly
because Plutarch lived in the time of Roman domination and partly because he was in far closer sympathy with the masters of practical affairs than
with artists in stone like Phidias or artists in
thought like Plato. The true explanation of Shakespeare's caricatures of Greek life, whether Homeric
or Athenian, is to be found in the fact that he was
not only entirely ignorant of it but prejudiced

against it. And this prejudice in him had an obvious root. Chapman had just translated and published the first books of his Iliad, and Chapman was the poet whom Shakespeare speaks of as his rival in Sonnets 78 86. He cannot help smiling at the " strained touches " of Chapman's rhetoric and his heavy learning. Those who care to remember the first scene of " Love's Labour's Lost " will recall how Shakespeare in that early work mocked at learning and derided study. When he first reached London he was no doubt despised for his ignorance of Greek and Latin; he had had to bear the sneers and flouts of the many who appraised learning, an university training and gentility above genius. He took the first opportunity of answering his critics:

> " Small have continual plodders ever won,
>   Save bare authority from others' books."

But the taunts rankled, and when the bitter days came of disappointment and disillusion he took up that Greek life which his rival had tried to depict in its fairest colours, and showed what he thought was the seamy side of it. But had he known anything of Greek life and Greek art it would have been his pleasure to outdo his rival by giving at once a truer and a fairer presentation of Greece than Chapman could conceive. It is the rivalry of Chapman that irritates Shakespeare into pouring contempt on Greek life in " Troilus and Cressida." As Chapman was for the Greeks, Shakespeare took sides with the Trojans.

But why do I assume that " Troilus and Cressida " is earlier than " Antony and Cleopatra? " Some critics, and among them Dr. Brandes, place it later, and they have some reason for their belief.

Troilus and Cressida

The bitterness in " Troilus and Cressida," they say
rightly, is more intense; and as Shakespeare's disappointment with men and things appears to have
increased from " Hamlet " to " Timon," or from
1602 to 1607-8, they put the bitterer play later.
Cogent as is this reasoning, I cannot believe that
Shakespeare could have painted Cressida after having painted Cleopatra.   The same model has evidently served for both women; but while Cleopatra
is perhaps the most superb portrait of a courtesan
in all literature, Cressida is a crude and harsh sketch
such as a Dumas or a Pinero might have conceived.

It is more than probable, I think, that " Troilus
and Cressida " was planned and the love-story at
least written about 1603, while Shakespeare's memory of one of his mistress's betrayals was still vivid
and sharp.   The play was taken up again four or
five years later and the character of Ulysses deepened
and strengthened.   In this later revision the outlook is so piercing-sad, the phrases of such preg-
nancy, that the work must belong to Shakespeare's
ripest maturity.   Moreover, he has grown compara-
tively careless of characterization as in all his later
work; he gives his wise sayings almost as freely to
Achilles as to Ulysses.

" Troilus and Cressida " is interesting because it
establishes the opinion that Chapman was indeed
the rival poet whom Shakespeare referred to in the
sonnets, and especially because it shows us the poet's
mistress painted in a rage of erotic passion so
violent that it defeats itself and the portrait becomes an incredible caricature—that way madness
lies: " Troilus and Cressida " points to " Lear "
and " Timon."

CHAPTER X

Antony and Cleopatra

WE now come to the finest work of Shakespeare's maturity, to the drama in which his passion for Mary Fitton finds supreme expression.

"Antony and Cleopatra" is an astonishing production not yet fairly appreciated even in England, and perhaps not likely to be appreciated anywhere at its full worth for many a year to come. But when we English have finally left that dark prison of Puritanism and lived for some time in the sunlight where the wayside crosses are hidden under climbing roses, we shall probably couple "Antony and Cleopatra" with "Hamlet" in our love as Shakespeare's supremest works. It was fitting that the same man who wrote "Romeo and Juliet," the incomparable symphony of first love, should also write "Antony and Cleopatra," the far more wonderful and more terrible tragedy of mature passion.

Let us begin with the least interesting part of the play, and we shall see that all the difficulties in it resolve themselves as soon as we think of it as Shakespeare's own confession. Wherever he leaves Plutarch, it is to tell his own story.

Some critics have reproached Shakespeare with the sensualism of "Romeo and Juliet"; no one, so far as I can remember, has blamed the Sapphic intensity of "Antony and Cleopatra," where the lust of the flesh and desire of the eye reign triumphant. Professor Dowden indeed says: "The spirit of the

298

play, though superficially it appear voluptuous, is essentially severe. That is to say, Shakespeare is faithful to the fact." Antony and Cleopatra kill themselves, forsooth, and thus conventional virtue is justified by self-murder. So superficial and false a judgement is a quaint example of mid-Victorian taste: it reminds me of the horsehair sofa and the antimacassar. Would Professor Dowden have had Shakespeare alter the historical facts, making Antony conquer Caesar and Cleopatra triumph over death? Would this have been sufficient to prove to the professor that Shakespeare's morals are not his, and that the play is certainly the most voluptuous in modern literature? Well, this is just what Shakespeare has done. Throughout the play Caesar is a subordinate figure while Antony is the protagonist and engages all our sympathies; whenever they meet Antony shows as the larger, richer, more generous nature. In every act he conquers Caesar; leaving on us the gorgeous ineffaceable impression of a great personality whose superb temperament moves everyone to admiration and love; Caesar, on the other hand, affects one as a calculating machine.

But Shakespeare's fidelity to the fact is so extraordinary that he gives Caesar one speech which shows his moral superiority to Antony. When his sister weeps on hearing that Antony has gone back to Cleopatra, Caesar bids her dry her tears,

> ". . . . .
> But let determined things to destiny
> Hold unbewailed their way . . ."

This line alone suffices to show why Antony was defeated; the force of imperial Rome is in the great phrase; but Shakespeare will not admit his favourite's inferiority, and in order to explain Antony's defeat Shakespeare represents luck as being against him, luck or fate, and this is not the only or even the chief proof of the poet's partiality. Pompey, who scarcely notices Caesar when Antony is by, says of Antony:

> "his soldiership
> Is twice the other twain."

And, indeed, Antony in the play appears to be able to beat Caesar whenever he chooses or whenever he is not betrayed.

All the personages of the play praise Antony, and when he dies the most magnificent eulogy of him is pronounced by Agrippa, Caesar's friend:

> "A rarer spirit never
> Did steer humanity; but you, Gods, will give us
> Some faults to make us men."

Antony is even permitted at the last to console himself; he declares exultantly that in the other world the ghosts shall come to gaze at him and Cleopatra, and:

> "Dido and her Aeneas shall want troops."

Shakespeare makes conquering Caesar admit the truth of this boast:

> "No grave upon the earth shall clip in it
> A pair so famous."

To win in life universal admiration and love, and in death imperishable renown, is to succeed in spite of failure and suicide, and this is the lesson which Shakespeare read into Plutarch's story. Even Enobarbus is conquered at the last by Antony's noble magnanimity. But why does Shakespeare show this extraordinary, this extravagant liking for him who was " the bellows and the fan to cool a gipsy's lust," for that Marc Antony who might have been the master of the world, and who threw away empire, life, and honour to be " a strumpet's fool"? There is only one possible explanation: Shakespeare felt the most intense, the most intimate sympathy with Antony because he, too, was passion's slave, and had himself experienced with his dark mistress, Mary Fitton, the ultimate degradation of lust. For this reason he took Plutarch's portrait of Antony, and, by emphasizing the kingly traits, transformed it. In the play, as Dr. Brandes sees, Antony takes on something of the " artist-nature." It is Antony's greatness and weakness; the spectacle of a high intellect struggling with an overpowering sensuality; of a noble nature at odds with passionate human frailty, that endeared him to Shakespeare. The pomp of Antony's position, too, and his kingly personality pleased our poet. As soon as Shakespeare reached maturity, he began to depict himself as a monarch; from " Twelfth Night " on he assumed royal state in his plays, and surely in this figure of Antony he must for the moment have satisfied his longing for regal magnificence and domination. From the first scene to the last Antony is a king of men by right divine of nature.

It is, however, plain that Antony's pride, his superb mastery of life, the touch of imperious brutality in him, are all traits taken from Plutarch, and are indeed wholly inconsistent with Shakespeare's own character. Had Shakespeare possessed these qualities his portraits of men of action would have been infinitely better than they are, while his portraits of the gentle thinker and lover of the arts, his Hamlets and his Dukes, would have been to seek.

The personal note of every one of his great tragedies is that Shakespeare feels he has failed in life, failed lamentably. His Brutus, we feel, failed of necessity because of his aloofness from practical life; his Coriolanus, too, had to fail, and almost forgoes sympathy by his faults; but this Antony ought not to have failed: we cannot understand why the man leaves the sea-battle to follow Cleopatra's flight, who but an act or two before, with lesser reason, realized his danger and was able to break off from his enchantress. Yet the passion of desire that sways Antony is so splendidly portrayed; is, too, so dominant in all of us, that we accept it at once as explaining the inexplicable.

In measure as Shakespeare ennobled Antony, the historical fact of ultimate defeat and failure allowed him to degrade Cleopatra. And this he did willingly enough, for from the moment he took up the subject he identified the Queen of Egypt with his own faithless mistress, Mary Fitton, whom he had already tried to depict as "false Cressid." This identification of himself and his own experience of passion with the persons and passions of the story explains some of the faults of the drama; while being the source, also, of its singular splendour.

In this play we have the finest possible example of the strife between Shakespeare's yielding poetic temperament and the severity of his intellect. He heaps praises on Antony, as we have seen, from all sides; he loved the man as a sort of superb *alter ego*, and yet his intellectual fairness is so extraordinary that it compelled him to create a character who should uphold the truth even against his heart's favourite. Dr. Brandes speaks of Enobarbus as a

302

" sort of chorus "; he is far more than that; he is
the intellectual conscience of the play, a weight, so
to speak, to redress the balance which Shakespeare
used this once and never again. What a confession
this is of personal partiality! A single instance will
suffice to prove my point: Shakespeare makes Antony cast the blame for the flight at Actium on Cleopatra, and manages almost to hide the unmanly
weakness of the plaint by its infinitely pathetic
wording:

> " Whither hast thou led me, Egypt? "

A little later Cleopatra asks:

> " Is Antony or we in fault for this? "

and at once Enobarbus voices the exact truth:

> " Antony only, that would make his will
> Lord of his reason. What though you fled
>
> .   .   .   .   .   .
> .   .   .   why should he follow? "

Again and again Antony reproaches Cleopatra,
and again and again Enobarbus is used to keep
the truth before us. Some of these reproaches, it
seems to me, are so extravagant and so ill-founded
that they discover the personal passion of the poet.
For example, Antony insults Cleopatra:

> " You have been a boggler ever."

And the proof forsooth is:

> " I found you as a morsel cold upon
> Dead Caesar's trencher."

But to have been Caesar's mistress was Cleopatra's

chief title to fame. Shakespeare is here probably re-
viling Mary Fitton for being deserted by some early
lover. Curiously enough, this weakness of Antony
increases the complexity of his character, while the
naturalistic passion of his words adds enormously
to the effect of the play. Again and again in this
drama Shakespeare's personal vindictiveness serves
an artistic purpose. The story of " Troilus and
Cressida " is in itself low and vile, and when loaded
with Shakespeare's bitterness outrages probability;
but the love of Antony and Cleopatra is so overwhelming that it goes to ruin and suicide and beyond, and when intensified by Shakespeare's personal feeling becomes a world's masterpiece.

We have already seen that the feminine railing
Shakespeare puts in the mouth of Antony increases
the realistic effect, and just in the same way the
low cunning, temper, and mean greed which he attributes to Cleopatra, transform her from a somewhat incomprehensible historical marionette into the
most splendid specimen of the courtesan in the
world's literature. Heine speaks of her contemptuously as a " kept woman," but the epithet only shows
how Heine in default of knowledge fell back on his
racial gift of feminine denigration. Even before she
enters we see that Shakespeare has not forgiven his
dark scornful mistress; Cleopatra is the finest picture he ever painted of Mary Fitton; but Antony's
friends tell us, at the outset, she is a " lustful gipsy,"
a " strumpet," and at first she merely plays on Antony's manliness; she sends for him, and when he
comes, departs. A little later she sends again, telling her messenger:

" I did not send you: if you find him sad,
Say, I am dancing; if in mirth, report
That I am sudden sick: quick, and return."

And when Charmian, her woman, declares that
the way to keep a man is to " cross him in nothing,"
she replies scornfully:

" Thou teachest, like a fool, the way to lose him."

She uses a dozen taunts to prevent her lover from
leaving her; but when she sees him resolved, she
wishes him victory and success.   And so through
a myriad changes of mood and of cunning wiles we
discover that love for Antony which is the anchor
to her unstable nature.

The scene with the eunuch Mardian is a little
gem.   She asks:

> " Hast thou affections?
> *Mar.* Yes, gracious madam.
> *Cleo.*   Indeed?
> *Mar.* Not in deed, madam; for I can do nothing.
> But what indeed is honest to be done;
> Yet have I fierce affections, and think
> What Venus did with Mars.
> *Cleo.*   O, Charmian!
> Where think'st thou he is now? Stands he, or sits he? "

She is with her lover again, and recalls his phrase
for her, " my serpent of old Nile," and feeds herself
with love's " delicious poison."

No sooner does she win our sympathy by her
passion for Antony than Shakespeare chills our
admiration by showing her as the courtesan:

> " *Cleo.*   Did I, Charmian,
> Ever love Caesar so?
> *Char.*   O, that brave Caesar!
> *Cleo.* Be choked with such another emphasis!
> Say, the brave Antony.
> *Char.*   The valiant Caesar!

Cleo. By Isis, I will give thee bloody teeth
If thou with Caesar paragon again
My man of men.
 Char.   By your most gracious pardon,
I sing but after you.
 Cleo.   My salad days,
When I was green in judgement: cold in blood,
To say as I said then!"

Already we see and know her, her wiles, her passion, her quick temper, her chameleon-like changes, her subtle charms of person and of word, and yet we have not reached the end of the first act. Next to Falstaff and to Hamlet, Cleopatra is the most astonishing piece of portraiture in all Shakespeare. Enobarbus gives the soul of her:

"*Ant.* She is cunning past man's thought.
Eno. Alack, sir, no; her passions are made of nothing but the finest part of pure love . . .
Ant. Would I had never seen her!
Eno. O, sir, you had then left unseen a wonderful piece of work; which not to have been blest withal would have discredited your travel."

Here Shakespeare gives his true opinion of Mary Fitton: then comes the miraculous expression:

"Age cannot wither her, nor custom stale
Her infinite variety. Other women cloy
The appetites they feed; but she makes hungry
Where most she satisfies."

Act by act Shakespeare makes the portrait more complex and more perfect. In the second act she calls for music, like the dark lady of the Sonnets:

" Music—moody food of us that trade in love,"

and then she'll have no music, but will play billiards, and not billiards either, but will fish and think every fish caught an Antony. And again she flies to memory:

> "That time—O times!—
> I laughed him out of patience; and that night
> I laughed him into patience; and next morn,
> Ere the ninth hour, I drunk him to his bed;
> Then put my tires and mantles on him, whilst
> I wore his sword Philippan."

The charm of it all, the deathless charm and the astounding veracity! The messenger enters, and she promises him for good news "gold and her bluest veins to kiss." When she hears that Antony is well she pours more gold on him, but when he pauses in his recital she has a mind to strike him. When he tells that Caesar and Antony are friends, it is a fortune she'll give; but when she learns that Antony is betrothed to Octavia she turns to her women with "I am pale, Charmian," and when she hears that Antony is married she flies into a fury, strikes the messenger down and hales him up and down the room by his hair. When he runs from her knife she sends for him:

> "I will not hurt him.
> These hands do lack nobility, that they strike
> A meaner than myself."

She has the fascination of great pride and the magic of manners. When the messenger returns she is a queen again, most courteous-wise:

> "Come hither, sir.
> Though it be honest, it is never good
> To bring bad news."

She wants to know the features of Octavia, her years, her inclination, the colour of her hair, her height—everything.

A most veracious full-length portrait, with the minute finish of a miniature; it shows how Shakespeare had studied every fold and foible of Mary Fitton's soul. In the third act Cleopatra takes up again the theme of Octavia's appearance, only to run down her rival, and so salve her wounded vanity and cheat her heart to hope. The messenger, too, who lends himself to her humour now becomes a proper man. Shakespeare seizes every opportunity to add another touch to the wonderful picture.

Cleopatra appears next in Antony's camp at Actium talking with Enobarbus:

" *Cleo.* I will be even with thee, doubt it not.
Eno. But why, why, why?
Cleo. Thou hast forspoke my being in these wars,
And say'st it is not fit."

Each phrase of the dialogue reveals her soul, dark fold on fold.

She is the only person who strengthens Antony in his quixotic-foolish resolve to fight at sea.

" *Cleo.* I have sixty sails, Caesar none better."

And then the shameful flight.

I have pursued this bald analysis thus far, not for pleasure merely, but to show the miracle of that portraiture the traits of which can bear examination one by one. So far Cleopatra is, as Enobarbus calls her, " a wonderful piece of work," a woman of women, inscrutable, cunning, deceitful, prodigal, with a good memory for injuries, yet as quick to forgiveness as to anger, a minion of the moon, fleet-

ing as water yet loving-true withal, a sumptuous
bubble, whose perpetual vagaries are but perfect
obedience to every breath of passion. But now
Shakespeare without reason makes her faithless to
Antony and to love. In the second scene of the
third act Thyreus comes to her with Caesar's mes-
sage:

> "*Thyr.* He knows that you embrace not Antony
> As you did love but as you feared him.
> *Cleo.*   O!
> *Thyr.* The scars upon your honour therefore he
> Does pity as constrainèd blemishes,
> Not as deserved.
> *Cleo.*   He is a god, and knows
> What is most right. Mine honour was not yielded,
> But conquered merely.
> *Eno.* [*Aside.*]   To be sure of that
> I will ask Antony.—Sir, sir, thou'rt so leaky
> That we must leave thee to thy sinking, for
> Thy dearest quit thee."

And when Thyreus asks her to leave Antony and
put herself under Caesar's protection, who " desires
to give," she tells him:

> " I am prompt
> To lay my crown at his feet, and there to kneel."

Thyreus then asks for grace to lay his duty on
her hand. She gives it to him with the words:

> " Your Caesar's father oft,
> When he hath mused of taking kingdoms in,
> Bestowed his lips on that unworthy place
> As it rained kisses."

It is as if Antony were forgotten, clean wiped

from her mind. The whole scene is a libel upon Cleopatra and upon womanhood. When betrayed, women are faithless out of anger, pique, desire of revenge; they are faithless out of fear, out of ambition, for fancy's sake—for fifty motives, but not without motive. It would have been easy to justify this scene. All the dramatist had to do was to show us that Cleopatra, a proud woman and scorned queen, could not forget Antony's faithlessness in leaving her to marry Octavia; but she never mentions Octavia, never seems to remember her after she has got Antony back. This omission, too, implies a slur upon her. Nor does she kiss Caesar's " conquering hand " out of fear. Thyreus has told her it would please Caesar if she would make of his fortunes a staff to lean upon; she has no fear, and her ambitions are wreathed round Antony: Caesar has nothing to offer that can tempt her, as we shall see later. The scene is a libel upon her. The more one studies it, the clearer it becomes that Shakespeare wrote it out of wounded personal feeling. Cleopatra's prototype, Mary Fitton, had betrayed him again and again, and the faithlessness rankled. Cleopatra, therefore, shall be painted as faithless, without cause, as Cressid was, from incurable vice of nature. Shakespeare tried to get rid of his bitterness in this way, and if his art suffered, so much the worse for his art. Curiously enough, in this instance, for reasons that will appear later, the artistic effect is deepened.

The conclusion of this scene, where Thyreus is whipped and Cleopatra overwhelmed with insults by Antony, does not add much to our knowledge of Cleopatra's character: one may notice, however, that it is the reproach of cold-heartedness that she catches up to answer. The scene follows in which she plays

squire to Antony and helps to buckle on his armour.
But this scene (invented by Shakespeare), which
might bring out the sweet woman-weakness in her,
and so reconcile us to her again, is used against her
remorselessly by the poet. When Antony wakes and
cries for his armour she begs him to " sleep a little "; the touch is natural enough, but coming after
her faithlessness to her lover and her acceptance of
Caesar it shows more than human frailty. It is plain
that, intent upon ennobling Antony, Shakespeare is
willing to degrade Cleopatra beyond nature. Then
comes Antony's victory, and his passion at length
finds perfect lyrical expression:

> " O thou day o' the world,
> Chain mine armed neck; leap thou, attire and all,
> Through proof of harness to my heart, and there
> Ride on the pants triumphing."

At once Cleopatra catches fire with that respon-
sive flame of womanhood which was surely her
chiefest charm:

> " Lord of lords!
> O infinite virtue! Com'st thou smiling from
> The world's great snare uncaught? "

What magic in the utterance, what a revelation of
Cleopatra's character and of Shakespeare's! To
Cleopatra's feminine weakness the world seems one
huge snare .which only cunning may escape.

Another day, and final irremediable defeat drives
her in fear to the monument and to that pretended
suicide which is the immediate cause of Antony's
despair:

> "Unarm, Eros: the long day's task is done,
> And we must sleep."

When Antony leaves the stage, Shakespeare's idealizing vision turns to Cleopatra. About this point, too, the historical fact fetters Shakespeare and forces him to realize the other side of Cleopatra. After Antony's death Cleopatra did kill herself. One can only motive and explain this suicide by self-immolating love. It is natural that at first Shakespeare will have it that Cleopatra's nobility of nature is merely a reflection, a light borrowed from Antony. She will not open the monument to let the dying man enter, but her sincerity and love enable us to forgive this:

> " I dare not, dear,—
> Dear my lord, pardon,—I dare not,
> Lest I be taken. . . ."

Here occurs a fault of taste which I find inexplicable. While Cleopatra and her women are drawing Antony up, he cries:

> " O quick, or I am gone."

And Cleopatra answers:

> " Here's sport, indeed!—How heavy weighs my lord!
> Our strength has all gone into heaviness,
> That makes the weight."

The " Here's sport, indeed! " seems to me a terrible fault, an inexcusable lapse of taste. I should like to think it a misprint or misreading, but it is unfortunately like Shakespeare in a certain mood, possible to him, at least, here as elsewhere.

Cleopatra's lament over Antony's dead body is a piece of Shakespeare's self-revealing made lyrical by beauty of word and image. The allusion to his

boy-rival, Pembroke, is unmistakable; for women are
not contemptuous of youth:

> " Young boys and girls
> Are level now with men; the odds is gone,
> And there is nothing left remarkable
> Beneath the visiting moon."

When Cleopatra comes to herself after swooning,
her anger is characteristic because wholly unexpected; it is one sign more that Shakespeare had
a living model in his mind:

> " It were for me
> To throw my sceptre at the injurious gods;
> To tell them that this world did equal theirs
> Till they had stolen our jewel. All's but naught."

Her resolve to kill herself is borrowed:

> " We 'll bury him; and then, what's brave, what's noble,
> Let's do it after the high Roman fashion,
> And make death proud to take us."

But the resolution holds:

> " It is great
> To do that thing that ends all other deeds,
> Which shackles accidents and bolts up change."

It is this greatness of soul in Cleopatra which
Shakespeare has now to portray. Caesar's messenger, Proculeius, whom Antony has told her to
trust, promises her everything in return for her
" sweet dependency." On being surprised she tries
to kill herself, and when disarmed shows again that
characteristic petulant anger:

" Sir, I will eat no meat, I'll not drink, sir;
.   .   .   . This mortal house I'll ruin,
Do Caesar what he can."

And her reasons are all of pride and hatred of
disgrace. She'll not be " chastised with the sober
eye of dull Octavia," nor shown " to the shouting
varletry of censuring Rome." Her imagination is
at work now, that quick forecast of the mind that
steels her desperate resolve:

" Rather on Nilus' mud
Lay me stark nak'd, and let the water-flies
Blow me into abhorring."

The heroic mood passes. She tries to deceive
Caesar as to her wealth, and is shamed by her
treasurer Seleucus. The scene is appalling; poor
human nature stripped to the skin—all imperfections exposed; Cleopatra cheating, lying, raging
like a drab; her words to Seleucus are merciless while
self-revealing:

" O slave, of no more trust
Than love that's hired."

This scene deepens and darkens the impression
made by her unmotived faithlessness to Antony.
It is, however, splendidly characteristic and I think
needful; but it renders that previous avowal of faithlessness to Antony altogether superfluous, the sole
fault in an almost perfect portrait. For, as I have
said already, Shakespeare's mistakes in characterization nearly always spring from his desire to idealize;
but here his personal vindictiveness comes to help
his art. The historical fact compels him now to give
his harlot, Cleopatra, heroic attributes; in spite of

Caesar's threats to treat her sons severely if she dares to take her own life and thus deprive his triumph of its glory, she outwits him and dies a queen, a worthy descendant, as Charmian says, of " many royal kings." Nothing but personal bitterness could have prevented Shakespeare from idealizing such a woman out of likeness to humanity. But in this solitary and singular case his personal suffering bound him to realism though the history justified idealization. The high lights were for once balanced by the depths of shadow, and a masterpiece was the result.

Shakespeare leaves out Caesar's threats to put Cleopatra's sons to death; had he used these menaces he would have made Caesar more natural in my opinion, given a touch of characteristic brutality to the calculating intellect; but he omitted them probably because he felt that Cleopatra's pedestal was high enough without that addition.

The end is very characteristic of Shakespeare's temper. Caesar becomes nobly generous; he approves Cleopatra's wisdom in swearing falsehoods about her treasure; he will not reckon with her like " a merchant," and Cleopatra herself puts on the royal robes, and she who has played wanton before us so long becomes a queen of queens. And yet her character is wonderfully maintained; no cunning can cheat this mistress of duplicity:

" He words me, girls, he words me that I should not
Be noble to myself."

She holds to her heroic resolve; she will never be degraded before the base Roman public; she will not see

" Some squeaking Cleopatra boy my greatness."

It is, perhaps, worth noting here that Shakespeare lends Cleopatra, as he afterwards lent Coriolanus, his own delicate senses and neuropathic loathing for mechanic slaves with " greasy aprons " and " thick breaths rank of gross diet "; it is Shakespeare too and not Cleopatra who speaks of death as bringing " liberty." In " Cymbeline," Shakespeare's mask Posthumus dwells on the same idea. But these lapses are momentary; the superb declaration that follows is worthy of the queen:

> " My resolution's placed, and I have nothing
> Of woman in me: now from head to foot
> I am marble-constant; now the fleeting moon
> No planet is of mine."

The scene with the clown who brings the " pretty worm " is the solid ground of reality on which Cleopatra rests for a breathing space before rising into the blue:

> "*Cleo.* Give me my robe, put on my crown; I have
> Immortal longings in me. Now no more
> The juice of Egypt's grape shall moist this lip.—
> Yare, yare, good Iras! quick.—Methinks I hear
> Antony call; I see him rouse himself
> To praise my noble act; I hear him mock
> The luck of Caesar, which the gods give men
> To excuse their after-wrath. Husband, I come.
> Now to that name my courage prove my title!
> I am fire and air; my other elements
> I give to baser life."

The whole speech is miraculous in speed of mounting emotion, and when Iras dies first, this Cleopatra finds again the perfect word in which truth and beauty meet:

316

Antony and Cleopatra

> " This proves me base:
> If she first meet the curlèd Antony
> He'll make demand of her, and spend that kiss
> Which is my heaven to have.   Come, thou mortal wretch,
>   [*To the asp, which she applies to her breast.*
> With thy sharp teeth this knot intrinsicate
> Of life at once untie: poor venomous fool,
> Be angry, and despatch.   O, could'st thou speak,
> That I might hear thee call great Caesar, ass
> Unpolicied ! "

The characteristic high temper of Mary Fitton breaking out again—" ass unpolicied "—and then the end:

> " Peace, peace!
> Dost thou not see my baby at my breast,
> That sucks the nurse asleep? "

The final touch is of soft pleasure:

> " As sweet a balm, as soft as air, as gentle,—
> O, Antony!—Nay, I will take thee too.
>   [*Applying another asp to her arm.*
> What should I stay——"

For ever fortunate in her self-inflicted death Cleopatra thereby frees herself from the ignominy of certain of her actions: she is woman at once and queen, and if she cringes lower than other women, she rises, too, to higher levels than other women know.   The historical fact of her self-inflicted death forced the poet to make false Cressid a Cleopatra— and his wanton gipsy-mistress was at length redeemed by a passion of heroic resolve.

The majority of critics are still debating whether indeed Cleopatra is the " dark lady " of the sonnets or not.   Professor Dowden puts forward the theory

317

as a daring conjecture; but the identity of the two
cannot be doubted. It is impossible not to notice
that Shakespeare makes Cleopatra, who was a fair
Greek, gipsy-dark like his sonnet-heroine. He says,
too, of the " dark lady " of the sonnets:

"Whence hast thou this becoming of things ill,
   That in the very refuse of thy deeds
There is such strength and warrantise of skill,
   That in my mind, thy worst all best exceeds?"

Enobarbus praises Cleopatra in precisely the same
words:
                    "Vilest things,
      Become themselves in her."

Antony, too, uses the same expression:

                "Fie, wrangling queen!
Whom everything becomes—to chide, to laugh,
To weep; whose every passion fully strives
To make itself, in thee, fair and admired."

These professors have no distinct mental image
of the " dark lady " or of Cleopatra, or they would
never talk of " daring conjecture " in regard to this
simple identification. The points of likeness are
numberless. Ninety-nine poets and dramatists out
of a hundred would have followed Plutarch and made
Cleopatra's love for Antony the mainspring of her
being, the *causa causans* of her self-murder. But
Shakespeare does not do this; he allows the love of
Antony to count with her, but it is imperious pride
and hatred of degradation that force his Cleopatra
to embrace the Arch-fear. And just this same
quality of pride is attributed to the " dark lady."
Sonnet 131 begins:

"Thou art as tyrannous, so as thou art,
  As those whose beauties proudly make them cruel."

Both are women of infinite cunning and small
regard for faith or truth; hearts steeled with an insane pride, and violent tempers suited with scolding slanderous tongues. Prolonged analysis is not
needed. A point of seeming difference between them
establishes their identity. Cleopatra is beautiful,
" a lass unparalleled," as Charmian calls her, and
accordingly we can believe that all emotions became
her, and that when hopping on the street or pretending to die she was alike bewitching; beauty has
this magic. But how can all things become a woman
who is not beautiful, whose face some say " hath not
the power to make love groan," who cannot even
blind the senses with desire? And yet the " dark
lady " of the sonnets who is thus described, has the
" powerful might " of personality in as full measure as Egypt's queen. The point of seeming unlike-
ness is as convincing as any likeness could be; the
peculiarities of both women are the same and spring
from the same dominant quality. Cleopatra is cunning, wily, faithless, passionately unrestrained in
speech and proud as Lucifer, and so is the sonnet-
heroine. We may be sure that the faithlessness,
scolding, and mad vanity of his mistress were defects in Shakespeare's eyes as in ours; these, indeed,
were " the things ill " which nevertheless became her.
What Shakespeare loved in her was what he himself
lacked or possessed in lesser degree—that dæmonic
power of personality which he makes Enobarbus
praise in Cleopatra and which he praises directly in
the sonnet-heroine. Enobarbus says of Cleopatra:

"I saw her once
Hop forty paces through the public street,
319

And, having lost her breath, she spoke and panted,
That she did make defect perfection,
And, breathless, power breathe forth."

One would be willing to wager that Shakespeare
is here recalling a performance of his mistress; but
it is enough for my purpose now to draw attention
to the unexpectedness of the attribute "power."
The sonnet fastens on the same word:

" O, from what power hast thou this powerful might
With insufficiency my heart to sway? "

In the same sonnet he again dwells upon her
"strength": she was bold, too, to unreason, and of
unbridled tongue, for, "twice forsworn herself," she
had yet urged his "amiss," though guilty of the
same fault. What he admired most in her was force
of character. Perhaps the old saying held in her
case: *ex forti dulcedo;* perhaps her confident
strength had abandonments more flattering and
complete than those of weaker women; perhaps in
those moments her forceful dark face took on a soul-
ful beauty that entranced his exquisite susceptibil-
ity; perhaps—but the suppositions are infinite.

Though a lover and possessed by his mistress
Shakespeare was still an artist. In the sonnets he
brings out her overbearing will, boldness, pride—the
elemental force of her nature; in the play, on the
other hand, while just mentioning her "power," he
lays the chief stress upon the cunning wiles and
faithlessness of her whose trade was love. But just
as Cleopatra has power, so there can be no doubt
of the wily cunning—" the warrantise of skill "—of
the sonnet-heroine, and no doubt her faithlessness
was that " just cause of hate " which Shakespeare
bemoaned.

Antony and Cleopatra

It is worth while here to notice his perfect comprehension of the powers and limits of the different forms of his art. Just as he has used the sonnets in order to portray certain intimate weaknesses and maladies of his own nature that he could not present dramatically without making his hero ridiculously effeminate, so also he used the sonnets to convey to us the domineering will and strength of his mistress —qualities which if presented dramatically would have seemed masculine-monstrous.

By taking the sonnets and the play together we get an excellent portrait of Shakespeare's mistress. In person she was probably tall and vain of her height, as Cleopatra is vain of her superiority in this respect to Octavia, with dark complexion, black eyebrows and hair, and pitch-black eyes that mirrored emotion as the lakelet mirrors the ever-changing skies; her cheeks are " damask'd white "; her breath fragrant with health, her voice melodious, her movements full of dignity—a superb gipsy to whom beauty may be denied but not distinction.

If we have a very good idea of her person we have a still better idea of her mind and soul. I must begin by stating that I do not accept implicitly Shakespeare's angry declarations that his mistress was a mere strumpet. A nature of great strength and pride is seldom merely wanton; but the fact stands that Shakespeare makes a definite charge of faithlessness against his mistress; she is, he tells us, " the bay where all men ride "; no " several plot," but " the wide world's common place." The accusation is most explicit. But if it were well founded why should he devote two sonnets (135 and 136) to imploring her to be as liberal as the sea and to receive his love-offering as well as the tributes of others?

The Man Shakespeare

"Among a number one is reckon'd none
Then in the number let me pass untold."

It is plain that Mistress Fitton drew away from Shakespeare after she had given herself to his friend, and this fact throws some doubt upon his accusations of utter wantonness. A true " daughter of the game," as he says in " Troilus and Cressida," is nothing but " a sluttish spoil of opportunity " who falls to Troilus or to Diomedes in turn, knowing no reserve. It must be reckoned to the credit of Mary Fitton, or to her pride, that she appears to have been faithful to her lover for the time being, and able to resist even the solicitings of Shakespeare. But her desires seem to have been her sole restraint, and therefore we must add an extraordinary lewdness to that strength, pride, and passionate temper which Shakespeare again and again attributes to her. Her boldness is so reckless that she shows her love for his friend even before Shakespeare's face; she knows no pity in her passion, and always defends herself by attacking her accuser. But she is cunning in love's ways and dulls Shakespeare's resentment with " I don't hate you." Unwilling, perhaps, to lose her empire over him and to forego the sweetness of his honeyed flatteries, she blinded him to her faults by occasional caresses. Yet this creature, with the soul of a strumpet, the tongue of a fishwife and the " proud heart " of a queen, was the crown and flower of womanhood to Shakespeare, his counterpart and ideal. Hamlet in love with Cleopatra, the poet lost in desire of the wanton—that is the tragedy of Shakespeare's life.

In this wonderful world of ours dramatic writers are sure to live dramatic lives. Again and again in his disgrace Antony cries:

322

Antony and Cleopatra

"Whither hast thou led me, Egypt?"

Shakespeare's passion for Mary Fitton led him
to shame and madness and despair; his strength
broke down under the strain and he never won
back again to health. He paid the price of passion
with his very blood. It is Shakespeare and not
Antony who groans:

"O this false soul of Egypt! this grave charm,—

Like a right gipsy, hath, at fast and loose,
Beguil'd me to the very heart of loss."

Shakespeare's love for Mary Fitton is to me one
of the typical tragedies of life—a symbol for ever.
In its progress through the world genius is inevitably scourged and crowned with thorns and done
to death; inevitably, I say, for the vast majority
of men hate and despise what is superior to them:
Don Quixote, too, was trodden into the mire by the
swine. But the worst of it is that genius suffers
also through its own excess; is bound, so to speak,
to the stake of its own passionate sensibilities, and
consumed, as with fire.

CHAPTER XI

EVER since Lessing and Goethe it has been the fashion to praise Shakespeare as a demi-god; whatever he wrote is taken to be the rose of perfection. This senseless hero-worship, which reached idolatry in the superlatives of the " Encyclopædia Britannica " and elsewhere in England, was certain to provoke reaction, and the reaction has come to vigorous expression in Tolstoi, who finds nothing to praise in any of Shakespeare's works, and everything to blame in most of them, especially in " Lear." Lamb and Coleridge, on the other hand, have praised " Lear " as a world's masterpiece. Lamb says of it:

" While we read it, we see not Lear; but we are Lear, —we are in his mind, we are sustained by a grandeur which baffles the malice of daughters and storms; in the aberrations of his reason we discover a mighty irregular power of reasoning, immethodised from the ordinary purposes of life, but exerting its powers, as the wind bloweth where it listeth, at will upon the corruptions and abuses of mankind."

Coleridge calls " Lear," " the open and ample playground of Nature's passions."

These dithyrambs show rather the lyrical power of the writers than the thing described.

Tolstoi, on the other hand, keeps his eyes on the

object, and sets himself to describe the story of
"Lear" "as impartially as possible." He says of
the first scene:

"Not to mention the pompous, characterless language of King Lear, the same in which all Shakespeare's kings speak, the reader or spectator cannot
conceive that a king, however old and stupid he may
be, could believe the words of the vicious daughters
with whom he had passed his whole life, and not believe his favourite daughter, but curse and banish her;
and therefore, the spectator or reader cannot share the
feelings of the persons participating in this unnatural
scene."

He goes on to condemn the scene between
Gloucester and his sons in the same way. The
second act he describes as "absurdly foolish." The
third act is "spoiled, by the characteristic Shakespearean language." The fourth act is "marred in
the making," and of the fifth act, he says: "Again
begin Lear's awful ravings, at which one feels
ashamed, as at unsuccessful jokes." He sums up in
these words:

"Such is this celebrated drama. However absurd it
may appear in my rendering (which I have endeav-
oured to make as impartial as possible), I may con-
fidently say that in the original it is yet more absurd.
For any man of our time—if he were not under the
hypnotic suggestion that this drama is the height of
perfection—it would be enough to read it to its end
(were he to have sufficient patience for this) in order
to be convinced that, far from being the height of perfection, it is a very bad, carelessly-composed production, which, if it could have been of interest to a certain public at a certain time, cannot evoke amongst us
anything but aversion and weariness. Every reader

of our time who is free from the influence of suggestion will also receive exactly the same impression from all the other extolled dramas of Shakespeare, not to mention *the senseless dramatized tales, 'Pericles,' 'Twelfth Night,' 'The Tempest,' 'Cymbeline,' and 'Troilus and Cressida.' "

Every one must admit, I think, that what Tolstoi has said of the hypothesis of the play is justified. Shakespeare, as I have shown, was nearly always an indifferent playwright, careless of the architectural construction of his pieces, contemptuous of stage-craft. So much had already been said in England, if not with the authority of Tolstoi.

It may be conceded, too, that the language which Shakespeare puts into Lear's mouth in the first act is "characterless and pompous," even silly; but Tolstoi should have noticed that as soon as Lear realises the ingratitude of his daughters, his language becomes more and more simple and pathetic. Shakespeare's kings usually rant and mouth when first introduced; he appears to have thought that pomp of speech went with royal robes; but as soon as the action is engaged even his monarchs speak naturally.

The truth is, that just as the iambics of Greek drama were lifted above ordinary conversation, so Shakespeare's language, being the language mainly of poetic and romantic drama, is a little more measured and, if you will, more pompous than the small talk of everyday life, which seems to us, accustomed as we are to prose plays, more natural. Shakespeare, however, in his blank verse, reaches heights which are not often reached by prose, and when he pleases, his verse becomes as natural-easy as any prose, even that of Tolstoi himself.

Tolstoi finds everything Lear says " pompous," " artificial," " unnatural," but Lear's words:

> " Pray do not mock me,
> I am a very foolish-fond old man
> Fourscore and upward, not an hour more nor less,
> And, to deal plainly
> I fear I am not in my perfect mind,"

touch us poignantly, just because of their childish simplicity; we feel as if Lear, in them, had reached the heart of pathos. Tolstoi, I am afraid, has missed all the poetry of Lear, all the deathless phrases. Lear says:

> " I am a man,
> More sinn'd against than sinning,"

and the new-coined phrase passed at once into the general currency. Who, too, can ever forget his description of the poor?

> " Poor naked wretches, wheresoe'er you are,
> That bide the pelting of this pitiless storm,
> How shall your houseless heads and unfed sides,
> Your looped and windowed raggedness, defend you
> From seasons such as these? "

The like of that " looped and windowed raggedness " is hardly to be found in any other literature. In the fourth and fifth acts Lear's speech is simplicity itself, and even in that third act which Tolstoi condemns as " incredibly pompous and artificial," we find him talking naturally:

> " Ha! here's three on's are sophisticated: thou art the thing itself, unaccommodated man is no more but such a poor, bare, forked animal as thou art."

There is still another reason why some of us cannot read "Lear" with the cold eyes of reason, contemptuously critical. "Lear" marks a stage in Shakespeare's agony. We who know the happy ingenuousness of his youth undimmed by doubts of man or suspicions of woman, cannot help sympathizing with him when we see him cheated and betrayed, drinking the bitter cup of disillusion to the dregs. In "Lear" the angry brooding leads to madness; and it is only fitting that the keynote of the tragedy, struck again and again, should be the cry:

> "O, let me not be mad, not mad, sweet Heaven!
> Keep me in temper: I would not be mad."

"Lear" is the first attempt in all literature to paint madness, and not the worst attempt.

In "Lear," Shakespeare was intent only on expressing his own disillusion and naked misery. How blind Lear must have been, says Tolstoi; how incredibly foolish not to know his daughters better after living with them for twenty years; but this is just what Shakespeare wishes to express: How blind I was, he cries to us, how inconceivably trusting and foolish! How could I have imagined that a young noble would be grateful, or a wanton true? "Lear" is a page of Shakespeare's autobiography, and the faults of it are the stains of his blistering tears.

"Lear" is badly constructed, but worse was to follow. The next tragedy, "Timon," is merely a scream of pain, and yet it, too, has a deeper than artistic interest for us as marking the utmost limit of Shakespeare's suffering. The mortal malady of perhaps the finest spirit that has ever appeared

among men has an interest for us profounder than
any tragedy. And to find that in Shakespeare's
agony and bloody sweat he ignores the rules of
artistry is simply what might have been expected,
and, to some of us, deepens the personal interest in
the drama.

In "Lear" Edgar is peculiarly Shakespeare's
mouthpiece, and to Edgar Shakespeare gives some
of the finest words he ever coined:

> "The gods are just, and of our pleasant vices
> Make instruments to plague us."

Here, too, in what Edgar says of himself, is the
moral of all passion: it is manifestly Shakespeare's
view of himself:

> "A most poor man, made tame to Fortune's blows,
> Who by the art of knowing and feeling sorrows
> Am pregnant to good pity."

Then we find the supreme phrase—perhaps the
finest ever written:

> "Men must endure
> Their going hence even as their coming hither.
> Ripeness is all."

Of course Shakespeare speaks through Lear in
the last acts as plainly as through Edgar. In the
third scene of the fifth act Lear talks to Cordelia in
the very words Shakespeare gave to the saint Henry
VI. at the beginning of his career. Compare the
extracts on pages 117-8 with the following passage
and you will see the similarity and the astonishing
growth in his art:

" *Lear.*　　　　　　　Come, let's away to prison:
We two alone will sing like birds i' the cage:
When thou dost ask me blessing, I'll kneel down
And ask of thee forgiveness; so we'll live
And pray, and sing, and tell old tales, and laugh
At gilded butterflies and hear poor rogues
Talk of Court news. . . ."

More characteristic still of Shakespeare is the
fact that when Lear is at his bitterest in the fourth
act, he shows the erotic mania which is the source
of all Shakespeare's bitterness and misery; but which
is utterly out of place in Lear.　The reader will
note how "adultery" is dragged in:

　　　　　　　"Ay, every inch a King,
When I do stare see how the subject quakes.
I pardon that man's life.　What was thy cause?
Adultery?
Thou shalt not die: die for adultery!　No:
The wren goes to't, and the small gilded fly
Does lecher in my sight.
Let copulation thrive; . . .
　　　　・　　　　・　　　　・　　　　・　　　　・
Down from the waist they are Centaurs,
Though women all above;
But to the girdle do the gods inherit,
Beneath is all the fiends' . . ."

Thus Lear raves for a whole page:　Shakespeare
on his favourite hobby: in the same erotic spirit he
makes both Goneril and Regan lust after Edmund.
　　The note of this tragedy is Shakespeare's understanding of his insane blind trust in men; but
the passion of it springs from erotic mania and from
the consciousness that he is too old for love's lists.
Perhaps his imagination never carried him higher

than when Lear appeals to the heavens because they too are old:

> " . . . O heavens,
> If you do love old men, if your sweet sway
> Allow obedience, if yourselves are old,
> Make it your cause."

CHAPTER XII

"TIMON" marks the extremity of Shakespeare's suffering. It is not to be called a work of art, it is hardly even a tragedy; it is the causeless ruin of a soul, a ruin insufficiently motived by complete trust in men and spendthrift generosity. If there was ever a man who gave so lavishly as Timon, if there was ever one so senseless blind in trusting, then he deserved his fate. There is no gradation in his giving, and none in his fall; no artistic crescendo. The whole drama is, as I have said, a scream of suffering, or rather, a long curse upon all the ordinary conditions of life. The highest qualities of Shakespeare are not to be found in the play. There are none of the magnificent phrases which bejewel "Lear"; little of high wisdom, even in the pages which are indubitably Shakespeare's, and no characterization worth mentioning. The honest steward, Flavius, is the honest Kent again of "Lear," honest and loyal beyond nature; Apemantus is another Thersites. Words which throw a high light on Shakespeare's character are given to this or that personage of the play without discrimination. One phrase of Apemantus is as true of Shakespeare as of Timon and is worth noting:

"The middle of humanity thou never knewest, but the extremity of both ends."

The tragic sonnet-note is given to Flavius:

"What viler thing upon the earth than friends
Who can bring noblest minds to basest ends!"

In so far as Timon is a character at all he is
manifestly Shakespeare, Shakespeare who raves
against the world, because he finds no honesty in
men, no virtue in women, evil everywhere—" boundless thefts in limited professions." This Shake-
speare-Timon swings round characteristically as
soon as he finds that Flavius is honest:

" Had I a steward
So true, so just, and now so comfortable?
It almost turns my dangerous nature mild.
Let me behold thy face. Surely this man
Was born of woman.
Forgive my general and exceptless rashness,
You perpetual-sober gods! I do proclaim
One honest man—mistake me not—but one." . . .

I cannot help putting the great and self-revealing
line [1] in italics; a line Tolstoi would, no doubt, think
pompous. Timon ought to have known his steward,
one might say in Tolstoi's spirit, as Lear should
have known his daughters; but this is still the
tragedy, which Shakespeare wishes to emphasize,
that his hero was blind in trusting.

Towards the end Shakespeare speaks through
Timon quite unfeignedly. Richard II. said characteristically:

" Nor I nor any man that but man is
With nothing shall be pleased, till he be eased
With being nothing."

And Timon says to Flavius:

[1] This passage is among those rejected by the commentators as un-Shakespearean: " It does not stand the test,"
says the egregious Gollancz.

" My long sickness
Of health and living now begins to mend
And nothing brings me all things."

Then the end:

" Timon hath made his everlasting mansion
Upon the beachèd verge of the salt flood . . ."

We must not leave this play before noticing the
overpowering erotic strain in Shakespeare which
suits Timon as little as it suited Lear. The long
discussion with Phrynia and Timandra is simply
dragged in: neither woman is characterized: Shake-
speare-Timon eases himself in pages of erotic rav-
ing:

. . . " Strike me the counterfeit matron;
It is her habit only that is honest,
Herself's a bawd. . . ."

And then:

" Consumptions sow
In hollow bones of man . . . . .
. . . . . Down with the nose,
Down with it flat; take the bridge quite away."

The " damned earth " even is the common whore
of mankind.

" Timon " is the true sequel to " The Merchant of
Venice."   Antonio gives lavishly, but is saved at
the crisis by his friends.   Timon gives with both
hands; but when he appeals to his friends, is treated
as a bore.   Shakespeare had travelled far in the
dozen years which separate the two plays.

All Shakespeare's tragedies are phases of his own
various weaknesses, and each one brings the hero to
defeat and ruin.   Hamlet cannot carry revenge to

murder and fails through his own irresolution. Othello comes to grief through mad jealousy. Antony fails and falls through excess of lust; Lear through trust in men, and Timon through heedless generosity. All these are separate studies of Shakespeare's own weaknesses; but the ruin is irretrievable, and reaches its ultimate in Timon. Trust and generosity, Shakespeare would like to tell us, were his supremest faults. In this he deceived himself. Neither "Lear" nor "Timon" is his greatest tragedy; but "Antony and Cleopatra," for lust was his chief weakness, and the tragedy of lust his greatest play.

Much of "Timon" is not Shakespeare's, the critics tell us, and some of it is manifestly not his, though many of the passages rejected with the best reason have, I think, been touched up by him. The second scene of the first act is as bad as bad can be; but I hear his voice in the line:

"Methinks, I could deal kingdoms to my friends,
    And ne'er be weary."

At any rate, this is the keynote of the tragedy, which is struck again and again. Shakespeare probably exaggerated his own generosity out of aristocratic pose; but that he was careless of money and freehanded to a fault, is, I think, certain from his writings, and can be proved from the facts known to us of his life.

CHAPTER XIII

" Winter's Tale ": " Cymbeline ": " The Tempest "

THE wheel has swung full circle: Timon is almost as weak as " Titus Andronicus "; the pen falls from the nerveless hand. Shakespeare wrote nothing for some time. Even the critics make a break after " Timon," which closes what they are pleased to call his third period; but they do not seem to see that the break was really a breakdown in health. In " Lear " he had brooded and raged to madness; in " Timon " he had spent himself in futile, feeble cursings. His nerves had gone to pieces. He was now forty-five years of age, the forces of youth and growth had left him. He was prematurely old and feeble.

His recovery, it seems certain, was very slow, and he never again, if I am right, regained vigorous health. I am almost certain he went down to Stratford at this crisis and spent some time there, probably a couple of years, trying, no doubt, to staunch the wound in his heart, and win back again to life. The fear of madness had frightened him from brooding: he made up his mind to let the dead past bury its dead; he would try to forget and live sanely. After all, life is better than death.

It was probably his daughter who led him back from the brink of the grave. Almost all his latest works show the same figure of a young girl. He

seems now, for the first time, to have learned that
a maiden can be pure, and in his old idealizing way
which went with him to the end, he deified her.
Judith became a symbol to him, and he lent her
the ethereal grace of abstract beauty. In "Pericles" she is Marina; in "The Winter's Tale" Perdita; in "The Tempest" Miranda. It is probable,
when one comes to think of it, that Ward was right
when he says that Shakespeare spent his "elder
years" in Stratford; he was too broken to have
taken up his life in London again.

The assertion that Shakespeare broke down in
health, and never won back to vigorous life, will be
scorned as my imagining. The critics who have
agreed to regard "Cymbeline," "The Winter's
Tale," and "The Tempest" as his finest works are
all against me on this point, and they will call for
"Proofs, proofs. Give us proofs," they will cry,
"that the man who went mad and raved with Lear,
and screamed and cursed in 'Timon' did really
break down, and was not imagining madness and
despair." The proofs are to be found in these works
themselves, plain for all men to read.

The three chief works of his last period are
romances and are all copies; he was too tired to
invent or even to annex; his own story is the only
one that interests him. The plot of "The Winter's
Tale" is the plot of "Much Ado about Nothing."
Hero is Hermione. Another phase of "Much Ado
About Nothing" is written out at length in "Cymbeline"; Imogen suffers like Hero and Hermione,
under unfounded accusation. It is Shakespeare's
own history turned from this world to fairyland:
what would have happened, he asks, if the woman
whom I believed false, had been true? This, the
theme of "Much Ado," is the theme also of "The

Winter's Tale " and of " Cymbeline." The idealism
of the man is inveterate: he will not see that it was
his own sensuality which gave him up to suffering,
and not Mary Fitton's faithlessness. " The Tempest " is the story of " As you Like it." We have
again the two dukes, the exiled good Duke, who
is Shakespeare, and the bad usurping Duke, Shakespeare's rival, Chapman, who has conquered for a
time. Shakespeare is no longer able or willing to
discover a new play: he can only copy himself, and
in one of the scenes which he wrote into " Henry
VIII." the copy is slavish.

I allude to the third scene in the second act; the
dialogue between Anne Bullen and the Old Lady
is extraordinarily reminiscent. When Anne Bullen
says—

> " 'Tis better to be lowly born,
> And range with humble livers in content,
> Than to be perk'd up in a glistening grief
> And wear a golden sorrow "

I am reminded of Henry VI. And the contention
between Anne Bullen and the Old Lady, in which
Anne Bullen declares that she would not be a
queen, and the Old Lady scorns her:

> " Beshrew me, I would,
> And venture maidenhead for't; and so would you,
> For all this spice of your hypocrisy."

is much the same contention, and is handled in the
same way as the contention between Desdemona
and Emilia in " Othello."

There are many other proofs of Shakespeare's
weakness of hand throughout this last period, if
further proofs were needed. The chief character-

338

istics of Shakespeare's health are his humour, his gaiety, and wit—his love of life. A correlative characteristic is that all his women are sensuous and indulge in coarse expressions in and out of season. This is said to be a fault of his time; but only professors could use an argument which shows such ignorance of life. Homer was clean enough, and Sophocles, Spenser, too; sensuality is a quality of the individual man. Still another characteristic of Shakespeare's maturity is that his characters, in spite of being idealized, live for us a vigorous, pulsing life.

All these characteristics are lacking in the works after " Timon." There is practically no humour, no wit, the clowns even are merely boorish-stupid with the solitary exception of Autolycus, who is a pale reflex of one or two characteristics of Falstaff. Shakespeare's humour has disappeared, or is so faint as scarcely to be called humour; all the heroines, too, are now vowed away from sensuality: Marina passes through the brothel unsoiled; Perdita might have milk in her veins, and not blood, and Miranda is but another name for Perdita. Imogen, too, has no trace of natural passion in her: she is a mere washing-list, so to speak, of sexless perfections. In this last period Shakespeare will have nothing to do with sensuality, and his characters, and not the female characters alone, are hardly more than abstractions; they lack the blood of emotion; there is not one of them could cast a shadow. How is it that the critics have mistaken these pale, bloodless silhouettes for Shakespeare's masterpieces?

In his earliest works he was compelled, as we have seen, to use his own experiences perpetually, not having had any experience of life, and in these, his latest plays, he also uses when he can his own experiences to give his pictures of the world from which he had withdrawn, some sense of vivid life. For example, in " The Winter's Tale " his account of the death of the boy Mamillius is evidently a reflex of his own emotion when he lost his son, Hamnet, an emotion which at the time he pictured deathlessly in Arthur and the grief of the Queen-mother, Constance. Similarly, in " Cymbeline," the joy of the brothers in finding the sister is an echo of his own pleasure in getting to know his daughter.

I have an idea about the genesis of these last three plays as regards their order which may be wholly false, though true, I am sure, to Shakespeare's character. I imagine he was asked by the author to touch up " Pericles." On reading the play, he saw the opportunity of giving expression to the new emotion which had been awakened in him by the serious sweet charm of his young daughter, and accordingly he wrote the scenes in which Marina figures. Judith's modesty was a perpetual wonder to him.

His success induced him to sketch out " The Winter's Tale," in which tale he played sadly with what might have been if his accused love, Mary Fitton, had been guiltless instead of guilty. I imagine he saw that the play was not a success, or, supreme critic as he was, that his hand had grown weak, and seeking for the cause he probably came to the conclusion that the comparative failure was due to the fact that he did not put himself into " The Winter's Tale," and so he determined in the next play to draw a full-length portrait of himself again, as he had done in " Hamlet," and accordingly he sketched Posthumus, a staider, older, idealized Hamlet, with lymph in his veins, instead of blood. In the same idealizing spirit, he pictured

340

his rose of womanhood for us in Imogen, who is, however, not a living woman at all, any more than his earliest ideal, Juliet, was a woman. The contrast between these two sketches is the contrast between Shakespeare's strength and his weakness. Here is how the fourteen-year-old Juliet talks of love:

> "Spread thy close curtain, love-performing night,
> That runaways' eyes may wink, and Romeo
> Leap to these arms, untalk'd of and unseen.
> Lovers can see to do their amorous rites
> By their own beauties."

And here what Posthumus says of Imogen:

> "Me of my lawful pleasure she restrain'd,
> And pray'd me oft forbearance: did it with
> A pudency so rosy, the sweet view on't
> Might well have warmed old Saturn."

When Shakespeare praises restraint in love he must have been very weak; in full manhood he prayed for excess of it, and regarded a surfeit as the only rational cure.

I think Shakespeare liked Posthumus and Imogen; but he could not have thought "Cymbeline" a great work, and so he pulled himself together for a masterpiece. He seems to have said to himself, "All that fighting of Posthumus is wrong; men do not fight at forty-eight; I will paint myself simply in the qualities I possess now; I will tell the truth about myself so far as I can." The result is the portrait of Prospero in "The Tempest."

Let me just say before I begin to study Prospero that I find the introduction of the Masque in the fourth act extraordinarily interesting. Ben Jonson had written classic masques for this and that occasion; masques which were very successful, we are told; they had " caught on," in fact, to use our modern slang. Shakespeare will now show us that he, too, can write a masque with classic deities in it, and better Jonson's example. It is pitiful, and goes to prove, I think, that Shakespeare was but little esteemed by his generation.

Jonson answered him conceitedly, as Jonson would, in the Introduction to his " Bartholomew Fair " (1612-14), " If there be never a *Servant monster* i' the Fayre, who can help it, he sayes; nor a nest of *Antiques*. He is loth to make nature afraid in his *Playes,* like those that beget *Tales, Tempests,* and such like *Drolleries.*"

At the very end, the creator of Hamlet, the finest mind in the world, was eager to show that he could write as well in any style as the author of " Every Man in his Humour." To me the bare fact is full of interest, and most pitiful.

Let us now turn to " The Tempest," and see how our poet figures in it. It is Shakespeare's last work, and one of his very greatest; his testament to the English people; in wisdom and high poetry a miracle.

The portrait of Shakespeare we get in Prospero is astonishingly faithful and ingenuous, in spite of its idealization. His life's day is waning to the end, and shadows of the night are drawing in upon him, yet he is still the same bookish, melancholy student, the lover of all courtesies and generosities, whom we met first as Biron in " Love's Labour's Lost." The gaiety is gone and the sensuality; the spiritual outlook is infinitely sadder—that is what the years have done with our gentle Shakespeare.

Prospero's first appearance in the second scene

of the first act is as a loving father and magician;
he says to Miranda:

> " I have done nothing but in care of thee,
> Of thee, my dear one! thee, my daughter."

He asks Miranda what she can remember of her
early life, and reaches magical words:

> "What seest thou else
> In the dark backward and abysm of time?"

Miranda is only fifteen years of age. Shakespeare
turned Juliet, it will be remembered, from a girl of
sixteen into one of fourteen; now, though the sensuality has left him, he makes Miranda only fifteen;
clearly he is the same admirer of girlish youth at
forty-eight as he was twenty years before. Then
Prospero tells Miranda of himself and his brother,
the " perfidious " Duke:

> "And Prospero, the prime Duke, being so reputed
> In dignity, and for the liberal arts
> Without a parallel; those being all my study."

He will not only be a Prince now, but a master
" without a parallel " in the liberal arts. He must
explain, too, at undue length, how he allowed himself to be supplanted by his false brother, and speaks
about himself in Shakespeare's very words:

> "I thus neglecting worldly ends, all dedicate
> To closeness, and the bettering of my mind
> With that, which, but by being so retired,
> O'erprized all popular rate, in my false brother
> Awaked an evil nature: and my trust,
> Like a good parent, did beget of him,
> A falsehood, in its contrary as great
> As my trust was; which had, indeed, no limit,
> A confidence sans bound."

Shakespeare, too, "neglecting worldly ends," had
dedicated himself to "bettering of his mind," we
may be sure. Prospero goes on to tell us explicitly
how Shakespeare loved books, which we were only
able to infer from his earlier plays:

> "Me, poor man, my library
> Was dukedom large enough."

And again, Gonzalo (another name for Kent and
Flavius) having given him some books, he says:

> "Of his gentleness,
> Knowing I loved my books, he furnished me
> From my own library, with volumes that
> I prize above my dukedom."

His daughter grieves lest she had been a trouble
to him: forthwith Shakespeare-Prospero answers:

> "O, a cherubim
> Thou wast, that did preserve me. Thou didst smile
> Infused with a fortitude from heaven,
> When I have deck'd the sea with drops full salt
> Under my burden groan'd; which raised in me
> An undergoing stomach, to bear up
> Against what should ensue."

But why should the magician weep or groan under
a burden? had he no confidence in his miraculous
powers? All this is Shakespeare's confession.
Every word is true; his daughter did indeed "pre-
serve" Shakespeare, and enable him to bear up
under the burden of life's betrayals.

No wonder Prospero begins to apologize for this
long-winded confession, which indeed is "most imper-
tinent" to the play, as he admits, though most
interesting to him and to us, for he is simply

Shakespeare telling us his own feelings at the time. The gentle magician then hears from Ariel how the shipwreck has been conducted without harming a hair of anyone.

The whole scene is an extraordinarily faithful and detailed picture of Shakespeare's soul. I find significance even in the fact that Ariel wants his freedom " a full year " before the term Prospero had originally proposed. Shakespeare finished " The Tempest," I believe, and therewith set the seal on his life's work a full year earlier than he had intended; he feared lest death might surprise him before he had put the pinnacle on his work. Ariel's torment, too, is full of meaning for me; for Ariel is Shakespeare's " shaping spirit of imagination," who was once the slave of " a foul witch," and by her "imprisoned painfully " for " a dozen years."

That " dozen years " is to me astonishingly true and interesting; it shows that my reading of the duration of his passion-torture was absolutely correct—Shakespeare's " delicate spirit " and best powers bound to Mary Fitton's " earthy " service from 1597 to 1608.

We can perhaps fix this latter date with some assurance. Mistress Fitton married for the second time a Captain or Mr. Polwhele late in 1607, or some short time before March, 1608, when the fact of her recent marriage is mentioned in the will of her great-uncle. It seems to me probable, or at least possible, that this event marks her complete separation from Shakespeare; she may very likely have left the Court and London on ceasing to be a Maid of Honour.

Shakespeare is so filled with himself in this last play, so certain that he is the most important per-

son in the world, that this scene is more charged
with intimate self-revealing than any other in all
his works. And when Ferdinand comes upon the
stage Shakespeare lends him, too, his own peculiar
qualities. His puppets no longer interest him; he
is careless of characterization. Ferdinand says:

> " This music crept by me upon the waters
> Allaying both their fury and my passion
> With its sweet air."

Music, it will be remembered, had precisely the
same peculiar effect upon Duke Orsino in " Twelfth
Night." Ferdinand, too, is extraordinarily conceited:

> "I am the best of them that speak this speech.
> .   .   .   Myself am Naples."

Shakespeare's natural aristocratic pride as a Prince
reinforced by his understanding of his own real
importance. Ferdinand then declares that he will
be content with a prison if he can see Miranda in it:

> " Space enough
> Have I in such a prison."

Which is Hamlet's:

> " I could be bounded in a nutshell, and count myself
> a king of infinite space."

The second act, with its foiled conspiracy, is
wretchedly bad, and the meeting of Caliban and
Trinculo with Stephanio does not improve it much.
Shakespeare has little interest now in anything outside himself: age and greatness are as self-centred as
youth.

In the third act the courtship of Ferdinand and
Miranda is pretty, but hardly more. Ferdinand is

bloodless, thin, and Miranda swears "by her modesty," as the jewel in her dower, which takes away a little from the charming confession of girl-love:

> " I would not wish
> Any companion in the world but you."

The comic relief which follows, is unspeakably dull; but the words of Ariel, warning the King of Naples and the usurping Duke that the wrong they have done Prospero is certain to be avenged unless blotted out by " heart-sorrow and a clear life ensuing," are most characteristic and memorable.

In the fourth act Prospero preaches, as we have seen, self-restraint to Ferdinand in words which, in their very extravagance, show how deeply he regretted his own fault with his wife before marriage. I shall consider the whole passage when treating of Shakespeare's marriage as an incident in his life. Afterwards comes the masque, and the marvellous speech of Prospero, which touches the highest height of poetry:

> " These our actors,
> As I foretold you, were all spirits, and
> Are melted into air, into thin air:
> And, like the baseless fabric of this vision
> The cloud-capped towers, the gorgeous palaces,
> The solemn temples, the great globe itself,
> Yea, all which it inhabit, shall dissolve
> And, like this insubstantial pageant faded,
> Leave not a rack behind. We are such stuff
> As dreams are made of; and our little life
> Is rounded with a sleep. Sir, I am vex'd;
> Bear with my weakness; my old brain is troubled:
> Be not disturb'd with my infirmity:
> If you be pleased, retire into my cell,
> And there repose: a turn or two I'll walk,
> To still my beating mind."

I have given the verses to the very end, for I find the insistence on his age and weakness (which are not in keeping with the character of a magician), a confession of Shakespeare himself: the words " beating mind " are extraordinarily characteristic, proving as they do that his thoughts and emotions were too strong for his frail body.

In the fifth act Shakespeare-Prospero shows himself to us at his noblest: he will forgive his enemies:

" Though with their high wrongs I am struck to the
    quick,
Yet with my nobler reason 'gainst my fury
Do I take part: the rarer action is
In virtue than in vengeance: they being penitent,
The sole drift of my purpose doth extend
Not a frown further."

In " The Two Gentlemen of Verona " we saw how Shakespeare-Valentine forgave his faithless friend as soon as he repented: here is the same creed touched to nobler expression.

And then, with all his wishes satisfied, his heart's desire accomplished, Prospero is ready to set out for Milan again and home. We all expect some expression of joy from him, but this is what we get:

" And thence retire me to my Milan, where
Every third thought shall be my grave."

The despair is wholly unexpected and out of place, as was the story of his weakness and infirmity, his " beating mind." It is evidently Shakespeare's own confession. After writing " The Tempest " he intends to retire to Stratford, where " every third thought shall be my grave."

I have purposely drawn special attention to Shakespeare's weakness and despair at this time, because the sad, rhymed Epilogue which has to be spoken by Prospero has been attributed to another hand by a good many scholars. It is manifestly Shakespeare's, out of Shakespeare's very heart indeed; though Mr. Israel Gollancz follows his leaders in saying that the " Epilogue to the play is evidently by some other hand than Shakespeare's ": " evidently " is good. Here it is:

> " Now my charms are all o'erthrown,
> And what strength I have's mine own,
> Which is most faint: now, 'tis true,
> I must be here confined by you,
> Or sent to Naples. Let me not
> Since I have my dukedom got,
> And pardon'd the deceiver, dwell
> In this bare island by your spell;
> But release me from my bands
> With the help of your good hands:
> Gentle breath of yours my sails
> Must fill, or else my project fails,
> Which was to please. Now I want,
> Spirits to enforce, art to enchant;
> And my ending is despair,
> Unless I be relieved by prayer,
> Which pierces so that it assaults
> Mercy itself, and frees all faults.
> As you from crimes would pardon'd be
> Let your indulgence set me free."

From youth to age Shakespeare occupied himself with the deepest problems of human existence; again and again we find him trying to pierce the darkness that enshrouds life. Is there indeed nothing beyond the grave—nothing? Is the noble fabric of human thought, achievement and endeavour to fade into nothingness and pass away like the pageant of a dream? He will not cheat himself with unfounded hopes, nor delude himself into belief; he resigns himself with a sigh—it is the undiscovered country, from whose bourn no traveller returns. But Shakespeare always believed in repentance and forgiveness, and now, world-weary, old and weak, he turns to prayer,[1] prayer that—

> " Assaults
> Mercy itself and frees all faults."

Poor, broken Shakespeare! " My ending is despair ": the sadness of it, and the pity, lie deeper than tears.

What a man! to produce a masterpiece in spite of such weakness. What a play is this " Tempest "! At length Shakespeare sees himself as he is, a monarch without a country, but master of a very " potent art," a great magician, with imagination as an attendant spirit, that can conjure up shipwrecks, or enslave enemies, or create lovers at will; and all his powers are used in gentle kindness. Ariel is a higher creation, more spiritual and charming than any other poet has ever attempted; and Caliban, the earth-born, half-beast, half-man—these are the poles of Shakespeare's genius.

[1] Hamlet, too, after speaking with his father's ghost, cries: " I'll go pray."

CHAPTER XIV

OUR long travail is almost at an end. We have watched Shakespeare painting himself at various periods of his life, and at full length in twenty dramas, as the gentle, sensuous poet-thinker. We have studied him when given over to wild passion in the sonnets and elsewhere, and to insane jealousy in " Othello "; we have seen him as Hamlet brooding on revenge and self-murder, and in " Lear," and " Timon " raging on the verge of madness, and in these ecstasies, when the soul is incapable of feigning, we have discovered his true nature as it differed from the ideal presentments which his vanity shaped and coloured. We have corrected his personal estimate by that " story of faults conceal'd " which Shakespeare himself referred to in sonnet 88. It only remains for me now to give a brief account of his life and the incidents of it to show that my reading of his character is borne out by the known facts, and thus put the man in his proper setting, so to speak.

On the other hand, our knowledge of Shakespeare's character will help us to reconstruct his life-story. What is known positively of his life could be given in a couple of pages; but there are traditions of him, tales about him, innumerable scraps of fact and fiction concerning him which are more or less interesting and authentic; and now that we know the man, we shall be able to

351

accept or reject these reports with some degree of confidence, and so arrive at a credible picture of his life's journey, and the changes which Time wrought in him. In all I may say about him I shall keep close to the facts as given in his works. When tradition seems consonant with what Shakespeare has told us about himself, or with what Ben Jonson said of him, I shall use it with confidence.

Shakespeare was a common name in Warwickshire; other Shakespeares besides the poet's family were known there in the sixteenth century, and at least one other William Shakespeare in the neighbourhood of Stratford. The poet's father, John Shakespeare, was of farmer stock, and seems to have had an adventurous spirit: he left Snitterfield, his birthplace, as a young man, for the neighbouring town of Stratford, where he set up in business for himself. Aubrey says he was a butcher; he certainly dealt in meat, skins, and leather, as well as in corn, wool, and malt—an adaptable, quick man, who turned his hand to anything—a Jack-of-all trades. He appears to have been successful at first, for in 1556, five years after coming to Stratford, he purchased two freehold tenements, one with a garden in Henley Street, and the other in Greenhill Street, with an orchard. In 1557 he was elected burgess, or town councillor, and shortly afterwards did the best stroke of business in his life by marrying Mary Arden, whose father had been a substantial farmer. Mary inherited the fee simple of Asbies, a house with some fifty acres of land at Wilmcote, and an interest in property at Snitterfield; the whole perhaps worth some £80 or £90, or, say, £600 of our money. His marriage turned John Shakespeare into a well-to-do citizen; he filled various offices in the borough, and in 1568 became a bailiff, the highest position in the corporation. During his year of office, we are told, he entertained two companies of actors at Stratford.

Mary Arden seems to have been her father's favourite child, and though she could not sign her own name, must have possessed rare qualities; for the poet, as we learn from " Coriolanus," held her in extraordinary esteem and affection, and mourned her after her death as " the noblest mother in the world."

William Shakespeare, the first son and third child of this couple, was born on the 22nd or 23rd April, 1564, no one knows which day; the Stratford parish registers prove that he was baptized on 26th April. And if the date of his birth is not known, neither is the place of it; his father owned two houses in Henley Street, and it is uncertain which he was born in.

John Shakespeare had, fortunately, nothing to pay for the education of his sons. They had free tuition at the Grammar School at Stratford. The poet went to school when he was seven or eight years of age, and received an ordinary education together with some grounding in Latin. He probably spent most of 'his time at first making stories out of the frescoes on the walls. There can be no doubt that he learned easily all he was taught, and still less doubt that he was not taught much. He mastered Lyly's " Latin Grammar," and was taken through some conversation books like the " Sententiae Pueriles," and not much further, for he puts Latin phrases in the mouth of the schoolmasters, Holofernes in " Love's Labour's Lost," and Hugh Evans in " The Merry Wives of Windsor," and all these phrases are taken word for word either from Lyly's Grammar or from the " Sententiae Pueriles." In " Titus Andronicus," too, one of Tamora's sons, on reading a Latin couplet, says it

353

is a verse of Horace, but he " read it in the grammar," which was probably the author's case. Ben Jonson's sneer was well-founded, Shakespeare had " little Latine and lesse Greeke." His French, as shown in his " Henry V.," was anything but good, and his Italian was probably still slighter.

It was lucky for Shakespeare that his father's increasing poverty withdrew him from school early, and forced him into contact with life. Aubrey says that " when he was a boy he exercised his father's trade [of butcher]; but when he kill'd a calfe he would doe it in high style and make a speech." I daresay young Will flourished about with a knife and made romantic speeches; but I am pretty sure he never killed a calf. Killing a calf is not the easiest part of a butcher's business; nor a task which Shakespeare at any time would have selected. The tradition is simply sufficient to prove that the town folk had already noticed the eager, quick, spouting lad.

Of Shakespeare's life after he left school, say from thirteen to eighteen, we know almost nothing. He probably did odd jobs for his father from time to time; but his father's business seems to have run rapidly from bad to worse; for in 1586 a creditor informed the local Court that John Shakespeare had no goods on which distraint could be levied, and on 6th September of the same year he was deprived of his alderman's gown. During this period of steadily increasing poverty in the house it was only to be expected that young Will Shakespeare would run wild.

The tradition as given by Rowe says that he fell " into low company, and amongst them some that made a frequent practice of deer-stealing engaged him with them more than once in robbing

the park of Sir Thomas Lucy of Charlecot, near
Stratford. For this he was prosecuted by that
gentleman, as he then thought somewhat too
severely, and in order to revenge that ill-usage he
made a ballad upon him."

Another story has it that Sir Thomas Lucy got
a lawyer from Warwick to prosecute the boys, and
that Shakespeare stuck his satirical ballad to the
park gates at Charlecot. The ballad is said to have
been lost, but certain verses were preserved which
fit the circumstances and suit Shakespeare's character so perfectly that I for one am content to
accept them. I give the first and the last verses as
most characteristic:

SONG

" A parliament member, a Justice of peace,
 At home a poor scarecrow, in London an asse,
 If Lowsie is lucy, as some volke miscalle it
 Then Lucy is lowsie, whatever befalle it.
  He thinks himself greate
  Yet an asse in his state,
 We allowe by his ears but with asses to mate.
 If Lucy is lowsie, as some volke miscalle it
 Sing lowsie Lucy whatever befalle it.

" If a juvenile frolick he cannot forgive,
 We'll sing lowsie Lucy as long as we live,
 And Lucy, the lowsie, a libel may calle it
 Sing lowsie Lucy whatever befalle it.
  He thinks himself greate
  Yet an asse in his state,
 We allowe by his ears but with asses to mate.
 If Lucy is lowsie, as some volke miscalle it
 Sing lowsie Lucy, whatever befalle it."

The last verse, so out of keeping in its curious

impartiality with the scurrilous refrain, appears to me to carry its own signature. There can be no doubt that the verses give us young Shakespeare's feelings in the matter. It was probably reading ballads and tales of "Merrie Sherwood" that first inclined him to deer-stealing; and we have already seen from his "Richard II." and "Henry IV." and "Henry V." that he had been led astray by low companions.

In his idle, high-spirited youth, Shakespeare did worse than break bounds and kill deer; he was at a loose end and up to all sorts of mischief. At eighteen he had already courted and won Anne Hathaway, a farmer's daughter of the neighbouring village of Shottery. Anne was nearly eight years older than he was. Her father had died a short time before and left Anne, his eldest daughter, £6 13s. 4d., or, say, £50 of our money. The house at Shottery, now shown as Anne Hathaway's cottage, once formed part of Richard Hathaway's farmhouse, and there, and in the neighbouring lanes, the lovers did their courting. The wooing on Shakespeare's side was nothing but pastime, though it led to marriage.

His marriage is perhaps the first serious mistake that Shakespeare made, and it certainly influenced his whole life. It is needful, therefore, to understand it as accurately as may be, however we may judge it. A man's life, like a great river, may be limpid-pure in the beginning, and when near its source; as it grows and gains strength it is inevitably sullied and stained with earth's soilure.

The ordinary apologists would have us believe that the marriage was happy; they know that Shakespeare was not married in Stratford, and, though a minor, his parents' consent to the marriage

was not obtained; but they persist in talking about
his love for his wife, and his wife's devoted affection
for him. Mr. Halliwell-Phillipps, the bell-wether of
the flock, has gone so far as to tell us how on the
morning of the day he died " his wife, who had
smoothed the pillow beneath his head for the last
time, felt that her right hand was taken from her."
Let us see if there is any foundation for this senti-
mental balderdash. Here are some of the recorded
facts.

In the Bishop of Worcester's register a licence was
issued on 27th November, 1582, authorizing the marriage of William Shakespeare with Anne Whately,
of Temple Grafton. On the very next day in the
register of the same Bishop there is a deed, wherein
Fulk Sandells and John Richardson, farmers of
Shottery, bound themselves in the Bishop's court
under a surety of £40 to free the Bishop of all
liability should a lawful impediment—" by reason
of any pre-contract or consanguinity "—be subse-
quently disclosed to imperil the validity of the marriage, then in contemplation, of William Shakespeare
with Anne Hathaway.

Dryasdust, of course, argues that there is no connection whatever between these two events. He is
able to persuade himself easily that the William
Shakespeare who got a licence to marry Anne
Whately, of Temple Grafton, on 27th November,
1582, is not the same William Shakespeare who is
being forced to marry Anne Hathaway on the next
day by two friends of Anne Hathaway's father.
Yet such a coincidence as two William Shakespeares
seeking to be married by special licence in the same
court at the same moment of time is too extraordinary to be admitted. Besides, why should Sandells and Richardson bind themselves as sureties

in £40 to free the Bishop of liability by reason of any pre-contract if there were no pre-contract? The two William Shakespeares are clearly one and the same person. Sandells was a supervisor of the will of Richard Hathaway, and was described in the will as " my trustie friende and neighbour." He showed himself a trusty friend of the usual sort to his friend's daughter, and when he heard that loose Will Shakespeare was attempting to marry Anne Whately, he forthwith went to the same Bishop's court which had granted the licence, pledged himself and his neighbour, Richardson, as sureties that there was no pre-contract, and so induced the Bishop, who no doubt then learned the unholy circumstances for the first time, to grant a licence in order that the marriage with Anne Hathaway could be celebrated, " with once asking of the bannes," and without the consent of the father of the bridegroom, which was usually required when the bridegroom was a minor.

Clearly Fulk Sandells was a masterful man; young Will Shakespeare was· forced to give up Anne Whately, poor lass, and marry Anne Hathaway, much against his will. Like many another man, Shakespeare married at leisure, and repented in hot haste. Six months later a daughter was born to him, and was baptized in the name of Susanna at Stratford Parish Church on the 26th of May, 1583. There was, therefore, an importunate reason for the wedding, as Sandells, no doubt, made the Bishop understand.

The whole story, it seems to me, is in perfect consonance with Shakespeare's impulsive, sensual nature ; is, indeed, an excellent illustration of it. Hot, impatient, idle Will got Anne Hathaway into trouble, was forced to marry her, and at once came to regret. Let us see how far these inferences from plain facts are borne out from his works.

The most important passages seem to have escaped critical scholarship. I have already said that the earliest works of Shakespeare, and the latest, are the most fruitful in details about his private life. In the earliest works he was compelled to use his own experience, having no observation of life to help him, and at the end of his life, having said almost everything he had to say, he again went back to his early experience for little vital facts to lend a colour to the fainter pictures of age. In " The Winter's Tale," a shepherd finds the child Perdita, who has been exposed; one would expect him to stumble on the child by chance and express surprise; but this shepherd of Shakespeare begins to talk in this way:

" I would there were no age between ten and three-and-twenty, or that youth would sleep out the rest; for there is nothing in the between but getting wenches with child, wronging the ancientry, stealing, fighting. Hark you now! Would any but these boiled brains of nineteen and two-and-twenty hunt this weather? "

Now this passage has nothing to do with the play, nor with the shepherd's occupation; nor is it at all characteristic of a shepherd boy. Between ten and three-and-twenty a poor shepherd boy is likely to be kept hard at work; he is not idle and at a loose end like young Shakespeare, free to rob the ancientry, steal, fight, and get wenches with child. That, in my opinion, is Shakespeare's own confession.

Of course, every one has noticed how Shakespeare again and again in his plays declares that a woman should take in marriage an " elder than herself,"

and that intimacy before marriage is productive of
nothing but "barren hate and discord." In
"Twelfth Night" he says:

> "Let still the woman take
> An elder than herself; so wears she to him
> So sways she level in her husband's heart."

In "The Tempest" he writes again:

> "If thou dost break her virgin knot before
> All sanctimonious ceremonies may
> With full and holy rite be minister'd,
> No sweet aspersions shall the heavens let fall
> To make this contract grow; but barren hate,
> Sour-ey'd disdain, and discord, shall bestrew
> The union of your bed with weeds so loathly
> That you shall hate it both."

These admonitions are so far-fetched and so
emphatic that they plainly discover personal feeling.
We have, besides, those quaint, angry passages in
"The Comedy of Errors," to which we have already
drawn attention, which show that the poet detested
his wife.

The known facts, too, all corroborate this inference: let us consider them a little. The first child
was born within six months of the marriage; twins
followed in 1585; a little later Shakespeare left
Stratford not to return to it for eight or nine years,
and when he did return there was probably no
further intimacy with his wife; at any rate, there
were no more children. Yet Shakespeare, one fancies, was fond of children. When his son Hamnet
died his grief showed itself in his work—in "King
John" and in "The Winter's Tale." He was full
of loving kindness to his daughters, too, in later

life; it was his wife alone for whom he had no affection, no forgiveness.

There are other facts which establish this conclusion. While Shakespeare was in London he allowed his wife to suffer the extremes of poverty. Sometime between 1585 and 1595 she appears to have borrowed forty shillings from Thomas Whittington, who had formerly been her father's shepherd. The money was still unpaid when Whittington died, in 1601, and he directed his executor to recover the sum from the poet, and distribute it among the poor of Stratford. Now Shakespeare was rich when he returned to Stratford in 1595, and always generous. He paid off his father's heavy debts; how came it that he did not pay this trifling debt of his wife? The mere fact proves beyond doubt that Shakespeare disliked her and would have nothing to do with her.

Even towards the end of his life, when suffering from increasing weakness, which would have made most men sympathetic, even if it did not induce them completely to relent, Shakespeare shows the same aversion to his poor wife. In 1613, when on a short visit to London, he bought a house in Blackfriars for £140; in the purchase he barred his wife's dower, which proceeding seems even to Dryasdust " pretty conclusive proof that he had the intention of excluding her from the enjoyment of his possessions after his death."

In the first draft of his will Shakespeare did not mention his wife. The apologists explain this by saying that, of course, he had already given her all that she ought to have. But if he loved her he would have mentioned her with affection, if only to console her in her widowhood. Before the will was signed he inserted a bequest to her of his " second-best bed," and the apologists have been at pains to explain that the best bed was kept for guests, and that Shakespeare willed to his wife the bed they both occupied. How inarticulate poor William Shakespeare must have become! Could the master of language find no better word than the contemptuous one? Had he said " our bed " it would have been enough; " the second-best bed " admits of but one interpretation. His daughters, who had lived with their mother, and who had not been afflicted by her jealousy and scolding tongue, begged the dying man to put in some mention of her, and he wrote in that " second-best bed "—bitter to the last. If his own plain words and these inferences, drawn from indisputable facts, are not sufficient, then let us take one fact more, and consider its significance; one fact, so to speak, from the grave.

When Shakespeare died he left some lines to be placed over his tomb. Here they are:

> "Good friend for Jesus sake forbeare
> To Digg the dust enclosed heare.
> Blessed be ye man yt spares thes stones
> And Curst be ye yt moves my bones."

Now, why did Shakespeare make this peculiar request? No one seems to have seen any meaning in it. It looks to me as if Shakespeare wrote the verses in order to prevent his wife being buried with him. He wanted to be free of her in death as in life. At any rate, the fact is that she was not buried with him, but apart from him; he had seen to that. His grave was never opened, though his wife expressed a desire to be buried with him. The man who needs further proofs would not be persuaded though one came from the dead to convince him.

The marriage was an unfortunate one for many reasons, as an enforced marriage is apt to be, even when it is not the marriage of a boy in his teens to a woman some eight years his senior. Shakespeare takes trouble to tell us in " The Comedy of Errors " that his wife was spitefully jealous, and a bitter scold. She must have injured him, poisoned his life with her jealous nagging, or Shakespeare would have forgiven her. There is some excuse for him, if excuse be needed. At the time the marriage must have seemed the wildest folly to him, seething as he was with inordinate conceits. He was wise beyond his years, and yet he had been forced to give hostages to fortune before he had any means of livelihood, before he had even found a place in life. What a position for a poet—penniless, saddled with a jealous wife and three children before he was twenty-one. And this poet was proud, and vain, and in love with all distinctions.

But why did Shakespeare nurse such persistent enmity all through his life to jealous, scolding Anne Hathaway? Shakespeare had wronged her; the keener his moral sense, the more certain he was to blame his partner in the fault, for in no other way could he excuse himself.

It was overpowering sensuality and rashness which had led Shakespeare into the noose, and now there was nothing for it but to cut the rope. He had either to be true to his higher nature or to the conventional view of his duty; he was true to himself and fled to London, and the world is the richer for his decision. The only excuse he ever made is to be found in the sonnet-line:

" Love is too young to know what conscience is."

For my part I do not see that any excuse is

needed: if Shakespeare had married Anne Whately he might never have gone to London or written a play. Shakespeare's hatred of his wife and his regret for having married her were alike foolish. Our brains are seldom the wisest part of us. It was well that he made love to Anne Hathaway; well, too, that he was forced to marry her; well, finally, that he should desert her. I am sorry he treated her badly and left her unsupplied with money; that was needlessly cruel; but it is just the kindliest men who have these extraordinary lapses; Shakespeare's loathing for his wife was measureless, was a part of his own self-esteem, and his self-esteem was founded on snobbish non-essentials for many years, if not, indeed, throughout his life.

There is a tradition preserved by Rowe that before going to London young Shakespeare taught school in the country; it may be; but he did not teach for long, we can be sure, and what he had to teach there were few scholars in the English country then or now capable of learning. Another tradition asserts that he obtained employment as a lawyer's clerk, probably because of the frequent use of legal phrases in his plays. But these apologists all forget that they are speaking of men like themselves, and of times like ours. Politics is the main theme of talk in our day; but in the time of Elizabeth it was rather dangerous to show one's wisdom by criticizing the government: law was then the chief subject of conversation: every educated man was therefore familiar with law and its phraseology, as men are familiar in our day with the jargon of politics.

When did Shakespeare fly to London? Some say when he was twenty-one, as soon as his wife presented him with twins, in 1585. Some say as soon as Sir Thomas Lucy's persecution became intolerable.

Both causes no doubt worked together, and yet another cause, given in "The Two Gentlemen of Verona," was the real *causa causans*. Shakespeare was naturally ambitious; eager to measure himself with the best and try his powers. London was the arena where all great prizes were to be won: Shakespeare strained towards the Court like a greyhound in leash. But when did he go? Again in doubt I take the shepherd's words in "The Winter's Tale" as a guide. Most men would have said from fourteen to twenty was the dangerous age for a youth; but Shakespeare had perhaps a personal reason for the peculiar "ten to twenty-three." He was, no doubt, astoundingly precocious, and probably even at ten he had learned everything of value that the grammar school had to teach, and his thoughts had begun to play truant. Twenty-three, too, is a significant date in his life; in 1587, when he was twenty-three, two companies of actors, under the nominal patronage of the Queen and Lord Leicester, returned to London from a provincial tour, during which they visited Stratford. In Lord Leicester's company were Burbage and Heminge, with whom we know that Shakespeare was closely connected in later life. It seems to me probable that he returned with this company to London, and arrived in London, as he tells us in "The Comedy of Errors," "stiff and weary with long travel," and at once went out to view the town and "peruse the traders."

There is a tradition that when he came to London in 1587 he held horses outside the doors of the theatre. This story was first put about by the compiler of "The Lives of the Poets," in 1753. According to the author the story was related by D'Avenant to Betterton; but Rowe, to whom Betterton must have told it, does not transmit it. Rowe was perhaps right to forget it or leave it out; though the story is not in itself incredible. Such work must have been infinitely distasteful to Shakespeare, but necessity is a hard master, and Greene, who talks of him later as "Shake-scene," also speaks in the same connection of these "grooms." Dr. Johnson's amplified version of the story that Shakespeare organized a service of boys to hold the horses is hardly to be believed. The great Doctor was anything but a poet, or a good judge of the poetic temperament.

The Shakespeares of this world are not apt to take up menial employs, and this one had already shown that he preferred idle musings and parasitic dependence to uncongenial labour. Whoever reads the second scene of the second act of " The Comedy of Errors," will see that Shakespeare, even at the beginning, had an uncommonly good opinion of himself. He plays gentleman from the first, and despises trade; he snubs his servant and will not brook familiarity from him. In " The Two Gentlemen of Verona," he tells us that he left the country and came to London seeking " honour," intending, no doubt, to make a name for himself by his writings. He had probably " Venus and Adonis " in his pocket when he first reached London. This would inspire a poet with the self-confidence which a well-filled purse lends to an ordinary man.

I am inclined to accept Rowe's statement that Shakespeare was received into an actor-company at first in a very mean rank. The parish clerk of Stratford at the end of the seventeenth century used to tell the visitors that Shakespeare entered the playhouse as a servitor; but, however he entered it, it is pretty certain he was not long in a subordinate position.

What manner of man was William Shakespeare

when he first fronted life in London somewhere about 1587? Aubrey tells us that he was " a handsome, well-shap't man, very good company, and of a very readie and pleasant smooth witt." The bust of him in Stratford Church was coloured; it gave him light hazel eyes, and auburn hair and beard. Rowe says of him that " besides the advantages of his witt, he was in himself a good-natured man, of too great sweetness in his manners, and a most agreeable companion."

I picture him to myself very like Swinburne—of middle height or below it, inclined to be stout; the face well-featured, with forehead domed to reverence and quick, pointed chin; a face lighted with hazel-clear vivid eyes and charming with sensuous-full mobile lips that curve easily to kisses or gay ironic laughter; an exceedingly sensitive, eager speaking face that mirrors every fleeting change of emotion. . . .

I can see him talking, talking with extreme fluency in a high tenor voice, the reddish hair flung back from the high forehead, the eyes now dancing, now aflame, every feature quick with the " beating mind."

And such talk—the groundwork of it, so to speak, very intimate-careless; but gemmed with thoughts, diamonded with wit, rhythmic with feeling: don't we know how it ran—" A hundred and fifty tattered prodigals. . . . No eye hath seen such scare-crows, . . . discarded, unjust serving-men, younger sons to younger brothers, revolted tapsters, and ostlers trade-fallen : the cankers of a calm world and a long peace." And after the thought the humour again—" food for powder, food for powder."

Now let us consider some of his other qualities.

In 1592 he published his " Venus and Adonis,"

which he had no doubt written in 1587 or even earlier, for he called it " the first heir of my invention " when he dedicated it to Lord Southampton. This work is to me extremely significant. It is all concerned with the wooing of young Adonis by Venus, an older woman. Now, goddesses have no age, nor do women, as a rule, woo in this sensual fashion. The peculiarities point to personal experience. " I, too," Shakespeare tells us practically, " was wooed by an older woman against my will." He seems to have wished the world to accept this version of his untimely marriage. Young Shakespeare in London was probably a little ashamed of being married to some one whom he could hardly introduce or avow. The apologists who declare that he made money very early in his career give us no explanation of the fact that he never brought his wife or children to London. Wherever we touch Shakespeare's intimate life, we find proof upon proof that he detested his wife and was glad to live without her.

Looked at in this light " Venus and Adonis " is not a very noble thing to have written; but I am dealing with a young poet's nature, and the majority of young poets would like to forget their Anne Hathaway if they could; or, to excuse themselves, put the blame of an ill-sorted union upon the partner to it.

There is a certain weakness, however, shown in the whole story of his marriage; a weakness of character, as well as a weakness of *morale*, which it is impossible to ignore; and there were other weaknesses in Shakespeare, especially a weakness of body which must necessarily have had its correlative delicacies of mind.

I have pointed out in the first part of this book

that sleeplessness was a characteristic of Shakespeare, even in youth; he attributes it to Henry IV. in old age, and to Henry V., a youth at the time, who probably never knew what a sleepless night meant. Shakespeare's *alter ego*, Valentine, in " The Two Gentlemen of Verona," suffers from it, and so do Macbeth and Hamlet, and a dozen other of his chief characters, in particular his impersonations—all of which shows, I think, that from the beginnning the mind of Shakespeare was too strong for his body. As we should say to-day, he was too emotional, and lived on his nerves. I always think of him as a ship over-engined; when the driving-power is working at full speed it shakes the ship to pieces.

One other weakness is marked in him, and that is that he could not drink, could not carry his liquor like a man—to use our accepted phrase. Hamlet thought drinking a custom more honoured in the breach than in the observance; Cassius, Shakespeare's incarnation in "Othello," confessed that he had " poor unhappy brains for drinking": tradition informs us that Shakespeare himself died of a " feavour " from drinking—all of which confirms my opinion that Shakespeare was delicate rather than robust. He was, also, extraordinarily fastidious: in drama after drama he rails against the " greasy " caps and " stinking " breath of the common people. This overstrained disgust suggests to me a certain delicacy of constitution.

But there is still another indication of bodily weakness which in itself would be convincing to those accustomed to read closely; but which would carry little or no weight to the careless. In sonnet 129 Shakespeare tells us of lust and its effects, and the confession seems to me purely personal. Here are four lines of it:

" Enjoy'd no sooner but despised straight;
Past reason hunted; and no sooner had,
Past reason hated, as a swallowed bait,
On purpose laid to make the taker mad."

Now, this is not the ordinary man's experience
of passion and its effects. " Past reason hunted,"
such an one might say, but he would certainly not
go on " No sooner had, Past reason hated." He is
not moved to hate by enjoyment, but to tenderness;
it is your weakling who is physically exhausted by
enjoyment who is moved to hatred. This sonnet
was written by Shakespeare in the prime of manhood at thirty-four or thirty-five at latest.

Shakespeare was probably healthy as a young
man, but intensely sensitive and highly strung; too
finely constituted ever to have been strong. One
notices that he takes no pleasure in fighting; his
heroes are, of course, all " valiant," but he shows no
loving interest in the game of fighting as a game.
In fact, we have already seen that he found no
wonderful phrase for any of the manly virtues; he
was a neuropath and a lover, and not a fighter, even
in youth, or Fulk Sandells might have rued his in-
terference.

The dominating facts to be kept ever in mind
about Shakespeare are that he was delicate in body,
and over-excitable; yielding and irresolute in character; with too great sweetness of manners and inordinately given to the pleasures of love.

How would such a man fare in the world of
London in 1587? It was a wild and wilful age;
eager English spirits were beginning to take a part
in the opening up of the new world; the old, limiting horizons were gone; men dared to think for
themselves and act boldly; ten years before Drake
had sailed round the world—the adventurer was the

characteristic product of the time. In ordinary company a word led to a blow, and the fight was often brought to a fatal conclusion with dagger or sword or both. In those rough days actors were almost outlaws; Ben Jonson is known to have killed two or three men; Marlowe died in a tavern brawl. Courage has always been highly esteemed in England, like gentility and a university training. Shakespeare possessed none of these passports to public favour. He could not shoulder his way through the throng. The wild adventurous life of the time was not to his liking, even in early manhood; from the beginning he preferred " the life removed " and his books; all given over to the " bettering of his mind " he could only have been appreciated at any time by the finer spirits.

Entering the theatre as a servitor he no doubt made such acquaintances as offered themselves, and spent a good deal of his leisure perforce with second-rate actors and writers in common taverns and studied his Bardolph and Pistol, and especially his Falstaff at first hand. Perhaps Marlowe was one of his *ciceroni* in rough company. Shakespeare had almost certainly met Marlowe very early in his career, for he worked with him in the " Third Part of Henry VI.," and his " Richard III." is a conscious imitation of Marlowe, and Marlowe was dissipated enough and wild enough to have shown him the wildest side of life in London in the '80's. It was the very best thing that could have happened to delicate Shakespeare, to come poor and unknown to London, and be soused in common rowdy life like this against his will by sheer necessity; for if left to his own devices he would probably have grown up a bookish poet—a second Coleridge. Fate takes care of her favourites.

It was all in his favour that he should have been forced at first to win his spurs as an actor. He must have been too intelligent, one would think, ever to have brought it far as a mummer; he looked upon the half-art of acting with disdain and disgust, as he tells us in the sonnets, and if in Hamlet he condescends to give advice to actors, it is to admonish them not to outrage the decencies of nature by tearing a passion to tatters. He had at hand a surer ladder to fame than the mummer's art. As soon as he felt his feet in London he set to work adapting plays, and writing plays, while reading his own poetry to all and sundry who would listen, and I have no doubt that patrons of the stage, who were also men of rank, were willing to listen to Shakespeare from the beginning. He was of those who require no introductions.

In 1592, four or five years after his arrival in London, he had already come to the front as a dramatist, or at least as an adapter of plays, for Robert Greene, a scholar and playwright, attacked him in his " Groatsworth of Wit " in this fashion:

" There is an upstart Crow, beautified in our feathers that, with his tiger's heart wrapt in a player's hide, supposes he is as well able to bombast out a blank verse as the best of you, and, being an absolute Johannes factotum, is, in his own conceit, the only Shakescene in a country. Oh, that I might intreat your rare wits to be employed in more profitable courses, and let these apes imitate your past excellence, and never more acquaint them with your admired inventions."

It is plain from this weird appeal that Shakespeare had already made his mark.

There are further proofs of his rapid success. One of Chettle's references to Shakespeare (I take

Chettle to be the original of Falstaff) throws light upon the poet's position in London in these early days. Shortly after Greene had insulted Shakespeare as "Shake-scene" Chettle apologized for the insult in these terms:

"I am as sorry," Chettle wrote, "as if the original fault had beene my fault, because myselfe have seen his (*i. e.,* Shakespeare's) demeanour no less civill than he (is) exelent in the qualitie he professes. Besides, divers of worship have reported his uprightnes of dealing, which argues his honesty, and his facetious grace in writing that aprooves his art."

In 1592, then, Shakespeare was most "civill in demeanour," and had won golden opinions from people of importance.

Actors and poets of that time could not help knowing a good many of the young nobles who came to the theatre and sat round the stage listening to the performances. And Shakespeare, with his aristocratic sympathies and charming sweetness of nature, must have made friends with the greatest ease. Chettle's apology proves that early in his career he had the art or luck to win distinguished patrons who spoke well of him. While still new to town he came to know Lord Southampton, to whom he dedicated "Venus and Adonis"; the fulsome dedication of "Lucrece" to the same nobleman two years later shows that deference had rapidly ripened into affectionate devotion; no wonder Rowe noticed the "too great sweetness in his manners."

Thinking of his intimacy with Southampton on the one hand and Bardolph on the other, one is constrained to say of Shakespeare what Apemantus says of Timon:

The Man Shakespeare

> " The middle of humanity thou never knewest,
> But the extremity of both ends."

In the extremes characters show themselves more clearly than they do in the middle classes; at both ends of society speech and deed are unrestrained. Falstaff and Bardolph and the rest were free of convention by being below it, just as Bassanio and Mercutio were free because they were above it, and made the rules. The young lord did what he pleased, and spoke his mind as plainly as the foot-pad. Life at both ends was the very school for quick, sympathetic Shakespeare. But even in early manhood, as soon as he came to himself and found his work, one other quality is as plain in Shakespeare as even his humour—high impartial intellect with honest ethical judgement. He judges even Falstaff severely, to the point of harshness, indeed; as he judged himself later in Enobarbus. This high critical faculty pervades all his work. But it must not be thought that his conduct was as scrupulous as his principles, or his will as sovereign as his intelligence. That he was a loose-liver while in London is well attested. Contemporary anecdotes generally hit off a man's peculiarities, and the only anecdote of Shakespeare that is known to have been told about him in his lifetime illustrates this master trait of his character. Burbage, we are told, when playing Richard III., arranged with a lady in the audience to visit her after the performance. Shakespeare overheard the rendezvous, anticipated the fellow's visit, and met Burbage on his arrival with the jibe that " William the Conqueror came before Richard III." The lightness is no doubt as characteristic of Shakespeare as the impudent humour.

There is another fact in Shakespeare's life which

throws almost as much light on his character as his marriage. He seems to have come to riches very early and very easily. As we have seen, he was never able to paint a miser, which confirms Jonson's testimony that he was " of an open and free nature." In 1597 he went down to Stratford and bought New Place, then in ruinous condition, but the chief house in the town, for £60; he spent at least as much more between 1597 and 1599 in rebuilding the house and stocking the barns with grain. In 1602 we find that he purchased from William and John Combe, of Stratford, a hundred and seven acres of arable land near the town, for which he paid £320; in 1605, too, he bought for £440 a moiety of the tithes of Stratford for an unexpired term of thirty-one years, which investment seems to have brought him in little except a wearisome lawsuit.

Now how did the poet obtain this thousand pounds or so? English apologists naturally assume that he was a " good business man "; with delicious unconscious irony they one and all picture the man who hated tradesmen as himself a sort of thrifty tradesman-soul—a master of practical life who looked after the pennies from the beginning. These commentators all treat Shakespeare as the Hebrews treated God; they make him in their own likeness. In Shakespeare's case this practice leads to absurdity. Let us take the strongest advocate of the accepted view. Dryasdust is at pains to prove that Shakespeare's emoluments, even as an actor in the '90's, were not likely to have fallen below a hundred a year; but even Dryasdust admits that his large earnings came after 1599, from his shares in the Globe Theatre, and is inclined " to accept the tradition that Shakespeare received from the Earl of Southampton a large gift of money." As Southampton came of age in 1595, he may well out of his riches have helped the man who had dedicated his poems to him with servile adulation. Moreover, the statement is put forward by Rowe, who is certainly more trustworthy than the general run of gossip-mongers, and his account of the matter proves that he did not accept the story with eager credulity, but as one compelled by authority. Here is what he says:

"There is one story so singular in magnificence of this patron of Shakespeare that if I had not been assured that the story was handed down by Sir Wm. D'Avenant, who was probably very well acquainted with his affairs, I should not have ventured to insert that my lord Southampton, at one time, gave him a thousand pounds to enable him to go through with a purchase to which he heard he had a mind. A bounty very great, and very rare at any time, almost equal to that profuse generosity the present age has shown to French dancers and Italian Eunuchs."

It seems to me a great deal more likely that this munificent gift of Southampton was the source of Shakespeare's wealth than that he added coin to coin in saving, careful fashion. It may be said at once that all the evidence we have is in favour of Shakespeare's extravagance, and against his thrift. As we have seen, when studying " The Merchant of Venice," the presumption is that he looked upon saving with contempt, and was himself freehanded to a fault. The Rev. John Ward, who was Vicar of Stratford from 1648 to 1679, tells us " that he spent at the rate of a thousand a year, as I have heard."

It is impossible to deny that Shakespeare got rid of a great deal of money even after his retirement to Stratford; and men accustomed to save are not likely to become prodigal in old age.

Shakespeare's Life

On the 10th March, 1613, Shakespeare bought a house in Blackfriars for £140; the next day he executed another deed, now in the British Museum, which stipulated that £60 of the purchase-money was to remain on mortgage until the following Michaelmas: the money was unpaid at Shakespeare's death, which seems to me to argue a certain carelessness, to say the least of it.

Dryasdust makes out that Shakespeare, in the years from 1600 to 1612, was earning about six hundred a year in the money of the period, or nearly five thousand a year of our money, and yet he was unable or unwilling to pay off a paltry £60.

After passing the last five years of his life in village Stratford, where he could not possibly have found many opportunities of extravagance, he was only able to leave a little more than one year's income. He willed New Place to his elder daughter, Susanna Hall, together with the land, barns, and gardens at and near Stratford (except the tenement in Chapel Lane), and the house in Blackfriars, London, all together equal, at the most, to five or six hundred pounds; and to his younger daughter, Judith, he bequeathed the tenement in Chapel Lane, £150 in money, and another £150 to be paid if she was alive three years after the date of the will. Nine hundred pounds, or so, of the money of the period, would cover all he possessed at death. When we consider these things, it becomes plain, I think, that Shakespeare was extravagant to lavishness even in cautious age. While in London he no doubt earned and was given large sums of money; but he was free-handed and careless, and died far poorer than one would have expected from an ordinarily thrifty man. The loose-liver is usually a spendthrift.

There are worse faults to be laid to his account than lechery and extravagance. Every one who has

read his works with any care must admit that
Shakespeare was a snob of the purest English
water. Aristocratic tastes were natural to him;
inherent, indeed, in the delicate sensitiveness of his
beauty-loving temperament; but he desired the
outward and visible signs of gentility as much as
any podgy millionaire of our time, and stooped as
low to get them as man could stoop. In 1596, his
young son, Hamnet, died at Stratford, and was
buried on 11th August in the parish church. This
event called Shakespeare back to his village, and
while he was there he most probably paid his father's
debts, and certainly tried to acquire for himself and
his successors the position of gentlefolk. He induced his father to make application to the College
of Heralds for a coat of arms, on the ground not
only that his father was a man of substance, but
that he had also married into a "worshipful"
family. The draft grant of arms was not executed
at the time. It may have been that the father's
pecuniary position became known to the College, or
perhaps the profession of the son created difficulties;
but in any case nothing was done for some time.
In 1597, however, the Earl of Essex became Earl
Marshal and Chief of the Heralds' College, and the
scholar and antiquary, William Camden, joined the
College as Clarenceux King of Arms. Shakespeare
must have been known to the Earl of Essex, who was
an intimate friend of the Earl of Southampton; he
was indeed almost certainly a friend and admirer of
Essex. The Shakespeares' second application to be
admitted to the status of gentlefolk took a new form.
They asserted roundly that the coat as set out in
the draft of 1596 had been assigned to John Shakespeare while he was bailiff, and the heralds were
asked to give him a "recognition" of it. At the

same time John Shakespeare asked for permission to quarter on his "ancient coat of arms" that of the Ardens of Wilmscote, his wife's family. But this was going too far, even for a friend of Essex. To grant such a request might have got the College into trouble with the influential Warwickshire family of Arden, and so it was refused; but the grant was "recognized," and Shakespeare's peculiar ambition was satisfied.

Every single incident in his life bears out what we have learned from his works. In all his writings he praises lords and gentlemen, and runs down the citizens and common people, and in his life he spent some years, a good deal of trouble, and many impudent lies in getting for his father a grant of arms and recognition as a gentleman—a very pitiful ambition, but peculiarly English. Shakespeare, one fancies, was a gentleman by nature, and a good deal more.

But his snobbishness had other worse results. Partly because of it he never got to know the middle classes in England. True, even in his time they were excessively Puritanical, which quality hedged them off, so to speak, from the playwright-poet. With his usual gentleness or timidity, Shakespeare never tells us directly what he thought of the Puritans, but his half-averted, contemptuous glance at them in passing, is very significant. Angelo, the would-be Puritan ruler, was a "false seemer," Malvolio was a "chough." The peculiar virtues of the English middle class, its courage and sheepishness; its good conduct and respect for duties; its religious sense and cocksure narrow-mindedness, held no attraction for Shakespeare, and, armoured in snobbishness, he utterly missed what a knowledge of the middle classes might have given him.

Let us take one instance of his loss. Though he lived in an age of fanaticism, he never drew a fanatic or reformer, never conceived a man as swimming against the stream of his time. He had but a vague conception of the few spirits in each age who lead humanity to new and higher ideals; he could not understand a Christ or a Mahomet, and it seems as if he took but small interest in Jeanne d'Arc, the noblest being that came within the ken of his art. For even if we admit that he did not write the first part of "Henry VI.," it is certain that it passed through his hands, and that in his youth, at any rate, he saw nothing to correct in that vile and stupid libel on the greatest of women. Even the English fanatic escaped his intelligence; his Jack Cade, as I have already noticed, is a wretched caricature; no Cade moves his fellows save by appealing to the best in them, to their sense of justice, or what they take for justice. The Cade who will wheedle men for his own gross ambitions may make a few dupes, but not thousands of devoted followers. These elementary truths Shakespeare never understood. Yet how much greater he would have been had he understood them; had he studied even one Puritan lovingly and depicted him sympathetically. For the fanatic is one of the hinges which swing the door of the modern world. Shakespeare's "universal sympathy"—to quote Coleridge—did not include the plainly-clad tub-thumper who dared to accuse him to his face of serving the Babylonish Whore. Shakespeare sneered at the Puritan instead of studying him; with the result that he belongs rather to the Renaissance than to the modern world, in spite even of his Hamlet. The best of a Wordsworth or a Turgenief is outside him; he would never have understood a Mariana or a Bazarof, and the noble faith of the sonnet to " Toussaint l'Ouverture " was quite beyond him. He could never have written :

> " Thou hast left behind
> Powers that will work for thee, air, earth and skies;
> There's not a breathing of the common wind
> That will forget thee; thou hast great allies;
> Thy friends are exultations, agonies,
> And love, and man's unconquerable mind."

It is time to speak of him frankly; he was gentle, and witty; gay, and sweet-mannered, very studious, too, and fair of mind; but at the same time he was weak in body and irresolute, hasty and wordy, and took habitually the easiest way out of difficulties; he was ill-endowed in the virile virtues and virile vices. When he showed arrogance it was always of intellect and not of character; he was a parasite by nature. But none of these faults would have brought him to ruin; he was snared again in full manhood by his master-quality, his overpowering sensuality, and thrown in the mire.

CHAPTER XV

SHAKESPEARE'S life seems to fall sharply into two halves. Till he met Mistress Fitton, about 1597, he must have been happy and well content, I think, in spite of his deep underlying melancholy. According to my reckoning he had been in London about ten years, and no man has ever done so much in the time and been so successful even as the world counts success. He had not only written the early poems and the early plays, but in the last three or four years half-a-dozen masterpieces: " A Midsummer Night's Dream," " Romeo and Juliet," " Richard II.," " King John," " The Merchant of Venice," " The Two Parts of Henry IV." At thirty-three he was already the greatest poet and dramatist of whom Time holds any record.

Southampton's bounty had given him ease, and allowed him to discharge his father's debts, and place his dearly loved mother in a position of comfort in the best house in Stratford.

He had troops of friends, we may be sure, for there was no gentler, gayer, kindlier creature in all London, and he set store by friendship. Ten years before he had neither money, place, nor position; now he had all these, and was known even at Court. The Queen had been kind to him. He ended the epilogue to the " Second Part of Henry IV.," which he had just finished, by kneeling " to pray for the Queen." Essex or Southampton had no doubt brought his work to Elizabeth's notice: she had approved his "Falstaff" and encouraged him to continue. Of all his successes, this royal recognition was surely the one which pleased him most. He was at the topmost height of happy hours when he met the woman who was to change the world for him.

In the lives of great men the typical tragedies are likely to repeat themselves. Socrates was condemned to drain many a poisoned cup before he was given the bowl of hemlock: Shakespeare had come to grief with many women before he fell with Mary Fitton. It was his ungovernable sensuality which drove him in youth to his untimely and unhappy marriage; it was his ungovernable sensuality, too, which in his maturity led him to worship Mary Fitton, and threw him into those twelve years of bondage to earthy, coarse service which he regretted so bitterly when the passion-fever had burned itself out.

One can easily guess how he came to know the self-willed and wild-living maid-of-honour. Like many of the courtiers, Mistress Fitton affected the society of the players. Kemp, the clown of his company, knew her, and dedicated a book to her rather familiarly. I have always thought that Shakespeare resented Kemp's intimacy with Mistress Fitton, for when Hamlet advises the players to prevent the clown from gagging, he adds, with a snarl of personal spite:

"a most pitiful ambition in the fool that uses it."

Mary Fitton's position, her proud, dark beauty, her daring of speech and deed took Shakespeare by storm. She was his complement in every failing; her strength matched his weakness; her resolution

383

his hesitation, her boldness his timidity; besides, she was of rank and place, and out of pure snobbery he felt himself her inferior. He forgot that humble worship was not the way to win a high-spirited girl. He loved her so abjectly that he lost her; and it was undoubtedly his overpowering sensuality and snobbishness which brought him to his knees, and his love to ruin. He could not even keep her after winning her; desire blinded him. His love was too fleshly-coarse to be perfect. He would not see that Mary Fitton was not a wanton through mere lust. As soon as her fancy was touched she gave herself; but she was true to the new lover for the time. We know that she bore a son to Pembroke and two daughters to Sir Richard Leveson. Her slips with these men wounded Shakespeare's vanity, and he persisted in underrating her. Let us probe to the root of the secret sore. Here is a page of " Troilus and Cressida," a page from that terrible fourth scene of the fourth act, when Troilus, having to part with Cressida, warns her against the Greeks and their proficience in the arts of love:

> " *Troilus.* I cannot sing
> Nor heel the high lavolt, nor sweeten talk,
> Nor play at subtle games; fair virtues all,
> To which the Grecians are most prompt and pregnant:
> But I can tell thee in each grace of these
> There lurks a still and dumb-discoursive devil
> That tempts most cunningly: but be not tempted.
> *Cressida.* Do you think I will?
> *Troilus. No: but something may be done that we will not.*"

The first lines show that poor Shakespeare often felt out of it at Court. The suggestion I have put in italics, is unspeakable. Shakespeare made use of every sensual bait in hope of winning his love, liming

384

himself and not the woman. His vanity was so inordinate that instead of saying to himself, " it's natural that a high-born girl of nineteen should prefer a great lord of her own age to a poor poet of thirty-four ": he strives to persuade himself and us that Mary Fitton was won away from him by " subtle games," and in his rage of wounded vanity he wrote that tremendous libel on her, which he put in the mouth of Ulysses:

> " Fie, fie upon her!
> There's language in her eye, her cheek, her lip,
> Nay, her foot speaks; her wanton spirits look out
> At every joint and motive of her body.
> O, these encounterers, so glib of tongue,
> That give accosting welcome ere it comes,
> And wide unclasp the tables of their thoughts
> To every ticklish reader! set them down
> For sluttish spoils of opportunity
> And daughters of the game."

His tortured sensuality caricatures his mistress: that " ticklish reader " reveals him; Mary Fitton was finer than his portraits; we want her soul, and do not get it from him even in Cleopatra. It was the consciousness of his own age and physical inferiority that drove him to jealous denigration of his mistress.

Mary Fitton did not beguile Shakespeare to " the very heart of loss," as he cried; but to the innermost shrine of the temple of Fame. It was this absolute abandonment to passion which made Shakespeare the supreme poet. If it had not been for his excessive sensuality, and his mad passion for his " gipsy," we should never have had from him " Hamlet," " Macbeth," " Othello," " Antony and Cleopatra," or " Lear." He would still have been a poet and a dramatic writer of the first rank; but he would not have stood alone above all others: he would not have been Shakespeare.

His passion for Mary Fitton lasted some twelve years. Again and again he lived golden hours with her like those Cleopatra boasted of and regretted. Life is wasted quickly in such orgasms of passion; lust whipped to madness by jealousy. Mary Fitton was the only woman Shakespeare ever loved, or at least, the only woman he loved with such intensity as to influence his art. She was Rosaline, Cressid, Cleopatra, and the " dark lady " of the sonnets. All his other women are parts of her or reflections of her, as all his heroes are sides of Hamlet, or reflections of him. Portia is the first full-length sketch of Mary Fitton, taken at a distance: Beatrice and Rosalind are mere reflections of her high spirits, her aristocratic pride and charm: her strength and resolution are incarnate in Lady Macbeth. Ophelia, Desdemona, Cordelia, are but abstract longings for purity and constancy called into life by his mistress's faithlessness and passion.

Shakespeare admired Mary Fitton as intensely as he desired her, yet he could not be faithful to her for the dozen years his passion lasted. Love and her soft hours drew him irresistibly again and again: he was the ready spoil of opportunity. Here is one instance: it was his custom, Aubrey tells us, to visit Stratford every year, probably every summer: on his way he was accustomed to put up at an inn in Oxford, kept by John D'Avenant. Mrs. D'Avenant, we are told, was " a very beautiful woman, and of a very good witt and of conversation extremely agreeable." No doubt Shakespeare made up to her from the first. Her second son, William, who afterwards became the celebrated playwright, was born in March, 1605, and according to a tradi-

tion long current in Oxford, Shakespeare was his
father. In later life Sir William D'Avenant himself
was " contented enough to be thought his (Shakespeare's) son." There is every reason to accept the
story as it has been handed down. Shakespeare, as
Troilus, brags of his constancy; talks of himself as
" plain and true "; but it was all boasting: from
eighteen to forty-five he was as inconstant as the
wind, and gave himself to all the " subtle games "
of love with absolute abandonment, till his health
broke under the strain.

In several of the Sonnets, notably in 36 and 37,
Shakespeare tells us that he was " poor and despised
. . . made lame by fortune's dearest spite." He
will not even have his friend's name coupled with
his for fear lest his " bewailed guilt " should do him
shame:

> " Let me confess that we two must be twain,
> Although our undivided loves are one:
> So shall those blots that do with me remain
> Without thy help, by me be borne alone. . . ."

Spalding and other critics believe that this " guilt "
of Shakespeare refers to his profession as an actor,
but that stain should not prevent Lord Herbert
from honouring him with " public kindness." It is
clear, I think, from the words themselves, that the
guilt refers to the fact that both Herbert and he
were in love with the same woman. Jonson, as we
have seen, had poked fun at their connection, and
this is how Shakespeare tries to take the sting out
of the sneer.

Shakespeare had many of the weaknesses of the
neurotic and artistic temperament, but he had assuredly the noblest virtues of it: he was true to his
friends, and more than generous to their merits.

387

If his ethical conscience was faulty, his aesthetical conscience was of the very highest. Whenever we find him in close relations with his contemporaries we are struck with his kindness and high impartial intelligence. Were they his rivals, he found the perfect word for their merits and shortcomings. How can one better praise Chapman than by talking of

" The proud full sail of his great verse "?

How can one touch his defect more lightly than by hinting that his learning needed feathers to lift it from the ground? And if Shakespeare was fair even to his rivals, his friends could always reckon on his goodwill and his unwearied service. All his fine qualities came out when as an elder he met churlish Ben Jonson. Jonson did not influence him as much as Marlowe had influenced him; but these were the two greatest living men with whom he was brought into close contact, and his relations with Jonson show him as in a glass. Rowe has a characteristic story which must not be forgotten:

" His acquaintance with Ben Jonson began with a remarkable piece of humanity and good-nature; Mr. Jonson, who was at that time altogether unknown, had offered one of his playes to the Players, in order to have it acted; but the persons into whose hands it was put, after having turned it carelessly and superciliously over, were just upon returning it to him, with an ill-natured answer, that it would be of no service to their company, when Shakespeare luckily cast his eye upon it, and found something so well in it as to encourage him to read through and afterwards to recommend Ben Jonson and his writings to the publick. After this they were professed friends; though I don't know whether the other ever made him an equal return of gentleness and sincerity. Ben was naturally proud and indolent,

388

and in the days of his reputation did so far take upon him the premier in witt that he could not but look with an evil eye upon anyone that seemed to stand in competition with him. And if at times he has affected to commend him, it has always been with some reserve, insinuating his incorrectness, a careless manner of writing and a want of judgment; the praise of seldom altering or blotting out what he writt which was given him by the players over the first publish of his works after his death was what Jonson could not bear. . . ."

The story reads exactly like the story of Goethe and Schiller. It was Schiller who held aloof and was full of fault-finding criticism: it was Goethe who made all the advances and did all the kindnesses. It was Goethe who obtained for Schiller that place as professor of history at Jena which gave Schiller the leisure needed for his dramatic work. It is always the greater who gives and forgives.

I believe, of course, too, in the traditional account of the unforgettable evenings at the Mermaid. "Many were the wit-combats," wrote Fuller of Shakespeare in his "Worthies" (1662), "betwixt him and Ben Jonson, which too I behold like a Spanish great galleon and an English man-of-war. Master Jonson (like the former) was built far higher in learning, solid but slow in his performances. Shakespeare, with the English man-of-war, lesser in bulk, but lighter in sailing, could turn with all sides, tack about, and take advantage of all winds by the quickness of his wit and invention."

It was natural for the onlooker to compare Ben Jonson and his "mountainous belly" to some Spanish galleon, and Shakespeare, with his quicker wit, to the more active English ship. It was Jonson's great size—a quality which has always been too highly esteemed in England—his domineering temper and desperate personal courage that induced the gossip to even him with Shakespeare.

Beaumont described these meetings, too, in his poetical letter to his friend Jonson:

> " What things have we seen
> Done at the Mermaid? Heard words that have been
> So nimble and so full of subtle flame,
> As if that every one from whence they came
> Had meant to put his whole wit in a jest,
> And had resolved to live a fool the rest
> Of his dull life."

In one respect at least the two men were antitheses. Jonson was exceedingly combative and quarrelsome, and seems to have taken a chief part in all the bitter disputes of his time between actors and men of letters. He killed one actor in a duel and attacked Marston and Dekker in " The Poetaster "; they replied to him in the " Satiromastix." More than once he criticized Shakespeare's writings; more than once jibed at Shakespeare, unfairly trying to wound him; but Shakespeare would not retort. It is to Jonson's credit that though he found fault with Shakespeare's " Julius Caesar " and " Pericles," he yet wrote of him in the " Poetaster " as a peacemaker, and, under the name of Virgil, honoured him as the greatest master of poetry.

Tradition gives us one witty story about the relations between the pair which seems to me extraordinarily characteristic. Shakespeare was godfather to one of Ben's children, and after the christening, being in a deep study, Jonson came to cheer him up, and asked him why he was so melancholy. " No, faith, Ben," says he; " not I, but I have been considering a great while what should be the fittest gift for me to bestow upon my godchild and I have

resolved at last." " I pr'ythee, what? " says he.
" I' faith, Ben, I'll e'en give him a dozen good Lattin
spoons, and thou shalt translate them." Lattin, as
everybody knows, was a mixed metal resembling
brass: the play upon words and sly fun poked at
Jonson's scholarship are in Shakespeare's best
manner. The story must be regarded as Shakespeare's answer to Jonson's sneer that he had " little
Latine and lesse Greeke."

Through the mist of tradition and more or less
uncertain references in his poetry, one sees that he
had come, probably through Southampton, to admire
Essex, and the fall and execution of Essex had an
immense effect upon him. It is certain, I think, that
the noble speech on mercy put into Portia's mouth
in " The Merchant of Venice," was primarily an
appeal to Elizabeth for Essex or for Southampton.
It is plainly addressed to the Queen, and not to a
Jew pariah:

> " . . . It becomes
> The throned monarch better than his crown;
> His sceptrè shows the force of temporal power,
> The attribute to awe and majesty,
> Wherein doth sit the dread and fear of kings;
> But mercy is above this scepter'd sway,
> It is enthroned in the heart of kings.
> It is an attribute of God Himself,
> And earthly power doth then show likest God's,
> When Mercy seasons Justice."

All this must have seemed the veriest irony when
addressed to an outcast Jew. It was clearly intended
as an appeal to Elizabeth, and shows how far gentle
Shakespeare would venture in defence of a friend.
Like a woman, he gained a certain courage through
his affections.

I feel convinced that he resented the condemnation of Essex and the imprisonment of Southampton very bitterly, for though he had praised Elizabeth in his salad days again and again, talked about her in " A Midsummer Night's Dream " as a " fair vestal throned by the west "; walking in " maiden meditation, fancy-free "; yet, when she died, he could not be induced to write one word about her. His silence was noticed, and Chettle challenged him to write in praise of the dead sovereign, because she had been kind to him; but he would not: he had come to dislike the harsh nature of Elizabeth, and he detested her ruthless cruelties. Like a woman, he found it difficult to forgive one who had injured those he loved.

Now that I have discussed at some length Shakespeare's character, its powers and its weaknesses, let us for a moment consider his intellect. All sorts and conditions of men talk of it in superlatives; but that does not help us much. It is as easy to sit in Shakespeare's brain and think from there, as it is from Balzac's. If we have read Shakespeare rightly, his intelligence was peculiarly self-centred; he was wise mainly through self-knowledge, and not, as is commonly supposed, through knowledge of others and observation; he was assuredly anything but worldly-wise. Take one little point. In nearly every play he discovers an intense love of music and of flowers; but he never tells you anything about the music he loves, and he only mentions a dozen flowers in all his works. True, he finds exquisite phrases for his favourites; but he only seems to have noticed or known the commonest. His knowledge of birds and beasts is similarly limited. But when Bacon praises flowers he shows at once the naturalist's gift of observation; he mentions hundreds of different kinds, enumerating them month by month; in April alone he names as many as Shakespeare has mentioned in all his writings. He used his eyes to study things outside himself, and memory to recall them; but Shakespeare's eyes were turned inward; he knew little of the world outside himself.

Shakespeare's knowledge of men and women has been overrated. With all his sensuality he only knew one woman, Mary Fitton, though he knew her in every mood, and only one man, himself, profoundly apprehended in every accident and moment of growth.

He could not construct plays or invent stories, though he selected good ones with considerable certainty. He often enriched the characters, seldom or never the incidents; even the characters he creates are usually sides of himself, or humorous masks without a soul. He must have heard of the statesman Burleigh often enough; but nowhere does he portray him; no hint in his works of Drake, or Raleigh, or Elizabeth, or Sidney. He has no care either for novelties; he never mentions forks or even tobacco or potatoes. A student by nature if ever there was one, all intent, as he tells us, on bettering his mind, he passes through Oxford a hundred times and never even mentions the schools: Oxford men had disgusted him with their *alma mater*.

The utmost reach of this self-student is extraordinary; the main puzzle of life is hidden from us as from him; but his word on it is deeper than most of ours, though we have had three centuries in which to climb above him.

> " Men must abide
> Their going hence even as their coming hither.
> Ripeness is all."

And if it be said that the men of the Renaissance occupied themselves more with such questions than we do, and therefore show better in relation to them, let us take another phrase which has always seemed to me of extraordinary insight. Antony has beaten Caesar, and returns to Cleopatra, who greets him with the astounding words:

> " Lord of lords,
> O, infinite virtue, com'st thou smiling from
> The world's great snare uncaught? "

This is all more or less appropriate in the mouth of Cleopatra; but it is to me Shakespeare's own comment on life; he is conscious of his failure; he has said to himself: " if I, Shakespeare, have failed, it is because every one fails; life's handicap searches out every weakness; to go through life as a conqueror would require ' infinite virtue.' " This is perhaps the furthest throw of Shakespeare's thought.

But his worldly wisdom is to seek. After he had been betrayed by Lord Herbert he raves of man's ingratitude, in play after play. Of course men are ungrateful; it is only the rarest and noblest natures who can feel thankful for help without any injury to vanity. The majority of men love their inferiors, those whom they help; to give flatters self-esteem; but they hate their superiors, and lend to the word " patron " an intolerable smirk of condescension. Shakespeare should have understood that at thirty.

When his vanity was injured, his blindness was almost inconceivable. He should have seen Mary Fitton as she was and given us a deathless-true portrait of her; but the noble side of her, the soul-side a lover should have cherished, is not even suggested. He deserves to lose her, seeking only the common, careless of the " silent, silver lights " she could have shown him. He was just as blind with his wife; she had been unwillingly the ladder to his advancement; he should have forgiven her on that ground, if not on a higher.

He was inordinately vain and self-centred. He talked incontinently, as he himself assures us, and as Ben Jonson complains. He was exceedingly quick and witty and impatient. His language shows his speed of thought; again and again the images tumble over each other, and the mere music of his verse is breathlessly rapid, just as the movement of Tennyson's verse is extremely slow.

More than once in his works I have shown how, at the crisis of fate, he jumps to conclusions like a woman. He seems often to have felt the faults of his own haste. His Othello says:

" How poor are they that have not patience."

With this speed of thought and wealth of language and of wit, he naturally loved to show off in conversation; but as he wished to get on and make a figure in the world, he should have talked less and encouraged his patrons to show off. Poor heedless, witty, charming Shakespeare! One threat which he used again and again, discovers all his world-blindness to me. Gravely, in sonnet 140, he warns Mary Fitton that she had better not provoke him or he will write the truth about her—just as if the maid of honour who could bear bastard after bastard, while living at court, cared one straw what poor Shakespeare might say or write or sing of her. And Hamlet runs to the same weapon: he praises the players to Polonius as

" Brief chronicles of the time; after your death you

were better have a bad epitaph than their ill report while you live."

It is all untrue; actors were then, as now, only mummers without judgement. Shakespeare was thinking of himself, the dramatist-poet, who was indeed a chronicle of the time; but the courtier Lord Polonius would not care a dam for a rhymester's praise or blame. Posthumus, too, will write against the wantons he dislikes. Shakespeare's weapon of offence was his pen; but though he threatened, he seldom used it maliciously; he was indeed a " harmless opposite," too full of the milk of human kindness to do injury to any man. But these instances of misapprehension in the simple things of life, show us that gentle Shakespeare is no trustworthy guide through this rough all-hating world.

The time has now come for me to consider how Shakespeare was treated by the men of his own time, and how this treatment affected his character. The commentators, of course, all present him as walking through life as a sort of uncrowned king, fêted and reverenced on all sides during his residence in London, and in the fullness of years and honours retiring to Stratford to live out the remainder of his days in the bosom of his family as " a prosperous country gentleman," to use Dowden's unhappy phrase. As I have already shown, his works give the lie to this flattering fiction, which in all parts is of course absolutely incredible. It is your Tennyson, who is of his time and in perfect sympathy with it; Tennyson, with his May Queens, prig heroes and syrupy creed, who passes through life as a conqueror, and after death is borne in state to rest in the great Abbey.

The Shakespeares, not being of an age, but for

all time, have another guess sort of reception. From the moment young Will came to London, he was treated as an upstart, without gentle birth or college training: to Greene he was "Maister of Artes in Neither University." He won through, and did his work; but he never could take root in life; his children perished out of the land. He was in high company on sufferance. On the stage he met the highest, Essex, Pembroke, Southampton, on terms of equality; but at court he stood among the menials and was despitefully treated. Let no one misunderstand me: I should delight in painting the other picture if there were any truth in it: I should have joyed in showing how the English aristocracy for this once threw off their senseless pride and hailed the greatest of men at least as an equal. Frederic the Great would have done this, for he put Voltaire at his own table, and told his astonished chamberlains that "privileged spirits rank with sovereigns." Such wisdom was altogether above the English aristocracy of that or any time. Yet they might have arisen above the common in this one instance. For Shakespeare had not only supreme genius to commend him, but all the graces of manner, all the sweetness of disposition, all the exquisite courtesies of speech that go to ensure social success. His imperial intelligence, however, was too heavy a handicap. Men resent superiority at all times, and there is nothing your aristocrat so much dislikes as intellectual superiority, and especially intellect that is not hall-marked and accredited: the Southamptons and the Pembrokes must have found Shakespeare's insight and impartiality intolerable. It was Ben Jonson whom Pembroke made Poet Laureate; it was Chapman the learned, and not Shakespeare, who was regarded with reverence. How could these gen-

tlemen appreciate Shakespeare when it was his
" Venus and Adonis " and his " Lucrece " that they
chiefly admired? " Venus and Adonis " went through
seven editions in Shakespeare's lifetime, while
" Othello " was not thought worthy of type till the
author had been dead six years.

But badly as the aristocrats treated Shakespeare
they yet treated him better than any other class.
The shopkeepers in England are infinitely further
removed from art or poetry than the nobles; now
as in the time of Elizabeth they care infinitely more
for beef and beer and broadcloth than for any
spiritual enjoyment; while the masses of the people
prefer a dog-fight to any masterpiece in art or
letters.

Some will say that Shakespeare was perhaps condemned for dissolute living, and did not come to
honour because of his shortcomings in character.
Such a judgement misapprehends life altogether.
Had Shakespeare's character been as high as his
intellect he would not have been left contemptuously on one side; he would have been hated and
persecuted, pilloried or thrown into prison as Bunyan
was. It was his dissolute life that commended him
to the liking of the loose-living Pembroke and Essex.
Pembroke, we know from Clarendon, was " immod-
erately given to women." Four maids of honour,
we learn, were *enceintes* to Essex at the same time.
Shakespeare was hardly as dissolute as his noble
patrons. The truth was they could not understand
his genius; they had no measure wherewith to
measure it, for no one can see above his own head;
and so they treated him with much the same con-
descending familiarity that nobles nowadays show to
a tenor or a ballet dancer. In March, 1604, after

he had written " Hamlet " and " Macbeth," Shakespeare and some other actors walked from the Tower of London to Westminster in the procession which accompanied King James on his formal entry into London. Each of the actors received four and a half yards of scarlet cloth to wear as a cloak on the occasion. The scarlet cloak to Shakespeare must have been a sort of Nessus' shirt, or crown of thorns —the livery of derision.

Shakespeare, who measured both enemies and friends fairly, measured himself fairly, too. He usually praises his impersonations: Hamlet is " a noble heart "; Brutus " the noblest Roman of them all "; and speaking directly he said of himself in a sonnet:

" I am that I am, and they that level
    At my abuses reckon up their own;
    I may be straight though they themselves be bevel."

He knew his own greatness, none better, and as soon as he reached middle age and began to take stock of himself, he must have felt bitterly that he, the best mind in the world, had not brought it far in the ordinary estimation of men. No wonder he showed passionate sympathy with all those who had failed in life; he could identify himself with Brutus and Antony, and not with the Caesars.

Shakespeare's view of England and of Englishmen was naturally affected by their treatment of him. He is continually spoken of as patriotic, and it is true that he started in youth with an almost lyrical love of country. His words in " Richard II." are often quoted; but they were written before he had any experience or knowledge of men.

399

" *Gaunt.* This royal throne of kings, this scepter'd
isle,

   •   •   •   •   •

This happy breed of men, this little world;
This precious stone set in the silver sea,
Which serves it in the office of a wall,
Or as a moat, defensive to a house,
Against the envy of less happier lands;
This blessed plot, this earth, this realm, this England."

The apologists who rejoice in his patriotism never
realize that Shakespeare did not hold the same
opinions throughout his life; as he grew and developed, his opinions developed with him. In " The
Merchant of Venice " we find that he has already
come to saner vision; when Portia and Nerissa talk
of the English suitor, Portia says:

" You know I say nothing to him; for he understands
not me, nor I him: he hath neither Latin, French, nor
Italian; and you will come into the court and swear that
I have a poor pennyworth in the Englishman. He is a
proper man's picture; but, alas, who can converse with a
dumb show? How oddly he is suited! I think he
bought his doublet in Italy, his round hose in France,
his bonnet in Germany, and his behaviour everywhere."

What super-excellent criticism it all is; true, now
as then, " a proper man's picture but . . . a dumb
show." It proves conclusively that Shakespeare was
able to see around and over the young English
noble of his day. From this time on I find no praise
of England or of Englishmen in any of his works,
except " Henry V.," which was manifestly written
to catch applause on account of its jingoism. In
his maturity Shakespeare saw his countrymen as
they were, and mentioned them chiefly to blame their
love of drinking. Imogen says:

" Hath Britain all the sun that shines? Day, night,
Are they not but in Britain
.   .   .   .   .   .   prithee, think
There's livers out of Britain."

Whoever reads " Coriolanus " carefully will see
how Shakespeare loathed the common Englishman;
there can be no doubt at all that he incorporated
his dislike of him once for all in Caliban. The
qualities he lends Caliban are all characteristic.
Whoever will give him drink is to Caliban a god.
The brutish creature would violate and degrade art
without a scruple, and the soul of him is given in
the phrase that if he got the chance he would people
the world with Calibans. Sometimes one thinks
that if Shakespeare were living to-day he would be
inclined to say that his prediction had come true.

One could have guessed without proof that in
the course of his life Shakespeare, like Goethe,
would rise above that parochial vanity which is so
much belauded as patriotism. He was in love with
the ideal and would not confine it to any country.

There is little to tell of his life after he met Mary
Fitton, or rather the history of his life afterwards
is the history of his passion and jealousy and madness as he himself has told it in the great tragedies.
He appears to have grown fat and scant of breath
when he was about thirty-six or seven. In 1608
his mother died, and " Coriolanus " was written as
a sort of monument to the memory of " the noblest
mother in the world." His intimacy with Mary
Fitton lasted, I feel sure, up to his breakdown in
1608 or thereabouts, and was probably the chief
cause of his infirmity and untimely death.

It only remains for me now to say a word or
two about the end of his life. Rowe says that " the

latter part of his life was spent as all men of good sense will that theirs may be, in ease, retirement, and the conversation of his friends. He had the good fortune to gather an estate equal to his occasion, and, in that, to his wish, and is said to have spent some years before his death at his native Stratford." Rowe, too, tells us that it is a story " well remembered in that country, that he had a particular intimacy with Mr. Combe, an old gentleman noted thereabouts for his wealth and usury; it happened that in a pleasant conversation amongst their common friends Mr. Combe told Shakespeare, in a laughing manner, that he fancied he intended to write his epitaph, if he happened to outlive him; and since he did not know what might be said of him when he was dead, he desired it might be done immediately; upon which Shakespeare gave him these four lines :

> ' Ten in the Hundred lies here ingrav'd
> 'Tis a Hundred to Ten his soul is not sav'd:
> If any Man ask, ' Who lies in this tomb,'
> Oh! ho! quoth the Devil, 'tis my John-a-Combe.'

But the sharpness of the Satyr is said to have stung the man so severely that he never forgave him."

I have given all this because I want the reader to have the sources before him, and because the contempt of tradesman-gain and usury, even at the very end, is so characteristic.

It appears, too, from the Stratford records, and is therefore certain, that as early as the year 1614 a preacher was entertained at New Place—" Item, one quart of sack, and one quart of claret wine, given to a preacher at the New Place, twenty

pence." The Reverend John Ward, who was vicar
of Stratford, in a manuscript memorandum book
written in the year 1664, asserts that " Shakespeare,
Drayton and Ben Jhonson had a merie meeting,
and itt seems drank too hard, for Shakespeare died
of a feavour there contracted."

Shakespeare, as we have seen from " The Tempest," retired to Stratford—" where every third
thought shall be my grave "—in broken health and
in a mood of despairing penitence. I do not suppose the mood lasted long; but the ill-health and
persistent weakness explain to me as nothing else
could his retirement to Stratford. It is incredible
to me that Shakespeare should leave London at
forty-seven or forty-eight years of age, in good
health, and retire to Stratford to live as a " prosperous country gentleman "! What had Stratford
to offer Shakespeare—village Stratford with a mid-
den in the chief street and the charms of the village
usurer's companionship tempered by the ministra-
tions of a wandering tub-thumper?

There is abundant evidence, even in " The Winter's Tale " and " Cymbeline," to prove that the
storm which wrecked Shakespeare's life had not
blown itself out even when these last works were
written, in 1611-12; the jealousy of Leontes is as
wild and sensual as the jealousy of Othello; the
attitude of Posthumus towards women as bitter as
anything to be found in " Troilus and Cressida ":

> " Could I find out
> The woman's part in me! For there's no motion
> That tends to vice in man but I affirm
> It is the woman's part: be it lying, note it,
> The woman's; flattering, hers; deceiving, hers;
> Lust and rank thoughts, hers, hers; revenges, hers;
> Ambitions, covetings, change of prides, disdain,

Nice longing, slanders, mutability,
All faults that may be named, nay, that hell knows,
Why, hers, in part or all, but rather all;
For even to vice
They are not constant, but are changing still
One vice, but of a minute old, for one
Not half so old as that."

The truth is, that the passions of lust and jealousy
and rage had at length worn out Shakespeare's
strength, and after trying in vain to win to serenity
in "The Tempest," he crept home to Stratford to
die.

In his native air, I imagine, his health gradually
improved; but he was never strong enough to venture back to residence in London. He probably
returned once or twice for a short visit, and during
his absence his pious daughter, Mrs. Hall, entertained the wandering preacher in New Place.

As Shakespeare grew stronger he no doubt talked
with Combe, the usurer, for want of any one better.

It is probable, too, that on one of his visits to
London he took up Fletcher's "Henry VIII." and
wrote in some scenes for him and touched up others,
or Fletcher may have visited him in Stratford and
there have begged his help.

His youngest daughter, Judith, was married early
in 1616; it seems probable to me that this was the
occasion of the visit of Jonson and Drayton to
Stratford. No doubt Shakespeare was delighted to
meet them, talked as few men ever talked before
or since, and probably drank too much with those
"poor unhappy brains for drinking" which his
Cassius deplored. Thus fanned, the weak flame of
his life wasted quickly and guttered out. It is all
comprehensible enough, and more than likely, that
the greatest man in the world, after the boredom of

solitary years spent in Stratford, died through a
merry meeting with his friends; in his joy and
excitement he drank a glass or so of wine, which
brought on a fever. It is all true, true to character,
and pitiful beyond words.

Shakespeare to me is the perfect type of the
artist, and the artist is gradually coming to his
proper place in the world's esteem. In the introduction to one of his "Lives," Plutarch apologizes for
writing about a painter, a mere artist, instead of
about some statesman or general, who would be a
worthy object of ambition for a well-born youth.
But since Plutarch's time our view of the relative
merits of men has changed and developed: to-day we
put the artist higher even than the saint. Indeed, it
seems to us that the hero or statesman, or saint,
only ranks in proportion to the artist-faculty he
may possess. The winning of a battle is not enough
to engage all our admiration; it must be won by an
artist. In every department of life this faculty is
beginning to be appreciated as the finest possession
of humanity, and Shakespeare was an almost perfect
example of the self-conscious artist.

People talk as if his masterpieces were produced
at haphazard or by unconscious fruition; but masterpieces are not brought forth in this happy-go-
lucky fashion. They are of the sort that only come
to flower with perfect tendance. Even if we did not
know that Shakespeare corrected his finest verses
again and again with critical care, we should have
to assume it. But we know that he spared no pains
to better his finer inspirations, and he has told us in
a sonnet how anxiously he thought about his art
and the art of his rivals:

"Desiring this man's art, and that man's scope
With what I most enjoy contented least."

405

The Man Shakespeare

He has all the qualities and all the shortcomings of the reflective, humane, sensuous artist temperament, intensified by the fact that he had not had the advantage of a middle-class training.

In a dozen ways our Puritan discipline and the rubs and buffets one gets in this work-a-day world where money is more highly esteemed than birth or sainthood or genius, have brought us beyond Shakespeare in knowledge of men and things. The courage of the Puritan, his self-denial and self-control, have taught us invaluable lessons; Puritanism tempered character as steel is tempered with fire and ice, and the necessity of getting one's bread, not as a parasite, but as a fighter, has had just as important results on character. Shakespeare is no longer an ideal to us; no single man can now fill our mental horizon; we can see around and above the greatest of the past: the overman of to-day is only on the next round of the ladder, and our children will smile at the fatuity of his conceit.

But if we can no longer worship Shakespeare, it is impossible not to honour him, impossible not to love him. All men—Spenser as well as Jonson—found him gentle and witty, gay and generous. He was always willing to touch up this man's play or write in an act for that one. He never said a bitter or cruel word about any man. Compare him with Dante or even with Goethe, and you shall find him vastly superior to either of them in loving-kindness. He was more contemptuously treated in life than even Dante, and yet he never fell away to bitterness as Dante did: he complained, it is true; but he never allowed his fairness to be warped; he was of the noblest intellectual temper.

It is impossible not to honour him, for the truth is he had more virtue in him than any other son of man. " By their fruits ye shall know them." He produced more masterpieces than any other writer, and the finest sayings in the world's literature are his. Think of it: Goethe was perfectly equipped; he had a magnificent mind and body and temperament: he was born in the better middle classes; he was well off; splendidly handsome; thoroughly educated; his genius was recognized on all hands when he was in his teens; and it was developed by travel and princely patronage. Yet what did Goethe do in proof of his advantages? " Faust " is the only play he ever wrote that can rank at all with a dozen of Shakespeare's. Poor Shakespeare brought it further in the sixteenth century than even Goethe at full strain could bring it in the nineteenth. I find Shakespeare of surpassing virtue. Cervantes ranks with the greatest because he created Don Quixote and Sancho Panza; but Hamlet and Falstaff are more significant figures, and take Hamlet and Falstaff away from Shakespeare's achievement, and more still remains than any other poet ever produced.

Harvest after harvest Shakespeare brought forth of astounding quality. Yet he was never strong, and he died at fifty-two, and the last six years of his life were wasted with weakness and ill-health. No braver spirit has ever lived. After " Hamlet " and " Antony and Cleopatra " and " Lear " and " Timon " he broke down; yet as soon as he struggled back to sanity, he came to the collar again and dug " The Winter's Tale " out of himself, and " Cymbeline," and seeing they were not his best, took breath, and brought forth " The Tempest "—another masterpiece, though written with a heart of lead and with the death-sweat dank on his forehead. Think of it; the noblest autumn fruit ever produced; all kindly-sweet and warm, bathed so to speak in love's golden sunshine; his last word to men:

> " The rarer action is
> In virtue than in vengeance. . . ."

And then the master of many styles, including the simple, wins to a childlike simplicity, and touches the source of tears:

> " . . . . We are such stuff
> As dreams are made on, and our little life
> Is rounded with a sleep."

True, Shakespeare was not the kind of man Englishmen are accustomed to admire. By a curious irony of fate Jesus was sent to the Jews, the most unworldly soul to the most material of peoples, and Shakespeare to Englishmen, the most gentle sensuous charmer to a masculine, rude race. It may be well for us to learn what infinite virtue lay in that frail, sensual singer.

This dumb struggling world, all in travail between Thought and Being, longs above everything to realize itself and become articulate, and never has it found such width of understanding, such melody of speech, as in this Shakespeare. " I have often said, and will often repeat," writes Goethe, " that the final cause and consummation of all natural and human activity is dramatic poetry." Englishmen do not appear yet to understand what arrogance and what profound wisdom there is in this saying; but in a dull, half conscious way they are beginning dimly to realize that the biggest thing they have done in the world yet is to produce Shakespeare. When I think of his paltry education, his limiting circumstances, the scanty appreciation of his contemporaries, his indifferent health, and recall his stupendous achievement, I am fain to apply to him, as most appropriate, the words he gave to his *alter ego*, Antony, Antony who, like himself, was world-worn and passion-weary:

> " A rarer spirit never
> Did steer humanity; but you, gods, will give us
> Some faults to make us men."

Index

Index

413

Index

Berowne, 161.
Bertillon, M., 6.
Betterton, 365.
Bevis, George, 115.
Bianca, 282.
Birnam Wood, 32.
Biron, 160, 161, 162, 163, 164, 165, 166, 168, 175, 176, 217, 218, 219, 220, 221, 222, 223, 225, 252, 342.
Blackfriars, 361, 377.
Blount, Sir Walter, 88, 89.
Boaden, 201.
Bolingbroke, 65, 67, 68, 70, 71, 72, 74, 75, 81, 82, 251.
Borachio, 206.
Bottom, 143.
Bourbon, 98.
Boyet, 161, 164, 166, 218.
Brabant, 218.
Brabantio, 272.
Brandes, 16, 35, 124, 160, 165, 256, 296, 301, 302.
Bright, 201.
Britain, 401.
Browning, 3.
Brutus, 39, 76, 190, 249, 250, 251, 252, 253, 254, 255, 256, 257, 258, 259, 260, 261, 302, 399.
Bullen, Anne, 338.
Bunyan, 124, 125, 398.
Burbage, 365, 374.
Bushy, 67, 68.
Byron, 124.

Cade, 113, 115, 149, 380.
Cæsar, 124, 251, 253, 254, 255, 256, 257, 258, 276, 299, 300, 303, 305, 306, 307, 308, 309, 310, 313, 314, 315, 316, 317, 394, 399.
Caliban, 346, 350, 401.
Camden, William, 378.
"Campaspe," 243.
Canterbury, Archbishop of, 105.
Capulet, 11, 214.
Carlyle, Thomas, X, XlV, 4, 55, 107, 108, 124.
Cassio, 275, 276, 277, 279, 282, 285.

Cassius, 251, 252, 253, 257, 258, 259, 369, 404.
Cecil, Sir Robert, 213.
Cervantes, XIII, 407.
Cesario, 133, 209.
Chamberlain, the Lord, 247.
Chapel Lane, 377.
Chapman, 124, 246, 296, 297, 338, 388, 397.
Charlecot, 355.
Charmian, 305, 306, 307, 315, 319.
Chesterfield, 232.
Chettle, 150, 151, 372, 373, 392.
Chief Justice, 103, 151.
Chus, 190.
Cinna, 255.
Cinthio, 271, 277.
Clarenceux (King of Arms), 378
Clarendon, 398.
Claudio, 37, 38, 39, 40, 44, 137, 206, 207, 208, 211.
Claudius, King of Denmark, 19, 265, 266.
Cleopatra, XII, 8, 32, 228, 297, 299, 300, 302, 303, 304, 305, 306, 307, 308, 309, 310, 311, 312, 313, 314, 315, 316, 317, 318, 319, 320, 321, 322, 385, 386, 394.
Clifford, 115.
Cloten, 49.
"Colbourn's Magazine," 40.
Coleridge, XI, XII, 5, 6, 7, 9, 35, 45, 55, 63, 72, 104, 112, 118, 119, 120, 132, 141, 142, 160, 165, 166, 175, 201, 221, 253, 254, 276, 277, 281, 324, 371, 380.
College of Heralds, 378, 379.
Combe, John, 375, 402, 404.
"Comedy of Errors," 69, 167, 172, 175, 176, 177, 360, 363, 365.
Comic Muse, 152.
Condell, 112.
"Confessio Amantis," 64.
Constance, 340.
Cordelia, 292, 386.
"Coriolanus," 115, 119, 130, 242, 302, 316, 353, 401.

414

Index

415

Index

Fitton, Mary, 202, 209, 212, 213, 214, 221, 225, 226, 247, 264, 265, 266, 269, 270, 283, 290, 291, 292, 294, 298, 301, 302, 304, 306, 308, 310, 317, 322, 323, 338, 340, 345, 382, 383, 384, 385, 386, 393, 394, 395, 401.
Flavius, 332, 333, 344.
Fleance, 22.
Fleet Prison, 103.
Fletcher (the poet), 404.
Ford, 153.
Ford, Mrs., 152.
Forman's Diary, 63.
Fortinbras, 145.
France, 106, 400.
Frederic the Great, 397.
Fuller, 389.
Furnival, Mr., 127, 175, 214.

Gadshill, 93, 145.
Gauls, 254.
Gaunt, John of, 64, 65, 72, 400.
Germany, 104, 400.
Gertrude (Queen: "Hamlet"), 265, 266.
Gill, Sir David, XVII.
Gladstone, 229.
Glendower, 84, 85, 95.
Globe Theatre, 375.
Gloster, 64, 113, 114, 116.
Glostershire, 82.
Gloucester, 125, 325.
God, 64, 67, 68, 69, 70, 77, 86, 105, 106, 124, 146, 148, 149, 197, 375, 391.
Goethe, XI, XII, 7, 49, 55, 129, 142, 163, 261, 266, 324, 389, 401, 407.
Gollancz, Israel, 204, 333, 349.
Gonzalo, 344.
"Gorgias," 120.
Goneril ("Lear"), XII.
Gower, 64.
Gratiano, 183, 187, 192, 197, 198, 240.
Greece, 296.
Green ("Richard II"), 67, 68, 278.

Greene, Robert (the playwright), 150, 191, 366, 372, 397.
Greenhill Street, 352.
"Groatsworth of Wit, The," 372.
Guildenstern, 36, 76, 258.

Hal, Prince, 91, 144, 146, 148.
Hall, Susanna, 358, 377, 404.
Hallam, 3, 201, 227, 248.
Halliwell-Phillipps, 357.
Hamlet, XI, XIII, XIV, 4, 7, 8, 9, 10, 11, 12, 13, 14, 15, 16, 17, 18, 19, 20, 21, 22, 23, 24, 26, 28, 29, 31, 32, 33, 34, 35, 36, 37, 39, 40, 41, 42, 43, 44, 45, 46, 48, 49, 50, 51, 52, 53, 54, 55, 68, 69, 70, 73, 75, 76, 77, 89, 90, 100, 121, 122, 130, 134, 135, 138, 139, 140, 141, 144, 145, 149, 155, 159, 162, 193, 215, 228, 248, 250, 251, 252, 258, 259, 261, 262, 263, 264, 265, 266, 267, 268, 269, 271, 272, 279, 281, 288, 290, 297, 298, 302, 306, 322, 334, 340, 342, 346, 350, 351, 369, 372, 380, 385, 395, 399, 407.
Hamnet, 58, 340, 360, 378.
Harfleur, 106.
Haroun-al-Raschid, 45.
Harrison, Rev. W. A., 202.
Hathaway, Anne, 178, 356, 357, 358, 363, 364, 368.
Hathaway, Richard, 356, 358.
Hazlitt, 10, 16, 35.
Hector, 295.
Heine, 227, 248, 304.
Helen, 290.
Hellicon, 151.
Heminge, 112, 365.
Henley Street, 352, 353.
Henry IV., King, 64, 66, 67, 79, 81, 83, 88, 89, 97, 101, 104, 110, 128, 138, 215, 356, 369.
—— First Part, 94, 152, 153, 155, 382.
—— Second Part, 99, 150, 152, 153, 155, 382.
Henry V., King, 98, 102, 103, 104, 105, 106, 107, 108, 109,

416

Index

Laban, 195.
Laertes, 12, 18, 32, 33, 42, 262, 268.
Lamb, 324.
Langland, William, 64.
Launce, 141.
Leander, 244.
Lear, King, X, 17, 26, 40, 66, 70,
  75, 167, 190, 251, 324, 325, 326,
  327, 328, 329, 330, 331, 332,
  333, 334, 335, 336, 337, 351,
  385, 407.
Leatherhead, 244, 245.
Lee, Sidney, 45.
Leicester, Lord, 365.
Leontes, 281, 403.
Lessing, 324.
Leveson, Sir Richard, 213.
Lieutenant of the Tower, 117.
"Lives" (Plutarch), 405.
"Lives of the Poets, The," 365.
Lodge, 14.
Lodovico, 280.
London, X, 77, 110, 162, 169,
  177, 178, 229, 296, 337, 355,
  361, 363, 364, 365, 366, 368,
  370, 371, 372, 374, 377, 382,
  396, 397, 399, 404.
Longaville, 218.
Lope de Vega, XIII.
Lord Governor of England, 65.
Lord of Comedy, 144.
Lord of Humour, 154.
Lorenzo, 136, 137, 193, 240.
"Love's Labour's Lost," 127, 160,
  161, 165, 166, 167, 168, 175,
  176, 177, 184, 217, 222, 224,
  296, 342, 353.
Lucetta, 175.
Luciana, 171, 172, 174.
Lucifer, 319.
Lucio, 41, 42, 44, 45, 100.
Lucius ("Julius Cæsar"), 259.
"Lucrece," 127, 373, 398.
Lucy, Sir Thomas, 154, 355, 364.
Luther, 124.
Lyly, 243, 353.

Macbeth, 16, 17, 18, 19, 20, 21,
  22, 23, 24, 25, 26, 27, 28, 29,
  30, 31, 32, 33, 34, 39, 40, 44, 45,

49, 54, 55, 70, 130, 135, 138,
  139, 155, 251, 256, 259, 271,
  279, 285, 288, 369, 385, 399.
Macbeth, Lady, 18, 19, 20, 23,
  24, 25, 26, 27, 28, 30, 31.
Macduff, 27, 29, 30, 31, 32, 33.
Malcolm, 30, 31.
Malvolio, 143, 379.
Mamillius, 340.
Marcus ("Titus Andronicus"),
  126.
Mardian ("Antony and Cleo-
  patra"), 305.
Margaret, 112.
Maria, 141, 155, 166.
Mariana, 380.
Marie, 57.
Marina, 337, 339, 340.
Marlowe, 5, 117, 119, 121, 128,
  371, 388.
Mars, 216, 305.
Marston, 390.
Masque, 342.
Master of the Revels, 232, 247.
May Queen, 61, 396.
"Measure for Measure," 35, 36,
  37, 45, 54, 76, 104.
"Merchant of Venice, The," 136,
  180, 183, 185, 239, 242, 334,
  376, 382, 391, 400.
Mercury, 216.
Mercutio, 164, 187, 215, 216, 218,
  221, 230, 374.
Meredith, George, 290.
Meres, 214.
Mermaid, 389, 390.
"Merry Wives of Windsor, The,"
  153, 154, 155, 215, 353.
"Midsummer Night's Dream,
  A," 135, 175, 382, 392.
Milan, 176, 179, 348.
Milton, 88, 124.
Miranda, 337, 339, 343, 346, 347.
Molière, XVIII.
Montaigne, 4.
Mortimer, 80, 81, 82, 95, 112.
Motley, 14.
"Much Ado About Nothing,"
  129, 140, 165, 206, 207, 210,
  211, 243, 337.

Index

Index

Thyrcus, 309, 310.
Timbuctoo, 108.
Timon, 104, 138, 143, 190, 251, 295, 297, 328, 332, 333, 334, 335, 336, 337, 339, 351, 373, 407.
Titania, 138.
Titian, XVIII, 271.
Titus, 126.
"Titus Andronicus," XIII, 69, 104, 126, 336, 353.
Tolstoi, XVIII, 324, 326, 327, 328, 333,
Tourgenief, 61, 380.
Toussaint l'Ouverture, 381.
Tower of London, 399.
Tree, Beerbohm, 267.
"Trial Table of the order of Shakespeare's Plays," 127, 175.
Trinculo, 346.
Triton, 152.
Troilus, 251, 292, 293, 322, 384, 387.
"Troilus and Cressida," 291, 294, 295, 296, 297, 304, 322, 326, 384, 403.
Trojans, 296.
"Troublesome Raigne of King John, The," 57, 58, 59.
Troy, 295.
"True Tragedie of Richard," 116, 117.
Tubal, 190.
"Twelfth Night," 129, 130, 135, 136, 137, 138, 140, 181, 210, 211, 228, 229, 249, 301, 326, 346, 360.
"Two Gentlemen of Verona, The," 127, 167, 175, 176, 184, 203, 204, 210, 211, 241, 242, 348, 365, 366, 369.
"Two Noble Kinsmen, The," 149, 180.
Tyler, Mr., 201, 202, 221.

Ulysses, 293, 297, 385.

Valentine, 131, 167, 175, 176, 177, 178, 179, 180, 181, 182, 183, 184, 204, 205, 241, 249, 252, 348.
Valiant-for-Truth, 125.
Venice, 280.
Venus, 305, 368.
"Venus and Adonis," 127, 172, 232, 233, 366, 367, 368, 373, 398.
Vernon, 97.
Veronese, 271.
Vienna, 36.
Villon, 227.
Vincentio, Duke, 35, 36, 37, 38, 39, 40, 41, 42, 43, 44, 45, 49, 53, 76, 100, 133.
Viola, 132, 133, 136, 210.
Virgil, 390.
"Vision of Piers Plowman," 64.
Voltaire, 397.

Ward, Rev. John, 337, 376, 403.
Warwick, 355.
Warwickshire, 352, 379.
Watts-Dunton, Theodore, 40.
Westminster, 399.
Westmoreland, 108.
Whately, Anne, 357, 358, 364.
Whittington, Thomas, 361.
William the Conqueror, 374.
Wilmcote, 352, 379.
"Winter's Tale, The," 281, 337, 338, 340, 359, 360, 365, 403, 407.
"Wit's Commonwealth," 243.
Wittenberg, 18, 19, 31.
Worcester, Bishop of, 357, 358.
Worcester, Lord, 82, 85, 87, 111.
Wordsworth, 3, 199, 201, 380.
"Worthies" (Fuller's), 389.